Free Software, Free Society

Selected Essays of Richard M. Stallman
Third Edition

Richard M. Stallman

This is the third edition of *Free Software, Free Society: Selected Essays of Richard M. Stallman.*

Free Software Foundation
51 Franklin Street, Fifth Floor
Boston, MA 02110-1335

ISBN 978-0-9831592-5-4

Cover design and photograph by Kyle Winfree.

Table of Contents

Foreword to the Third Edition

A love letter to Richard Stallman, by Jacob Appelbaum

We live in information societies where machines intermediate our lives.

Software and hardware are as important to our information age as the internet itself. Free Software is the political theory born from the mind of a revolutionary who believes that, just as we should have control over our own lives, we should also be able to understand and control the machines that are extensions of ourselves. This theory, as supported by the Free Software Foundation, has become a practice and a tradition for millions of people over the last three decades.

Free Software as a political theory acknowledges the role of software and hardware systems in our societies. Critiquing past and present systems is necessary. We may find ourselves unable to understand or modify these systems. We become beholden to others in ways that produce injustices and are themselves an injustice. The outcomes of these systems are not always obvious, particularly when one is forced into using them, and especially when they are normalized and branded as the standard. Free Software as a practice is not merely a critique: it is an alternative that provides liberty, resting on free standards, freely available to all.

Free Software is a paradigm shift where we are at liberty to understand and learn from those who have come before us, where we are free to grow and share, to learn from mistakes, to benefit as we learn, and to share those benefits with everyone. When we use copyleft, we ensure that all future users of our work get the same liberty. Free Software ensures that future generations will also be able to decode entire histories of data. It ensures not only our liberties, but theirs as well.

In times of mass surveillance, Free Software brings much needed transparency and with it verifiability. Free Software enables us to encrypt, to ensure integrity, to authorize, and to anonymize ourselves. In a world of ever increasing privatization, we find in Free Software a pillar of communal action towards free societies. The benefits of Free Software are impossible to fully enumerate as they vary as much as the benefits of liberty itself. Advancing the cause of Free Software is never ending, like all struggles for justice, and requires eternal vigilance. Advancing the cause of Free Software is difficult, and those advocating and implementing Free Software are often carrying essential ideas forward against all odds.

This is the foreword to *Free Software, Free Society: Selected Essays of Richard M. Stallman*, 3rd ed. (Boston: GNU Press, 2015).

Foreword to the First Edition

Every generation has its philosopher—a writer or an artist who captures the imagination of a time. Sometimes these philosophers are recognized as such; often it takes generations before the connection is made real. But recognized or not, a time gets marked by the people who speak its ideals, whether in the whisper of a poem, or the blast of a political movement.

Our generation has a philosopher. He is not an artist, or a professional writer. He is a programmer. Richard Stallman began his work in the labs of MIT, as a programmer and architect building operating system software. He has built his career on a stage of public life, as a programmer and an architect founding a movement for freedom in a world increasingly defined by "code."

"Code" is the technology that makes computers run. Whether inscribed in software or burned in hardware, it is the collection of instructions, first written in words, that directs the functionality of machines. These machines—computers—increasingly define and control our life. They determine how phones connect, and what runs on TV. They decide whether video can be streamed across a broadband link to a computer. They control what a computer reports back to its manufacturer. These machines run us. Code runs these machines.

What control should we have over this code? What understanding? What freedom should there be to match the control it enables? What power?

These questions have been the challenge of Stallman's life. Through his works and his words, he has pushed us to see the importance of keeping code "free." Not free in the sense that code writers don't get paid, but free in the sense that the control coders build be transparent to all, and that anyone have the right to take that control, and modify it as he or she sees fit. This is "free software"; "free software" is one answer to a world built in code.

"Free." Stallman laments the ambiguity in his own term. There's nothing to lament. Puzzles force people to think, and this term "free" does this puzzling work quite well. To modern American ears, "free software" sounds utopian, impossible. Nothing, not even lunch, is free. How could the most important words running the most critical machines running the world be "free." How could a sane society aspire to such an ideal?

Yet the odd clink of the word "free" is a function of us, not of the term. "Free" has different senses, only one of which refers to "price." A much more fundamental sense of "free" is the "free," Stallman says, in the term "free speech," or perhaps better in the term "free labor." Not free as in costless, but free as in limited in its control by others. Free software is control that is transparent, and open to change, just as free laws, or the laws of a "free society," are free when

---

This foreword was originally published, in 2002, as the introduction to the first edition. This, the original version, is part of *Free Software, Free Society: Selected Essays of Richard M. Stallman*, 3rd ed. (Boston: GNU Press, 2015).

they make their control knowable, and open to change. The aim of Stallman's "free software movement" is to make as much code as it can transparent, and subject to change, by rendering it "free."

The mechanism of this rendering is an extraordinarily clever device called "copyleft" implemented through a license called GPL. Using the power of copyright law, "free software" not only assures that it remains open, and subject to change, but that other software that takes and uses "free software" (and that technically counts as a "derivative") must also itself be free. If you use and adapt a free software program, and then release that adapted version to the public, the released version must be as free as the version it was adapted from. It must, or the law of copyright will be violated.

"Free software," like free societies, has its enemies. Microsoft has waged a war against the GPL, warning whoever will listen that the GPL is a "dangerous" license. The dangers it names, however, are largely illusory. Others object to the "coercion" in GPL's insistence that modified versions are also free. But a condition is not coercion. If it is not coercion for Microsoft to refuse to permit users to distribute modified versions of its product Office without paying it (presumably) millions, then it is not coercion when the GPL insists that modified versions of free software be free too.

And then there are those who call Stallman's message too extreme. But extreme it is not. Indeed, in an obvious sense, Stallman's work is a simple translation of the freedoms that our tradition crafted in the world before code. "Free software" would assure that the world governed by code is as "free" as our tradition that built the world before code.

For example: A "free society" is regulated by law. But there are limits that any free society places on this regulation through law: No society that kept its laws secret could ever be called free. No government that hid its regulations from the regulated could ever stand in our tradition. Law controls. But it does so justly only when visibly. And law is visible only when its terms are knowable and controllable by those it regulates, or by the agents of those it regulates (lawyers, legislatures).

This condition on law extends beyond the work of a legislature. Think about the practice of law in American courts. Lawyers are hired by their clients to advance their clients' interests. Sometimes that interest is advanced through litigation. In the course of this litigation, lawyers write briefs. These briefs in turn affect opinions written by judges. These opinions decide who wins a particular case, or whether a certain law can stand consistently with a constitution.

All the material in this process is free in the sense that Stallman means. Legal briefs are open and free for others to use. The arguments are transparent (which is different from saying they are good) and the reasoning can be taken without the permission of the original lawyers. The opinions they produce can be quoted in later briefs. They can be copied and integrated into another brief or opinion. The "source code" for American law is by design, and by principle, open and free for anyone to take. And take lawyers do—for it is a measure of a great brief that it achieves its creativity through the reuse of what happened before. The source is free; creativity and an economy is built upon it.

This economy of free code (and here I mean free legal code) doesn't starve lawyers. Law firms have enough incentive to produce great briefs even though the stuff they build can be taken and copied by anyone else. The lawyer is a craftsman; his or her product is public. Yet the crafting is not charity. Lawyers get paid; the public doesn't demand such work without price. Instead this economy flourishes, with later work added to the earlier.

We could imagine a legal practice that was different—briefs and arguments that were kept secret; rulings that announced a result but not the reasoning. Laws that were kept by the police but published to no one else. Regulation that operated without explaining its rule.

We could imagine this society, but we could not imagine calling it "free." Whether or not the incentives in such a society would be better or more efficiently allocated, such a society could not be known as free. The ideals of freedom, of life within a free society, demand more than efficient application. Instead, openness and transparency are the constraints within which a legal system gets built, not options to be added if convenient to the leaders. Life governed by software code should be no less.

Code writing is not litigation. It is better, richer, more productive. But the law is an obvious instance of how creativity and incentives do not depend upon perfect control over the products created. Like jazz, or novels, or architecture, the law gets built upon the work that went before. This adding and changing is what creativity always is. And a free society is one that assures that its most important resources remain free in just this sense.

This book collects the writing and lectures of Richard Stallman in a manner that will make their subtlety and power clear. The essays span a wide range, from copyright to the history of the free software movement. They include many arguments not well known, and among these, an especially insightful account of the changed circumstances that render copyright in the digital world suspect. They will serve as a resource for those who seek to understand the thought of this most powerful man—powerful in his ideas, his passion, and his integrity, even if powerless in every other way. They will inspire others who would take these ideas, and build upon them.

I don't know Stallman well. I know him well enough to know he is a hard man to like. He is driven, often impatient. His anger can flare at friend as easily as foe. He is uncompromising and persistent; patient in both.

Yet when our world finally comes to understand the power and danger of code—when it finally sees that code, like laws, or like government, must be transparent to be free—then we will look back at this uncompromising and persistent programmer and recognize the vision he has fought to make real: the vision of a world where freedom and knowledge survives the compiler. And we will come to see that no man, through his deeds or words, has done as much to make possible the freedom that this next society could have.

We have not earned that freedom yet. We may well fail in securing it. But whether we succeed or fail, in these essays is a picture of what that freedom could be. And in the life that produced these words and works, there is inspiration for anyone who would, like Stallman, fight to create this freedom.

Lawrence Lessig

Lawrence Lessig is a Professor of Law at Harvard Law School, the director of the Edmond J. Safra Foundation Center for Ethics, and the founder of Stanford Law School's Center for Internet and Society. For much of his career, he focused his work on law and technology, especially as it affects copyright. He is the author of numerous books and has served as a board member of many organizations, including the Free Software Foundation.

Preface

The third edition of *Free Software, Free Society* holds updated versions of most of the essays from the second edition, as well as many new essays. A third of the essays are new.

As it was in previous editions, the initial section of the book is devoted to the principles and philosophy of free software. It includes a more powerful presentation of why software ought to be free, an explanation of how our principles determine our practical decisions, and addresses the question of freedom and hardware designs.

The way we name and frame an issue affects how we think about it. Companies choose terminology to promote their framing; to accept that is to support them. Thus, this edition has new material about how we at the FSF name things and why.

The copyright section now presents a transcript of a speech that discusses the overall issue of copyright law and how it should be changed.

The patents section proposes a solution for the problem caused by patents in the computing field. I've kept essays about patents separate from those about copyright, since the two issues should not be lumped together.

The licensing section is largely unchanged, still presenting the GNU licenses, with an introduction written with Brett Smith giving their history and the motives for each of them, and an essay explaining why software projects should upgrade to version 3 of the GNU General Public License.

This edition continues to address dangers and traps that the free software community faces, including now the issues of nonfree games, e-books, and the growing threat of digital surveillance.

I hope this book can show you how you might lose your freedom, teach you how to protect it, and inspire you to value it.

Thank you to Jeanne Rasata for managing the project, editing the book, formatting the text, and creating the index. Thanks also to Karl Berry for technical assistance with Texinfo, and Kyle Winfree for designing and formatting the cover.

RICHARD STALLMAN

The efforts invested in Free Software are not merely about knowledge, they are about empowerment: empowerment to study, empowerment to modify, empowerment to share, and empowerment to enable sharing with others. Commitment to liberty in an information age requires a refusal to compromise on the core principles of Free Software, with a commitment and honesty that demands sacrifice. Many may refuse this burden, working only to enrich themselves in the present moment; others will work to increase the breadth and depth of human knowledge. Implemented as Free Software, we find a model of sustainability and long-term vision that increases not only knowledge but practical direct ability freely shared for all without exception. This is a worthy cause and its thoughtfulness has already enabled all of us; from the mundane to the most extraordinary, Free Software is involved.

Richard Stallman is the revolutionary and theorist who has given the world Free Software. His essays cover topics that have been essential reading for decades, widely read and understood by people creating systems for our information age and beyond. He has dedicated his life to the liberation of humanity, and this book explains how we might each help with this cause of liberation.

Jacob Appelbaum

Jacob Appelbaum is an independent computer-security researcher, journalist and artist. He is a co-founder of Noisebridge, a Debian GNU/Linux developer, a core member of the Tor Project, allegedly a WikiLeaks co-conspirator, and has collaborated on several high-profile research projects. Because of his political views and the recognition he's received in each of his fields of endeavor, he has been repeatedly targeted and detained by US law enforcement agencies. By birth an American, he works and lives in exile in Berlin.

Part I: The GNU Project and Free Software

1 What Is Free Software?

The Free Software Definition

> The free software definition presents the criteria for whether a particular software program qualifies as free software. From time to time we revise this definition, to clarify it or to resolve questions about subtle issues. For a list of the changes we've made to the definition of free software, please see the "History" section, following the definition, at `http://gnu.org/philosophy/free-sw.html`.

"Free software" means software that respects users' freedom and community. Roughly, it means that **the users have the freedom to run, copy, distribute, study, change and improve the software.** Thus, "free software" is a matter of liberty, not price. To understand the concept, you should think of "free" as in "free speech," not as in "free beer." We sometimes call it "libre software" to show we do not mean it is gratis.

We campaign for these freedoms because everyone deserves them. With these freedoms, the users (both individually and collectively) control the program and what it does for them. When users don't control the program, we call it a "nonfree" or "proprietary" program. The nonfree program controls the users, and the developer controls the program; this makes the program an instrument of unjust power.[1]

A program is free software if the program's users have the four essential freedoms:

- The freedom to run the program as you wish, for any purpose (freedom 0).
- The freedom to study how the program works, and change it so it does your computing as you wish (freedom 1). Access to the source code is a precondition for this.
- The freedom to redistribute copies so you can help your neighbor (freedom 2).
- The freedom to distribute copies of your modified versions to others (freedom 3). By doing this you can give the whole community a chance to benefit from your changes. Access to the source code is a precondition for this.

---

[1] See "Free Software Is Even More Important Now" (p. 28) for more on this issue.

The free software definition was first published in 1996, on `http://gnu.org`. This version is part of *Free Software, Free Society: Selected Essays of Richard M. Stallman,* 3rd ed. (Boston: GNU Press, 2015).

A program is free software if it gives users adequately all of these freedoms. Otherwise, it is nonfree. While we can distinguish various nonfree distribution schemes in terms of how far they fall short of being free, we consider them all equally unethical.

In any given scenario, these freedoms must apply to whatever code we plan to make use of, or lead others to make use of. For instance, consider a program A which automatically launches a program B to handle some cases. If we plan to distribute A as it stands, that implies users will need B, so we need to judge whether both A and B are free. However, if we plan to modify A so that it doesn't use B, only A needs to be free; we can ignore B.

The rest of this page clarifies certain points about what makes specific freedoms adequate or not.

Freedom to distribute (freedoms 2 and 3) means you are free to redistribute copies, either with or without modifications, either gratis or charging a fee for distribution, to anyone anywhere. Being free to do these things means (among other things) that you do not have to ask or pay for permission to do so.

You should also have the freedom to make modifications and use them privately in your own work or play, without even mentioning that they exist. If you do publish your changes, you should not be required to notify anyone in particular, or in any particular way.

The freedom to run the program means the freedom for any kind of person or organization to use it on any kind of computer system, for any kind of overall job and purpose, without being required to communicate about it with the developer or any other specific entity. In this freedom, it is the *user's* purpose that matters, not the *developer's* purpose; you as a user are free to run the program for your purposes, and if you distribute it to someone else, she is then free to run it for her purposes, but you are not entitled to impose your purposes on her.

The freedom to run the program as you wish means that you are not forbidden or stopped from doing so. It has nothing to do with what functionality the program has, or whether it is useful for what you want to do.

The freedom to redistribute copies must include binary or executable forms of the program, as well as source code, for both modified and unmodified versions. (Distributing programs in runnable form is necessary for conveniently installable free operating systems.) It is OK if there is no way to produce a binary or executable form for a certain program (since some languages don't support that feature), but you must have the freedom to redistribute such forms should you find or develop a way to make them.

In order for freedoms 1 and 3 (the freedom to make changes and the freedom to publish the changed versions) to be meaningful, you must have access to the source code of the program. Therefore, accessibility of source code is a necessary condition for free software. Obfuscated "source code" is not real source code and does not count as source code.

Freedom 1 includes the freedom to use your changed version in place of the original. If the program is delivered in a product designed to run someone else's modified versions but refuse to run yours—a practice known as "tivoization" or "lockdown," or (in its practitioners' perverse terminology) as "secure boot"—freedom 1 becomes an empty pretense rather than a practical reality. These binaries are not free software even if the source code they are compiled from is free.

One important way to modify a program is by merging in available free subroutines and modules. If the program's license says that you cannot merge in a suitably licensed existing module—for instance, if it requires you to be the copyright holder of any code you add—then the license is too restrictive to qualify as free.

Freedom 3 includes the freedom to release your modified versions as free software. A free license may also permit other ways of releasing them; in other words, it does not have to be a copyleft license. However, a license that requires modified versions to be nonfree does not qualify as a free license.

In order for these freedoms to be real, they must be permanent and irrevocable as long as you do nothing wrong; if the developer of the software has the power to revoke the license, or retroactively add restrictions to its terms, without your doing anything wrong to give cause, the software is not free.

However, certain kinds of rules about the manner of distributing free software are acceptable, when they don't conflict with the central freedoms. For example, copyleft (very simply stated) is the rule that when redistributing the program, you cannot add restrictions to deny other people the central freedoms. This rule does not conflict with the central freedoms; rather it protects them.

In the GNU Project, we use copyleft to protect the four freedoms legally for everyone. We believe there are important reasons why it is better to use copyleft. However, noncopylefted free software is ethical too. See "Categories of Free Software" (p. 68) for a description of how "free software," "copylefted software" and other categories of software relate to each other.

"Free software" does not mean "noncommercial." A free program must be available for commercial use, commercial development, and commercial distribution. Commercial development of free software is no longer unusual; such free commercial software is very important. You may have paid money to get copies of free software, or you may have obtained copies at no charge. But regardless of how you got your copies, you always have the freedom to copy and change the software, even to sell copies.

Whether a change constitutes an improvement is a subjective matter. If your right to modify a program is limited, in substance, to changes that someone else considers an improvement, that program is not free.

However, rules about how to package a modified version are acceptable, if they don't substantively limit your freedom to release modified versions, or your freedom to make and use modified versions privately. Thus, it is acceptable for the license to require that you change the name of the modified version, remove a logo, or identify your modifications as yours. As long as these requirements are not so burdensome that they effectively hamper you from releasing your changes, they are acceptable; you're already making other changes to the program, so you won't have trouble making a few more.

Rules that "if you make your version available in this way, you must make it available in that way also" can be acceptable too, on the same condition. An example of such an acceptable rule is one saying that if you have distributed a modified version and a previous developer asks for a copy of it, you must send one. (Note that such a rule still leaves you the choice of whether to distribute your version at all.) Rules that require release of source code to the users for versions that you put into public use are also acceptable.

A special issue arises when a license requires changing the name by which the program will be invoked from other programs. That effectively hampers you from releasing your changed version so that it can replace the original when invoked by those other programs. This sort of requirement is acceptable only if there's a suitable aliasing facility that allows you to specify the original program's name as an alias for the modified version.

Sometimes government export control regulations and trade sanctions can constrain your freedom to distribute copies of programs internationally. Software developers do not have the power to eliminate or override these restrictions, but what they can and must do is refuse to impose them as conditions of use of the program. In this way, the restrictions will not affect activities and people outside the jurisdictions of these governments. Thus, free software licenses must not require obedience to any nontrivial export regulations as a condition of exercising any of the essential freedoms.

Merely mentioning the existence of export regulations, without making them a condition of the license itself, is acceptable since it does not restrict users. If an export regulation is actually trivial for free software, then requiring it as a condition is not an actual problem; however, it is a potential problem, since a later change in export law could make the requirement nontrivial and thus render the software nonfree.

A free license may not require compliance with the license of a nonfree program. Thus, for instance, if a license requires you to comply with the licenses of "all the programs you use," in the case of a user that runs nonfree programs this would require compliance with the licenses of those nonfree programs; that makes the license nonfree.

It is acceptable for a free license to specify which jurisdiction's law applies, or where litigation must be done, or both.

Most free software licenses are based on copyright, and there are limits on what kinds of requirements can be imposed through copyright. If a copyright-based license respects freedom in the ways described above, it is unlikely to have some other sort of problem that we never anticipated (though this does happen occasionally). However, some free software licenses are based on contracts, and contracts can impose a much larger range of possible restrictions. That means there are many possible ways such a license could be unacceptably restrictive and nonfree.

We can't possibly list all the ways that might happen. If a contract-based license restricts the user in an unusual way that copyright-based licenses cannot, and which isn't mentioned here as legitimate, we will have to think about it, and we will probably conclude it is nonfree.

When talking about free software, it is best to avoid using terms like "give away" or "for free," because those terms imply that the issue is about price, not freedom. Some common terms such as "piracy" embody opinions we hope you won't endorse. See "Words to Avoid (or Use with Care) Because They Are Loaded or Confusing" (p. 89) for a discussion of these terms. We also have a list of proper translations of "free software" into various languages (p. 274).

Finally, note that criteria such as those stated in this free software definition require careful thought for their interpretation. To decide whether a specific software license qualifies as a free software license, we judge it based on these criteria to determine whether it fits their spirit as well as the precise words. If a license includes unconscionable restrictions, we reject it, even if we did not anticipate the issue in these criteria. Sometimes a license requirement raises an issue that calls for extensive thought, including discussions with a lawyer, before we can decide if the requirement is acceptable. When we reach a conclusion about a new issue, we often update these criteria to make it easier to see why certain licenses do or don't qualify.

If you are interested in whether a specific license qualifies as a free software license, see our list of licenses, at `http://gnu.org/licenses/license-list.html`. If the license you are concerned with is not listed there, you can ask us about it by sending us email at `licensing@gnu.org`.

If you are contemplating writing a new license, please contact the Free Software Foundation first by writing to that address. The proliferation of different free software licenses means increased work for users in understanding the licenses; we may be able to help you find an existing free software license that meets your needs.

If that isn't possible, if you really need a new license, with our help you can ensure that the license really is a free software license and avoid various practical problems.

Beyond Software

Software manuals must be free,[2] for the same reasons that software must be free, and because the manuals are in effect part of the software.

The same arguments also make sense for other kinds of works of practical use—that is to say, works that embody useful knowledge, such as educational works and reference works. Wikipedia is the best-known example.

Any kind of work *can* be free, and the definition of free software has been extended to a definition of free cultural works[3] applicable to any kind of works.

---

[2] See "Why Free Software Needs Free Documentation" (p. 40).
[3] See `http://freedomdefined.org`.

Open Source?

Another group users the term "open source" to mean something close (but not identical) to "free software." We prefer the term "free software" because, once you have heard that it refers to freedom rather than price, it calls to mind freedom. The word "open" never refers to freedom.[4]

[4] See "Why Open Source Misses the Point of Free Software" (p. 75).

2 The GNU Project

The First Software-Sharing Community

When I started working at the MIT Artificial Intelligence Lab in 1971, I became part of a software-sharing community that had existed for many years. Sharing of software was not limited to our particular community; it is as old as computers, just as sharing of recipes is as old as cooking. But we did it more than most.

The AI Lab used a timesharing operating system called ITS (the Incompatible Timesharing System) that the lab's staff hackers[1] had designed and written in assembler language for the Digital PDP-10, one of the large computers of the era. As a member of this community, an AI Lab staff system hacker, my job was to improve this system.

We did not call our software "free software," because that term did not yet exist; but that is what it was. Whenever people from another university or a company wanted to port and use a program, we gladly let them. If you saw someone using an unfamiliar and interesting program, you could always ask to see the source code, so that you could read it, change it, or cannibalize parts of it to make a new program.

The Collapse of the Community

The situation changed drastically in the early 1980s when Digital discontinued the PDP-10 series. Its architecture, elegant and powerful in the 60s, could not extend naturally to the larger address spaces that were becoming feasible in the 80s. This meant that nearly all of the programs composing ITS were obsolete.

The AI Lab hacker community had already collapsed, not long before. In 1981, the spin-off company Symbolics had hired away nearly all of the hackers from the AI Lab, and the depopulated community was unable to maintain itself. (The book *Hackers*, by Steve Levy, describes these events, as well as giving a

---

[1] The use of "hacker" to mean "security breaker" is a confusion on the part of the mass media. We hackers refuse to recognize that meaning, and continue using the word to mean someone who loves to program, someone who enjoys playful cleverness, or the combination of the two. See my article "On Hacking," at `http://stallman.org/articles/on-hacking.html`.

The original version of this essay was published in *Open Sources: Voices from the Open Source Revolution*, by Chris DiBona and others (Sebastopol: O'Reilly Media, 1999), under the title "The GNU Operating System and the Free Software Movement." Though I was never a supporter of "open source," I contributed this article anyway, so that the ideas of the free software movement would not be entirely absent from that book. This version is part of *Free Software, Free Society: Selected Essays of Richard M. Stallman*, 3rd ed. (Boston: GNU Press, 2015).

clear picture of this community in its prime.) When the AI Lab bought a new PDP-10 in 1982, its administrators decided to use Digital's nonfree timesharing system instead of ITS.

The modern computers of the era, such as the VAX or the 68020, had their own operating systems, but none of them were free software: you had to sign a nondisclosure agreement even to get an executable copy.

This meant that the first step in using a computer was to promise not to help your neighbor. A cooperating community was forbidden. The rule made by the owners of proprietary software was, "If you share with your neighbor, you are a pirate. If you want any changes, beg us to make them."

The idea that the proprietary software social system—the system that says you are not allowed to share or change software—is antisocial, that it is unethical, that it is simply wrong, may come as a surprise to some readers. But what else could we say about a system based on dividing the public and keeping users helpless? Readers who find the idea surprising may have taken the proprietary software social system as a given, or judged it on the terms suggested by proprietary software businesses. Software publishers have worked long and hard to convince people that there is only one way to look at the issue.

When software publishers talk about "enforcing" their "rights" or "stopping piracy,"[2] what they actually *say* is secondary. The real message of these statements is in the unstated assumptions they take for granted, which the public is asked to accept without examination. Let's therefore examine them.

One assumption is that software companies have an unquestionable natural right to own software and thus have power over all its users. (If this were a natural right, then no matter how much harm it does to the public, we could not object.) Interestingly, the US Constitution and legal tradition reject this view; copyright is not a natural right, but an artificial government-imposed monopoly that limits the users' natural right to copy.

Another unstated assumption is that the only important thing about software is what jobs it allows you to do—that we computer users should not care what kind of society we are allowed to have.

A third assumption is that we would have no usable software (or would never have a program to do this or that particular job) if we did not offer a company power over the users of the program. This assumption may have seemed plausible, before the free software movement demonstrated that we can make plenty of useful software without putting chains on it.

If we decline to accept these assumptions, and judge these issues based on ordinary commonsense morality while placing the users first, we arrive at very different conclusions. Computer users should be free to modify programs to fit their needs, and free to share software, because helping other people is the basis of society.

There is no room here for an extensive statement of the reasoning behind this conclusion, so I refer the reader to the articles "Why Software Should Not

[2] See p. 99 for more on the erroneous use of the term "piracy."

Have Owners," at http://gnu.org/philosophy/why-free.html, and "Free Software Is Even More Important Now" (p. 28).

A Stark Moral Choice

With my community gone, to continue as before was impossible. Instead, I faced a stark moral choice.

The easy choice was to join the proprietary software world, signing nondisclosure agreements and promising not to help my fellow hacker. Most likely I would also be developing software that was released under nondisclosure agreements, thus adding to the pressure on other people to betray their fellows too.

I could have made money this way, and perhaps amused myself writing code. But I knew that at the end of my career, I would look back on years of building walls to divide people, and feel I had spent my life making the world a worse place.

I had already experienced being on the receiving end of a nondisclosure agreement, when someone refused to give me and the MIT AI Lab the source code for the control program for our printer. (The lack of certain features in this program made use of the printer extremely frustrating.) So I could not tell myself that nondisclosure agreements were innocent. I was very angry when he refused to share with us; I could not turn around and do the same thing to everyone else.

Another choice, straightforward but unpleasant, was to leave the computer field. That way my skills would not be misused, but they would still be wasted. I would not be culpable for dividing and restricting computer users, but it would happen nonetheless.

So I looked for a way that a programmer could do something for the good. I asked myself, was there a program or programs that I could write, so as to make a community possible once again?

The answer was clear: what was needed first was an operating system. That is the crucial software for starting to use a computer. With an operating system, you can do many things; without one, you cannot run the computer at all. With a free operating system, we could again have a community of cooperating hackers—and invite anyone to join. And anyone would be able to use a computer without starting out by conspiring to deprive his or her friends.

As an operating system developer, I had the right skills for this job. So even though I could not take success for granted, I realized that I was elected to do the job. I chose to make the system compatible with Unix so that it would be portable, and so that Unix users could easily switch to it. The name GNU was chosen, following a hacker tradition, as a recursive acronym for "GNU's Not Unix."

An operating system does not mean just a kernel, barely enough to run other programs. In the 1970s, every operating system worthy of the name included command processors, assemblers, compilers, interpreters, debuggers, text editors, mailers, and much more. ITS had them, Multics had them, VMS had them, and Unix had them. The GNU operating system would include them too.

Later I heard these words, attributed to Hillel:[3]

> If I am not for myself, who will be for me?
> If I am only for myself, what am I?
> If not now, when?

The decision to start the GNU Project was based on a similar spirit.

Free as in Freedom

The term "free software" is sometimes misunderstood—it has nothing to do with price. It is about freedom. Here, therefore, is the definition of free software.

A program is free software, for you, a particular user, if:

- You have the freedom to run the program as you wish, for any purpose.
- You have the freedom to modify the program to suit your needs. (To make this freedom effective in practice, you must have access to the source code, since making changes in a program without having the source code is exceedingly difficult.)
- You have the freedom to redistribute copies, either gratis or for a fee.
- You have the freedom to distribute modified versions of the program, so that the community can benefit from your improvements.

Since "free" refers to freedom, not to price, there is no contradiction between selling copies and free software. In fact, the freedom to sell copies is crucial: collections of free software sold on CD-ROMs are important for the community, and selling them is an important way to raise funds for free software development. Therefore, a program which people are not free to include on these collections is not free software.

Because of the ambiguity of "free," people have long looked for alternatives, but no one has found a better term. The English language has more words and nuances than any other, but it lacks a simple, unambiguous, word that means "free," as in freedom—"unfettered" being the word that comes closest in meaning. Such alternatives as "liberated," "freedom," and "open" have either the wrong meaning or some other disadvantage.

GNU Software and the GNU System

Developing a whole system is a very large project. To bring it into reach, I decided to adapt and use existing pieces of free software wherever that was possible. For example, I decided at the very beginning to use TeX as the principal text formatter; a few years later, I decided to use the X Window System rather than writing another window system for GNU.

Because of these decisions, and others like them, the GNU system is not the same as the collection of all GNU software. The GNU system includes programs that are not GNU software, programs that were developed by other people and projects for their own purposes, but which we can use because they are free software.

---

[3] As an Atheist, I don't follow any religious leaders, but I sometimes find I admire something one of them has said.

Commencing the Project

In January 1984 I quit my job at MIT and began writing GNU software. Leaving MIT was necessary so that MIT would not be able to interfere with distributing GNU as free software. If I had remained on the staff, MIT could have claimed to own the work, and could have imposed their own distribution terms, or even turned the work into a proprietary software package. I had no intention of doing a large amount of work only to see it become useless for its intended purpose: creating a new software-sharing community.

However, Professor Winston, then the head of the MIT AI Lab, kindly invited me to keep using the lab's facilities.

The First Steps

Shortly before beginning the GNU Project, I heard about the Free University Compiler Kit, also known as VUCK. (The Dutch word for "free" is written with a *v*.) This was a compiler designed to handle multiple languages, including C and Pascal, and to support multiple target machines. I wrote to its author asking if GNU could use it.

He responded derisively, stating that the university was free but the compiler was not. I therefore decided that my first program for the GNU Project would be a multilanguage, multiplatform compiler.

Hoping to avoid the need to write the whole compiler myself, I obtained the source code for the Pastel compiler, which was a multiplatform compiler developed at Lawrence Livermore Lab. It supported, and was written in, an extended version of Pascal, designed to be a system-programming language. I added a C front end, and began porting it to the Motorola 68000 computer. But I had to give that up when I discovered that the compiler needed many megabytes of stack space, and the available 68000 Unix system would only allow 64k.

I then realized that the Pastel compiler functioned by parsing the entire input file into a syntax tree, converting the whole syntax tree into a chain of "instructions," and then generating the whole output file, without ever freeing any storage. At this point, I concluded I would have to write a new compiler from scratch. That new compiler is now known as GCC; none of the Pastel compiler is used in it, but I managed to adapt and use the C front end that I had written. But that was some years later; first, I worked on GNU Emacs.

GNU Emacs

I began work on GNU Emacs in September 1984, and in early 1985 it was beginning to be usable. This enabled me to begin using Unix systems to do editing; having no interest in learning to use vi or ed, I had done my editing on other kinds of machines until then.

At this point, people began wanting to use GNU Emacs, which raised the question of how to distribute it. Of course, I put it on the anonymous ftp server on the MIT computer that I used. (This computer, `prep.ai.mit.edu`, thus became the principal GNU ftp distribution site; when it was decommissioned a few years later, we transferred the name to our new ftp server.) But at that time, many of the interested people were not on the internet and could not get a copy by ftp. So the question was, what would I say to them?

I could have said, "Find a friend who is on the net and who will make a copy for you." Or I could have done what I did with the original PDP-10 Emacs: tell them, "Mail me a tape and a SASE (self-addressed stamped envelope), and I will mail it back with Emacs on it." But I had no job, and I was looking for ways to make money from free software. So I announced that I would mail a tape to whoever wanted one, for a fee of $150. In this way, I started a free software distribution business, the precursor of the companies that today distribute entire GNU/Linux system distributions.

Is a Program Free for Every User?

If a program is free software when it leaves the hands of its author, this does not necessarily mean it will be free software for everyone who has a copy of it. For example, public domain software[4] (software that is not copyrighted) is free software; but anyone can make a proprietary modified version of it. Likewise, many free programs are copyrighted but distributed under simple permissive licenses which allow proprietary modified versions.

The paradigmatic example of this problem is the X Window System. Developed at MIT, and released as free software with a permissive license, it was soon adopted by various computer companies. They added X to their proprietary Unix systems, in binary form only, and covered by the same nondisclosure agreement. These copies of X were no more free software than Unix was.

The developers of the X Window System did not consider this a problem—they expected and intended this to happen. Their goal was not freedom, just "success," defined as "having many users." They did not care whether these users had freedom, only that they should be numerous.

This led to a paradoxical situation where two different ways of counting the amount of freedom gave different answers to the question, "Is this program free?" If you judged based on the freedom provided by the distribution terms of the MIT release, you would say that X was free software. But if you measured the freedom of the average user of X, you would have to say it was proprietary software. Most X users were running the proprietary versions that came with Unix systems, not the free version.

---

[4] See p. 70 for more on public domain software.

Copyleft and the GNU GPL

The goal of GNU was to give users freedom, not just to be popular. So we needed to use distribution terms that would prevent GNU software from being turned into proprietary software. The method we use is called "copyleft."[5]

Copyleft uses copyright law, but flips it over to serve the opposite of its usual purpose: instead of a means for restricting a program, it becomes a means for keeping the program free.

The central idea of copyleft is that we give everyone permission to run the program, copy the program, modify the program, and distribute modified versions—but not permission to add restrictions of their own. Thus, the crucial freedoms that define "free software" are guaranteed to everyone who has a copy; they become inalienable rights.

For an effective copyleft, modified versions must also be free. This ensures that work based on ours becomes available to our community if it is published. When programmers who have jobs as programmers volunteer to improve GNU software, it is copyleft that prevents their employers from saying, "You can't share those changes, because we are going to use them to make our proprietary version of the program."

The requirement that changes must be free is essential if we want to ensure freedom for every user of the program. The companies that privatized the X Window System usually made some changes to port it to their systems and hardware. These changes were small compared with the great extent of X, but they were not trivial. If making changes were an excuse to deny the users freedom, it would be easy for anyone to take advantage of the excuse.

A related issue concerns combining a free program with nonfree code. Such a combination would inevitably be nonfree; whichever freedoms are lacking for the nonfree part would be lacking for the whole as well. To permit such combinations would open a hole big enough to sink a ship. Therefore, a crucial requirement for copyleft is to plug this hole: anything added to or combined with a copylefted program must be such that the larger combined version is also free and copylefted.

The specific implementation of copyleft that we use for most GNU software is the GNU General Public License, or GNU GPL for short. We have other kinds of copyleft that are used in specific circumstances. GNU manuals are copylefted also, but use a much simpler kind of copyleft, because the complexity of the GNU GPL is not necessary for manuals.[6]

---

[5] In 1984 or 1985, Don Hopkins (a very imaginative fellow) mailed me a letter. On the envelope he had written several amusing sayings, including this one: "Copyleft—all rights reversed." I used the word "copyleft" to name the distribution concept I was developing at the time.

[6] We now use the GNU Free Documentation License (p. 210) for documentation.

The Free Software Foundation

As interest in using Emacs was growing, other people became involved in the GNU project, and we decided that it was time to seek funding once again. So in 1985 we created the Free Software Foundation (FSF), a tax-exempt charity for free software development. The FSF also took over the Emacs tape distribution business; later it extended this by adding other free software (both GNU and non-GNU) to the tape, and by selling free manuals as well.

Most of the FSF's income used to come from sales of copies of free software and of other related services (CD-ROMs of source code, CD-ROMs with binaries, nicely printed manuals, all with the freedom to redistribute and modify), and Deluxe Distributions (distributions for which we built the whole collection of software for the customer's choice of platform). Today the FSF still sells manuals and other gear,[7] but it gets the bulk of its funding from members' dues. You can join the FSF at `http://fsf.org/join`.

Free Software Foundation employees have written and maintained a number of GNU software packages. Two notable ones are the C library and the shell. The GNU C Library is what every program running on a GNU/Linux system uses to communicate with Linux. It was developed by a member of the Free Software Foundation staff, Roland McGrath. The shell used on most GNU/Linux systems is BASH, the Bourne Again Shell,[8] which was developed by FSF employee Brian Fox.

We funded development of these programs because the GNU Project was not just about tools or a development environment. Our goal was a complete operating system, and these programs were needed for that goal.

Free Software Support

The free software philosophy rejects a specific widespread business practice, but it is not against business. When businesses respect the users' freedom, we wish them success.

Selling copies of Emacs demonstrates one kind of free software business. When the FSF took over that business, I needed another way to make a living. I found it in selling services relating to the free software I had developed. This included teaching, for subjects such as how to program GNU Emacs and how to customize GCC, and software development, mostly porting GCC to new platforms.

Today each of these kinds of free software business is practiced by a number of corporations. Some distribute free software collections on CD-ROM; others sell support at levels ranging from answering user questions, to fixing bugs, to adding major new features. We are even beginning to see free software companies based on launching new free software products.

---

[7] See our online shop, at `http://shop.fsf.org`.

[8] "Bourne Again Shell" is a play on the name "Bourne Shell," which was the usual shell on Unix.

Watch out, though—a number of companies that associate themselves with the term "open source" actually base their business on nonfree software that works with free software. These are not free software companies, they are proprietary software companies whose products tempt users away from freedom. They call these programs "value-added packages," which shows the values they would like us to adopt: convenience above freedom. If we value freedom more, we should call them "freedom-subtracted" packages.

Technical Goals

The principal goal of GNU is to be free software. Even if GNU had no technical advantage over Unix, it would have a social advantage, allowing users to cooperate, and an ethical advantage, respecting the user's freedom.

But it was natural to apply the known standards of good practice to the work—for example, dynamically allocating data structures to avoid arbitrary fixed size limits, and handling all the possible 8-bit codes wherever that made sense.

In addition, we rejected the Unix focus on small memory size, by deciding not to support 16-bit machines (it was clear that 32-bit machines would be the norm by the time the GNU system was finished), and to make no effort to reduce memory usage unless it exceeded a megabyte. In programs for which handling very large files was not crucial, we encouraged programmers to read an entire input file into core, then scan its contents without having to worry about I/O.

These decisions enabled many GNU programs to surpass their Unix counterparts in reliability and speed.

Donated Computers

As the GNU Project's reputation grew, people began offering to donate machines running Unix to the project. These were very useful, because the easiest way to develop components of GNU was to do it on a Unix system, and replace the components of that system one by one. But they raised an ethical issue: whether it was right for us to have a copy of Unix at all.

Unix was (and is) proprietary software, and the GNU Project's philosophy said that we should not use proprietary software. But, applying the same reasoning that leads to the conclusion that violence in self defense is justified, I concluded that it was legitimate to use a proprietary package when that was crucial for developing a free replacement that would help others stop using the proprietary package.

But, even if this was a justifiable evil, it was still an evil. Today we no longer have any copies of Unix, because we have replaced them with free operating systems. If we could not replace a machine's operating system with a free one, we replaced the machine instead.

The GNU Task List

As the GNU Project proceeded, and increasing numbers of system components were found or developed, eventually it became useful to make a list of the remaining gaps. We used it to recruit developers to write the missing pieces. This list became known as the GNU Task List. In addition to missing Unix components, we listed various other useful software and documentation projects that, we thought, a truly complete system ought to have.

Today,[9] hardly any Unix components are left in the GNU Task List—those jobs had been done, aside from a few inessential ones. But the list is full of projects that some might call "applications." Any program that appeals to more than a narrow class of users would be a useful thing to add to an operating system.

Even games are included in the task list—and have been since the beginning. Unix included games, so naturally GNU should too. But compatibility was not an issue for games, so we did not follow the list of games that Unix had. Instead, we listed a spectrum of different kinds of games that users might like.

The GNU Library GPL

The GNU C Library uses a special kind of copyleft called the GNU Library General Public License,[10] which gives permission to link proprietary software with the library. Why make this exception?

It is not a matter of principle; there is no principle that says proprietary software products are entitled to include our code. (Why contribute to a project predicated on refusing to share with us?) Using the LGPL for the C library, or for any library, is a matter of strategy.

The C library does a generic job; every proprietary system or compiler comes with a C library. Therefore, to make our C library available only to free software would not have given free software any advantage—it would only have discouraged use of our library.

One system is an exception to this: on the GNU system (and this includes GNU/Linux), the GNU C Library is the only C library. So the distribution terms of the GNU C Library determine whether it is possible to compile a proprietary program for the GNU system. There is no ethical reason to allow proprietary applications on the GNU system, but strategically it seems that disallowing them would do more to discourage use of the GNU system than to encourage development of free applications. That is why using the Library GPL is a good strategy for the C library.

---

[9] That was written in 1998. In 2009 we no longer maintain a long task list. The community develops free software so fast that we can't even keep track of it all. Instead, we have a list of High Priority Projects, a much shorter list of projects we really want to encourage people to write.

[10] This license is now called the GNU Lesser General Public License, to avoid giving the idea that all libraries ought to use it. See "Why You Shouldn't Use the Lesser GPL for Your Next Library," at `http://www.gnu.org/philosophy/why-not-lgpl.html`, for more information.

For other libraries, the strategic decision needs to be considered on a case-by-case basis. When a library does a special job that can help write certain kinds of programs, then releasing it under the GPL, limiting it to free programs only, is a way of helping other free software developers, giving them an advantage against proprietary software.

Consider GNU Readline, a library that was developed to provide command-line editing for BASH. Readline is released under the ordinary GNU GPL, not the Library GPL. This probably does reduce the amount Readline is used, but that is no loss for us. Meanwhile, at least one useful application has been made free software specifically so it could use Readline, and that is a real gain for the community.

Proprietary software developers have the advantages money provides; free software developers need to make advantages for each other. I hope some day we will have a large collection of GPL-covered libraries that have no parallel available to proprietary software, providing useful modules to serve as building blocks in new free software, and adding up to a major advantage for further free software development.

Scratching an Itch?

Eric Raymond[11] says that "Every good work of software starts by scratching a developer's personal itch."[12] Maybe that happens sometimes, but many essential pieces of GNU software were developed in order to have a complete free operating system. They come from a vision and a plan, not from impulse.

For example, we developed the GNU C Library because a Unix-like system needs a C library, BASH because a Unix-like system needs a shell, and GNU tar because a Unix-like system needs a tar program. The same is true for my own programs—the GNU C compiler, GNU Emacs, GDB and GNU Make.

Some GNU programs were developed to cope with specific threats to our freedom. Thus, we developed gzip to replace the Compress program, which had been lost to the community because of the LZW patents. We found people to develop LessTif, and more recently started GNOME and Harmony, to address the problems caused by certain proprietary libraries (see below). We are developing the GNU Privacy Guard to replace popular nonfree encryption software, because users should not have to choose between privacy and freedom.

Of course, the people writing these programs became interested in the work, and many features were added to them by various people for the sake of their own needs and interests. But that is not why the programs exist.

---

[11] Eric Raymond is a prominent open source advocate; see "Why Open Source Misses the Point of Free Software" (p. 75).

[12] Eric S. Raymond, *The Cathedral and the Bazaar: Musings on Linux and Open Source by an Accidental Revolutionary*, rev. ed. (Sebastopol, Calif.: O'Reilly, 2001), p. 23.

Unexpected Developments

At the beginning of the GNU Project, I imagined that we would develop the whole GNU system, then release it as a whole. That is not how it happened.

Since each component of the GNU system was implemented on a Unix system, each component could run on Unix systems long before a complete GNU system existed. Some of these programs became popular, and users began extending them and porting them—to the various incompatible versions of Unix, and sometimes to other systems as well.

The process made these programs much more powerful, and attracted both funds and contributors to the GNU Project. But it probably also delayed completion of a minimal working system by several years, as GNU developers' time was put into maintaining these ports and adding features to the existing components, rather than moving on to write one missing component after another.

The GNU Hurd

By 1990, the GNU system was almost complete; the only major missing component was the kernel. We had decided to implement our kernel as a collection of server processes running on top of Mach. Mach is a microkernel developed at Carnegie Mellon University and then at the University of Utah; the GNU Hurd is a collection of servers (i.e., a herd of GNUs) that run on top of Mach, and do the various jobs of the Unix kernel. The start of development was delayed as we waited for Mach to be released as free software, as had been promised.

One reason for choosing this design was to avoid what seemed to be the hardest part of the job: debugging a kernel program without a source-level debugger to do it with. This part of the job had been done already, in Mach, and we expected to debug the Hurd servers as user programs, with GDB. But it took a long time to make that possible, and the multithreaded servers that send messages to each other have turned out to be very hard to debug. Making the Hurd work solidly has stretched on for many years.

Alix

The GNU kernel was not originally supposed to be called the Hurd. Its original name was Alix—named after the woman who was my sweetheart at the time. She, a Unix system administrator, had pointed out how her name would fit a common naming pattern for Unix system versions; as a joke, she told her friends, "Someone should name a kernel after me." I said nothing, but decided to surprise her with a kernel named Alix.

It did not stay that way. Michael (now Thomas) Bushnell, the main developer of the kernel, preferred the name Hurd, and redefined Alix to refer to a certain part of the kernel—the part that would trap system calls and handle them by sending messages to Hurd servers.

Later, Alix and I broke up, and she changed her name; independently, the Hurd design was changed so that the C library would send messages directly to servers, and this made the Alix component disappear from the design.

But before these things happened, a friend of hers came across the name Alix in the Hurd source code, and mentioned it to her. So she did have the chance to find a kernel named after her.

Linux and GNU/Linux

The GNU Hurd is not suitable for production use, and we don't know if it ever will be. The capability-based design has problems that result directly from the flexibility of the design, and it is not clear whether solutions exist.

Fortunately, another kernel is available. In 1991, Linus Torvalds developed a Unix-compatible kernel and called it Linux. It was proprietary at first, but in 1992, he made it free software; combining Linux with the not-quite-complete GNU system resulted in a complete free operating system. (Combining them was a substantial job in itself, of course.) It is due to Linux that we can actually run a version of the GNU system today.

We call this system version GNU/Linux, to express its composition as a combination of the GNU system with Linux as the kernel. Please don't fall into the practice of calling the whole system "Linux," since that means attributing our work to someone else. Please give us equal mention.[13]

Challenges in Our Future

We have proved our ability to develop a broad spectrum of free software. This does not mean we are invincible and unstoppable. Several challenges make the future of free software uncertain; meeting them will require steadfast effort and endurance, sometimes lasting for years. It will require the kind of determination that people display when they value their freedom and will not let anyone take it away.

The following four sections discuss these challenges.

Secret Hardware

Hardware manufacturers increasingly tend to keep hardware specifications secret. This makes it difficult to write free drivers so that Linux and XFree86 can support new hardware. We have complete free systems today, but we will not have them tomorrow if we cannot support tomorrow's computers.

There are two ways to cope with this problem. Programmers can do reverse engineering to figure out how to support the hardware. The rest of us can choose the hardware that is supported by free software; as our numbers increase, secrecy of specifications will become a self-defeating policy.

Reverse engineering is a big job; will we have programmers with sufficient determination to undertake it? Yes—if we have built up a strong feeling that free software is a matter of principle, and nonfree drivers are intolerable. And will large numbers of us spend extra money, or even a little extra time, so we can use free drivers? Yes, if the determination to have freedom is widespread.

---

[13] See the "GNU/Linux FAQ," at `http://gnu.org/gnu/gnu-linux-faq.html`, and "Linux and the GNU System" (p. 64) for more on this issue.

[2008 note: this issue extends to the BIOS as well. There is a free BIOS, LibreBoot[14] (a distribution of coreboot); the problem is getting specs for machines so that LibreBoot can support them without nonfree "blobs."]

Nonfree Libraries

A nonfree library that runs on free operating systems acts as a trap for free software developers. The library's attractive features are the bait; if you use the library, you fall into the trap, because your program cannot usefully be part of a free operating system. (Strictly speaking, we could include your program, but it won't *run* with the library missing.) Even worse, if a program that uses the proprietary library becomes popular, it can lure other unsuspecting programmers into the trap.

The first instance of this problem was the Motif toolkit, back in the 80s. Although there were as yet no free operating systems, it was clear what problem Motif would cause for them later on. The GNU Project responded in two ways: by asking individual free software projects to support the free X Toolkit widgets as well as Motif, and by asking for someone to write a free replacement for Motif. The job took many years; LessTif, developed by the Hungry Programmers, became powerful enough to support most Motif applications only in 1997.

Between 1996 and 1998, another nonfree GUI toolkit library, called Qt, was used in a substantial collection of free software, the desktop KDE.

Free GNU/Linux systems were unable to use KDE, because we could not use the library. However, some commercial distributors of GNU/Linux systems who were not strict about sticking with free software added KDE to their systems—producing a system with more capabilities, but less freedom. The KDE group was actively encouraging more programmers to use Qt, and millions of new "Linux users" had never been exposed to the idea that there was a problem in this. The situation appeared grim.

The free software community responded to the problem in two ways: GNOME and Harmony.

GNOME, the GNU Network Object Model Environment, is GNU's desktop project. Started in 1997 by Miguel de Icaza, and developed with the support of Red Hat Software, GNOME set out to provide similar desktop facilities, but using free software exclusively. It has technical advantages as well, such as supporting a variety of languages, not just C++. But its main purpose was freedom: not to require the use of any nonfree software.

Harmony is a compatible replacement library, designed to make it possible to run KDE software without using Qt.

In November 1998, the developers of Qt announced a change of license which, when carried out, should make Qt free software. There is no way to be sure, but I think that this was partly due to the community's firm response to the problem that Qt posed when it was nonfree. (The new license is inconvenient and inequitable, so it remains desirable to avoid using Qt.)

---

[14] See `http://libreboot.org`.

[Subsequent note: in September 2000, Qt was rereleased under the GNU GPL, which essentially solved this problem.]

How will we respond to the next tempting nonfree library? Will the whole community understand the need to stay out of the trap? Or will many of us give up freedom for convenience, and produce a major problem? Our future depends on our philosophy.

Software Patents

The worst threat we face comes from software patents, which can put algorithms and features off limits to free software for up to twenty years. The LZW compression algorithm patents were applied for in 1983, and we still cannot release free software to produce proper compressed GIFs. [As of 2009 they have expired.] In 1998, a free program to produce MP3 compressed audio was removed from distribution under threat of a patent suit.

There are ways to cope with patents: we can search for evidence that a patent is invalid, and we can look for alternative ways to do a job. But each of these methods works only sometimes; when both fail, a patent may force all free software to lack some feature that users want. What will we do when this happens?

Those of us who value free software for freedom's sake will stay with free software anyway. We will manage to get work done without the patented features. But those who value free software because they expect it to be technically superior are likely to call it a failure when a patent holds it back. Thus, while it is useful to talk about the practical effectiveness of the "bazaar" model of development, and the reliability and power of some free software, we must not stop there. We must talk about freedom and principle.

Free Documentation

The biggest deficiency in our free operating systems is not in the software—it is the lack of good free manuals that we can include in our systems. Documentation is an essential part of any software package; when an important free software package does not come with a good free manual, that is a major gap. We have many such gaps today.

Free documentation, like free software, is a matter of freedom, not price. The criterion for a free manual is pretty much the same as for free software: it is a matter of giving all users certain freedoms. Redistribution (including commercial sale) must be permitted, online and on paper, so that the manual can accompany every copy of the program.

Permission for modification is crucial too. As a general rule, I don't believe that it is essential for people to have permission to modify all sorts of articles and books. For example, I don't think you or I are obliged to give permission to modify articles like this one, which describe our actions and our views.

But there is a particular reason why the freedom to modify is crucial for documentation for free software. When people exercise their right to modify the software, and add or change its features, if they are conscientious they will change the manual, too—so they can provide accurate and usable documentation with the modified program. A nonfree manual, which does not allow programmers to be conscientious and finish the job, does not fill our community's needs.

Some kinds of limits on how modifications are done pose no problem. For example, requirements to preserve the original author's copyright notice, the distribution terms, or the list of authors, are OK. It is also no problem to require modified versions to include notice that they were modified, even to have entire sections that may not be deleted or changed, as long as these sections deal with nontechnical topics. These kinds of restrictions are not a problem because they don't stop the conscientious programmer from adapting the manual to fit the modified program. In other words, they don't block the free software community from making full use of the manual.

However, it must be possible to modify all the *technical* content of the manual, and then distribute the result in all the usual media, through all the usual channels; otherwise, the restrictions do obstruct the community, the manual is not free, and we need another manual.

Will free software developers have the awareness and determination to produce a full spectrum of free manuals? Once again, our future depends on philosophy.

We Must Talk about Freedom

Estimates today are that there are ten million users of GNU/Linux systems such as Debian GNU/Linux and Red Hat "Linux." Free software has developed such practical advantages that users are flocking to it for purely practical reasons.

The good consequences of this are evident: more interest in developing free software, more customers for free software businesses, and more ability to encourage companies to develop commercial free software instead of proprietary software products.

But interest in the software is growing faster than awareness of the philosophy it is based on, and this leads to trouble. Our ability to meet the challenges and threats described above depends on the will to stand firm for freedom. To make sure our community has this will, we need to spread the idea to the new users as they come into the community.

But we are failing to do so: the efforts to attract new users into our community are far outstripping the efforts to teach them the civics of our community. We need to do both, and we need to keep the two efforts in balance.

"Open Source"

Teaching new users about freedom became more difficult in 1998, when a part of the community decided to stop using the term "free software" and say "open source software" instead.

Some who favored this term aimed to avoid the confusion of "free" with "gratis"—a valid goal. Others, however, aimed to set aside the spirit of principle that had motivated the free software movement and the GNU Project, and to appeal instead to executives and business users, many of whom hold an ideology that places profit above freedom, above community, above principle. Thus, the rhetoric of "open source" focuses on the potential to make high-quality, powerful software, but shuns the ideas of freedom, community, and principle.

The "Linux" magazines are a clear example of this—they are filled with advertisements for proprietary software that works with GNU/Linux. When the next Motif or Qt appears, will these magazines warn programmers to stay away from it, or will they run ads for it?

The support of business can contribute to the community in many ways; all else being equal, it is useful. But winning their support by speaking even less about freedom and principle can be disastrous; it makes the previous imbalance between outreach and civics education even worse.

"Free software" and "open source" describe the same category of software, more or less, but say different things about the software, and about values. The GNU Project continues to use the term "free software," to express the idea that freedom, not just technology, is important.

Try!

Yoda's aphorism ("There is no 'try' ") sounds neat, but it doesn't work for me. I have done most of my work while anxious about whether I could do the job, and unsure that it would be enough to achieve the goal if I did. But I tried anyway, because there was no one but me between the enemy and my city. Surprising myself, I have sometimes succeeded.

Sometimes I failed; some of my cities have fallen. Then I found another threatened city, and got ready for another battle. Over time, I've learned to look for threats and put myself between them and my city, calling on other hackers to come and join me.

Nowadays, often I'm not the only one. It is a relief and a joy when I see a regiment of hackers digging in to hold the line, and I realize, this city may survive—for now. But the dangers are greater each year, and now Microsoft has explicitly targeted our community. We can't take the future of freedom for granted. Don't take it for granted! If you want to keep your freedom, you must be prepared to defend it.

3 The Initial Announcement of the GNU Operating System

This is the original announcement of the GNU Project, posted by Richard Stallman on 27 September 1983.

The actual history of the GNU Project differs in many ways from this initial plan. For example, the beginning was delayed until January 1984. Several of the philosophical concepts of free software were not clarified until a few years later.

```
From mit-vax!mit-eddie!RMS@MIT-OZ
From: RMS%MIT-OZ@mit-eddie
Newsgroups: net.unix-wizards,net.usoft
Subject: new Unix implementation
Date: Tue, 27-Sep-83 12:35:59 EST
Organization: MIT AI Lab, Cambridge, MA
```

```
Free Unix!
```

```
Starting this Thanksgiving I am going to write a complete Unix-compatible
software system called GNU (for Gnu's Not Unix), and give it away free[1]
to everyone who can use it. Contributions of time, money, programs and
equipment are greatly needed.
```

```
To begin with, GNU will be a kernel plus all the utilities needed to write
and run C programs: editor, shell, C compiler, linker, assembler, and a few
other things. After this we will add a text formatter, a YACC, an Empire
game, a spreadsheet, and hundreds of other things. We hope to supply,
eventually, everything useful that normally comes with a Unix system, and
anything else useful, including on-line and hardcopy documentation.
```

```
GNU will be able to run Unix programs, but will not be identical to Unix. We
will make all improvements that are convenient, based on our experience with
other operating systems. In particular, we plan to have longer filenames,
file version numbers, a crashproof file system, filename completion perhaps,
terminal-independent display support, and eventually a Lisp-based window
system through which several Lisp programs and ordinary Unix programs can
share a screen. Both C and Lisp will be available as system programming
languages. We will have network software based on MIT's chaosnet protocol,
far superior to UUCP. We may also have something compatible with UUCP.
```

---

[1] The wording here was careless. The intention was that nobody would have to pay for *permission* to use the GNU system. But the words don't make this clear, and people often interpret them as saying that copies of GNU should always be distributed at little or no charge. That was never the intent.

Who Am I?

I am Richard Stallman, inventor of the original much-imitated EMACS editor, now at the Artificial Intelligence Lab at MIT. I have worked extensively on compilers, editors, debuggers, command interpreters, the Incompatible Timesharing System and the Lisp Machine operating system. I pioneered terminal-independent display support in ITS. In addition I have implemented one crashproof file system and two window systems for Lisp machines.

Why I Must Write GNU

I consider that the golden rule requires that if I like a program I must share it with other people who like it. I cannot in good conscience sign a nondisclosure agreement or a software license agreement.

So that I can continue to use computers without violating my principles, I have decided to put together a sufficient body of free software so that I will be able to get along without any software that is not free.

How You Can Contribute

I am asking computer manufacturers for donations of machines and money. I'm asking individuals for donations of programs and work.

One computer manufacturer has already offered to provide a machine. But we could use more. One consequence you can expect if you donate machines is that GNU will run on them at an early date. The machine had better be able to operate in a residential area, and not require sophisticated cooling or power.

Individual programmers can contribute by writing a compatible duplicate of some Unix utility and giving it to me. For most projects, such part-time distributed work would be very hard to coordinate; the independently-written parts would not work together. But for the particular task of replacing Unix, this problem is absent. Most interface specifications are fixed by Unix compatibility. If each contribution works with the rest of Unix, it will probably work with the rest of GNU.

If I get donations of money, I may be able to hire a few people full or part time. The salary won't be high, but I'm looking for people for whom knowing they are helping humanity is as important as money. I view this as a way of enabling dedicated people to devote their full energies to working on GNU by sparing them the need to make a living in another way.

For more information, contact me.
Arpanet mail:
  RMS@MIT-MC.ARPA

Usenet:
  ...!mit-eddie!RMS@OZ ...!mit-vax!RMS@OZ

US Snail:
  Richard Stallman
  166 Prospect St
  Cambridge, MA 02139

4 Free Software Is Even More Important Now

Since 1983, the Free Software Movement has campaigned for computer users' freedom—for users to control the software they use, rather than vice versa. When a program respects users' freedom and community, we call it "free software."

We also sometimes call it "libre software" to emphasize that we're talking about liberty, not price. Some proprietary (nonfree) programs, such as Photoshop, are very expensive; others, such as Flash Player, are available gratis—but that's a minor detail. Either way, they give the program's developer power over the users, power that no one should have.

Those two nonfree programs have something else in common: they are both *malware.* That is, both have functionalities designed to mistreat the user. Proprietary software nowadays is often malware because the developers' power corrupts them.[1] With free software, the users control the program, both individually and collectively. So they control what their computers do (assuming those computers are loyal and do what the users' programs tell them to do).

With proprietary software, the program controls the users, and some other entity (the developer or "owner") controls the program. So the proprietary program gives its developer power over its users. That is unjust in itself, and tempts the developer to mistreat the users in other ways.

Freedom means having control over your own life. If you use a program to carry out activities in your life, your freedom depends on your having control over the program. You deserve to have control over the programs you use, and all the more so when you use them for something important in your life.

Users' control over the program requires four essential freedoms.[2]

0. The freedom to run the program as you wish, for whatever purpose.

---

[1] See `http://gnu.org/proprietary/proprietary.html` for an evolving list of these threats.

[2] See p. 3 for the full definition of free software.

See `http://gnu.org/help` for ways to help the free software movement.

A substantially edited version of this article was published on the `Wired` web site as "Why Free Software Is More Important Now Than Ever Before" (*Wired*, 28 September 2013, `http://wired.com/opinion/2013/09/why-free-software-is-more-important-now-than-ever-before`). This version of this essay is part of *Free Software, Free Society: Selected Essays of Richard M. Stallman,* 3rd ed. (Boston: GNU Press, 2015).

1. The freedom to study the program's "source code," and change it, so the program does your computing as you wish. Programs are written by programmers in a programming language—like English combined with algebra—and that form of the program is the "source code." Anyone who knows programming, and has the program in source code form, can read the source code, understand its functioning, and change it too. When all you get is the executable form, a series of numbers that are efficient for the computer to run but extremely hard for a human being to understand, understanding and changing the program in that form are forbiddingly hard.
2. The freedom to make and distribute exact copies when you wish. (It is not an obligation; doing this is your choice. If the program is free, that doesn't mean someone has an obligation to offer you a copy, or that you have an obligation to offer him a copy. Distributing a program to users without freedom mistreats them; however, choosing not to distribute the program—using it privately—does not mistreat anyone.)
3. The freedom to make and distribute copies of your modified versions, when you wish.

The first two freedoms mean each user can exercise individual control over the program. With the other two freedoms, any group of users can together exercise *collective control* over the program. With all four freedoms, the users fully control the program. If any of them is missing or inadequate, the program is proprietary (nonfree), and unjust.

Other kinds of works are also used for practical activities, including recipes for cooking, educational works such as textbooks, reference works such as dictionaries and encyclopedias, fonts for displaying paragraphs of text, circuit diagrams for hardware for people to build, and patterns for making useful (not merely decorative) objects with a 3D printer. Since these are not software, the free software movement strictly speaking doesn't cover them; but the same reasoning applies and leads to the same conclusion: these works should carry the four freedoms.

A free program allows you to tinker with it to make it do what you want (or cease do to something you dislike). Tinkering with software may sound ridiculous if you are accustomed to proprietary software as a sealed box, but in the Free World it's a common thing to do, and a good way to learn programming. Even the traditional American pastime of tinkering with cars is obstructed because cars now contain nonfree software.

The Injustice of Proprietariness

If the users don't control the program, the program controls the users. With proprietary software, there is always some entity, the developer or "owner" of the program, that controls the program—and through it, exercises power over its users. A nonfree program is a yoke, an instrument of unjust power.

In outrageous cases (though this outrage has become quite usual) proprietary programs are designed to spy on the users, restrict them, censor them, and abuse them.[3] For instance, the operating system of Apple iThings does all of these, and so does Windows on mobile devices with ARM chips. Windows, mobile phone firmware, and Google Chrome for Windows include a universal back door that allows some company to change the program remotely without asking permission. The Amazon Kindle has a back door that can erase books.

The use of nonfree software in the "internet of things" would turn it into the "internet of telemarketers"[4] as well as the "internet of snoopers."

With the goal of ending the injustice of nonfree software, the free software movement develops free programs so users can free themselves. We began in 1984 by developing the free operating system GNU. Today, millions of computers run GNU, mainly in the GNU/Linux combination.[5]

Distributing a program to users without freedom mistreats those users; however, choosing not to distribute the program does not mistreat anyone. If you write a program and use it privately, that does no wrong to others. (You do miss an opportunity to do good, but that's not the same as doing wrong.) Thus, when we say all software must be free, we mean that every copy must come with the four freedoms, but we don't mean that someone has an obligation to offer you a copy.

Nonfree Software and SaaSS

Nonfree software was the first way for companies to take control of people's computing. Nowadays, there is another way, called Service as a Software Substitute, or SaaSS. That means letting someone else's server do your own computing tasks.

SaaSS doesn't mean the programs on the server are nonfree (though they often are). Rather, using SaaSS causes the same injustices as using a nonfree program: they are two paths to the same bad place. Take the example of a SaaSS translation service: The user sends text to the server, and the server translates it (from English to Spanish, say) and sends the translation back to the user. Now the job of translating is under the control of the server operator rather than the user.

---

[3] See footnote 1, on p. 28.

[4] Marcelo Rinesi, "The Telemarketer Singularity," 6 August 2015, `http://ieet.org/index.php/IEET/more/rinesi20150806`.

[5] See "The GNU Project" (p. 9), for more on the history of the GNU operating system, and `http://gnu.org/gnu/gnu-linux-faq.html`, for the "GNU/Linux FAQ."

If you use SaaSS, the server operator controls your computing. It requires entrusting all the pertinent data to the server operator, which will be forced to show it to the state as well—who does that server really serve, after all?[6]

Primary and Secondary Injustices

When you use proprietary programs or SaaSS, first of all you do wrong to yourself, because it gives some entity unjust power over you. For your own sake, you should escape. It also wrongs others if you make a promise not to share. It is evil to keep such a promise, and a lesser evil to break it; to be truly upright, you should not make the promise at all.

There are cases where using nonfree software puts pressure directly on others to do likewise. Skype is a clear example: when one person uses the nonfree Skype client software, it requires another person to use that software too—thus both surrender their freedom. (Google Hangouts have the same problem.) It is wrong even to suggest using such programs. We should refuse to use them even briefly, even on someone else's computer.

Another harm of using nonfree programs and SaaSS is that it rewards the perpetrator, encouraging further development of that program or "service," leading in turn to even more people falling under the company's thumb.

All the forms of indirect harm are magnified when the user is a public entity or a school.

Free Software and the State

Public agencies exist for the people, not for themselves. When they do computing, they do it for the people. They have a duty to maintain full control over that computing so that they can assure it is done properly for the people. (This constitutes the computational sovereignty of the state.) They must never allow control over the state's computing to fall into private hands.

To maintain control of the people's computing, public agencies must not do it with proprietary software (software under the control of an entity other than the state). And they must not entrust it to a service programmed and run by an entity other than the state, since this would be SaaSS.

Proprietary software has no security at all in one crucial case—against its developer. And the developer may help others attack. Microsoft shows Windows bugs to the NSA[7] (the US government digital spying agency) before fixing them. We do not know whether Apple does likewise, but it is under the same government pressure as Microsoft. If the government of any other country uses such software, it endangers national security.[8] Do you want the NSA to break into your government's computers?

---

[6] See "Who Does That Server Really Serve?" (p. 243) for more on this issue.

[7] Sean Gallagher, "NSA Gets Early Access to Zero-Day Data from Microsoft, Others," 14 June 2013, `http://arstechnica.com/security/2013/06/nsa-gets-early-access-to-zero-day-data-from-microsoft-others/`.

[8] See "Measures Governments Can User to Promote Free Software" (p. 36) for our suggested policies.

Free Software and Education

Schools (and this includes all educational activities) influence the future of society through what they teach. They should teach exclusively free software, so as to use their influence for the good. To teach a proprietary program is to implant dependence, which goes against the mission of education. By training in use of free software, schools will direct society's future towards freedom, and help talented programmers master the craft.

They will also teach students the habit of cooperating, helping other people. Each class should have this rule: "Students, this class is a place where we share our knowledge. If you bring software to class, you may not keep it for yourself. Rather, you must share copies with the rest of the class—including the program's source code, in case someone else wants to learn. Therefore, bringing proprietary software to class is not permitted except to reverse engineer it."

Proprietary developers would have us punish students who are good enough at heart to share software and thwart those curious enough to want to change it. This means a bad education.[9]

Free Software: More Than "Advantages"

I'm often asked to describe the "advantages" of free software. But the word "advantages" is too weak when it comes to freedom. Life without freedom is oppression, and that applies to computing as well as every other activity in our lives. We must refuse to give the developers of the programs or computing services control over the computing we do. This is the right thing to do, for selfish reasons; but not solely for selfish reasons.

Freedom includes the freedom to cooperate with others. Denying people that freedom means keeping them divided, which is the start of a scheme to oppress them. In the free software community, we are very much aware of the importance of the freedom to cooperate because our work consists of organized cooperation. If your friend comes to visit and sees you use a program, she might ask for a copy. A program which stops you from redistributing it, or says you're "not supposed to," is antisocial.

In computing, cooperation includes redistributing exact copies of a program to other users. It also includes distributing your changed versions to them. Free software encourages these forms of cooperation, while proprietary software forbids them. It forbids redistribution of copies, and by denying users the source code, it blocks them from making changes. SaaSS has the same effects: if your computing is done over the web in someone else's server, by someone else's copy of a program, you can't see it or touch the software that does your computing, so you can't redistribute it or change it.

---

[9] See `http://gnu.org/education` for more discussion of the use of free software in schools.

Conclusion

We deserve to have control of our own computing; how can we win this control? By rejecting nonfree software on the computers we own or regularly use, and rejecting SaaSS. By developing free software[10] (for those of us who are programmers). By refusing to develop or promote nonfree software or SaaSS. By spreading these ideas to others.[11]

We and thousands of users have done this since 1984, which is how we now have the free GNU/Linux operating system that anyone—programmer or not—can use. Join our cause, as a programmer or an activist. Let's make all computer users free.

[10] See "How to Choose a License for Your Own Work" (p. 174) for our licensing recommendations.

[11] See http://gnu.org/help for the various ways you could help.

5 Why Schools Should Exclusively Use Free Software

Educational activities (including schools) have a moral duty to teach only free software.

All computer users ought to insist on free software: it gives users the freedom to control their own computers—with proprietary software, the program does what its owner or developer wants it to do, not what the user wants it to do. Free software also gives users the freedom to cooperate with each other, to lead an upright life. These reasons apply to schools as they do to everyone. However, the purpose of this article is to present the additional reasons that apply specifically to education.

Free software can save schools money, but this is a secondary benefit. Savings are possible because free software gives schools, like other users, the freedom to copy and redistribute the software; the school system can give a copy to every school, and each school can install the program in all its computers, with no obligation to pay for doing so.

This benefit is useful, but we firmly refuse to give it first place, because it is shallow compared to the important ethical issues at stake. Moving schools to free software is more than a way to make education a little "better": it is a matter of doing good education instead of bad education. So let's consider the deeper issues.

Schools have a social mission: to teach students to be citizens of a strong, capable, independent, cooperating and free society. They should promote the use of free software just as they promote conservation and voting. By teaching students free software, they can graduate citizens ready to live in a free digital society. This will help society as a whole escape from being dominated by megacorporations.

In contrast, to teach a nonfree program is implanting dependence, which goes counter to the schools' social mission. Schools should never do this.

Why, after all, do some proprietary software developers offer gratis copies of their nonfree programs to schools? Because they want to *use* the schools to implant dependence on their products, like tobacco companies distributing gratis cigarettes to school children.[1] They will not give gratis copies to these students

[1] RJ Reynolds Tobacco Company was fined \$15m in 2002 for handing out free samples of cigarettes at events attended by children. See `http://bbc.co.uk/worldservice/sci_tech/features/health/tobaccotrial/usa.htm`.

This essay was originally published on `http://gnu.org`, in 2003. This version is part of *Free Software, Free Society: Selected Essays of Richard M. Stallman*, 3rd ed. (Boston: GNU Press, 2015).

once they've graduated, nor to the companies that they go to work for. Once you're dependent, you're expected to pay, and future upgrades may be expensive.

Free software permits students to learn how software works. Some students, natural-born programmers, on reaching their teens yearn to learn everything there is to know about their computer and its software. They are intensely curious to read the source code of the programs that they use every day.

Proprietary software rejects their thirst for knowledge: it says, "The knowledge you want is a secret—learning is forbidden!" Proprietary software is the enemy of the spirit of education, so it should not be tolerated in a school, except as an object for reverse engineering.

Free software encourages everyone to learn. The free software community rejects the "priesthood of technology," which keeps the general public in ignorance of how technology works; we encourage students of any age and situation to read the source code and learn as much as they want to know.

Schools that use free software will enable gifted programming students to advance. How do natural-born programmers learn to be good programmers? They need to read and understand real programs that people really use. You learn to write good, clear code by reading lots of code and writing lots of code. Only free software permits this.

How do you learn to write code for large programs? You do that by writing lots of changes in existing large programs. Free Software lets you do this; proprietary software forbids this. Any school can offer its students the chance to master the craft of programming, but only if it is a free software school.

The deepest reason for using free software in schools is for moral education. We expect schools to teach students basic facts and useful skills, but that is only part of their job. The most fundamental task of schools is to teach good citizenship, including the habit of helping others. In the area of computing, this means teaching people to share software. Schools, starting from nursery school, should tell their students, "If you bring software to school, you must share it with the other students. You must show the source code to the class, in case someone wants to learn. Therefore bringing nonfree software to class is not permitted, unless it is for reverse-engineering work."

Of course, the school must practice what it preaches: it should bring only free software to class (except objects for reverse-engineering), and share copies including source code with the students so they can copy it, take it home, and redistribute it further.

Teaching the students to use free software, and to participate in the free software community, is a hands-on civics lesson. It also teaches students the role model of public service rather than that of tycoons. All levels of school should use free software.

If you have a relationship with a school—if you are a student, a teacher, an employee, an administrator, a donor, or a parent—it's your responsibility to campaign for the school to migrate to free software. If a private request doesn't achieve the goal, raise the issue publicly in those communities; that is the way to make more people aware of the issue and find allies for the campaign.

6 Measures Governments Can Use to Promote Free Software

This article suggests policies for a strong and firm effort to promote free software within the state, and to lead the rest of the country towards software freedom.

The mission of the state is to organize society for the freedom and well-being of the people. One aspect of this mission, in the computing field, is to encourage users to adopt free software: software that respects the users' freedom.[1] A proprietary (nonfree) program tramples the freedom of those that use it; it is a social problem that the state should work to eradicate.

The state needs to insist on free software in its own computing for the sake of its computational sovereignty (the state's control over its own computing). All users deserve control over their computing, but the state has a responsibility to the people to maintain control over the computing it does on their behalf. Most government activities now depend on computing, and its control over those activities depends on its control over that computing. Losing this control in an agency whose mission is critical undermines national security.

Moving state agencies to free software can also provide secondary benefits, such as saving money and encouraging local software-support businesses.

In this text, "state entities" refers to all levels of government, and means public agencies including schools, public-private partnerships, largely state-funded activities such as charter schools, and "private" corporations controlled by the state or established with special privileges or functions by the state.

Education

The most important policy concerns education, since that shapes the future of the country:

- **Teach only free software**
  Educational activities, or at least those of state entities, must teach only free software (thus, they should never lead students to use a nonfree program), and should teach the civic reasons for insisting on free software. To teach a nonfree program is to teach dependence, which is contrary to the mission of the school.

[1] See p. 3 for the full definition of free software.

This article was first published on `http://gnu.org`, in 2011. This version is part of *Free Software, Free Society: Selected Essays of Richard M. Stallman*, 3rd ed. (Boston: GNU Press, 2015).

The State and the Public

Also crucial are state policies that influence what software individuals and organizations use:

- **Never require nonfree programs**
  Laws and public sector practices must be changed so that they never require or pressure individuals or organizations to use a nonfree program. They should also discourage communication and publication practices that imply such consequences (including Digital Restrictions Management[2]).
- **Distribute only free software**
  Whenever a state entity distributes software to the public, including programs included in or specified by its web pages, it must be distributed as free software, and must be capable of running on a platform containing exclusively free software.
- **State web sites**
  State entity web sites and network services must be designed so that users can use them, without disadvantage, by means of free software exclusively.
- **Free formats and protocols**
  State entities must use only file formats and communication protocols that are well supported by free software, preferably with published specifications. (We do not state this in terms of "standards" because it should apply to nonstandardized interfaces as well as standardized ones.) For example, they must not distribute audio or video recordings in formats that require Flash or nonfree codecs, and public libraries must not distribute works with Digital Restrictions Management.
- **Untie computers from licenses**
  Sale of computers must not require purchase of a proprietary software license. The seller should be required by law to offer the purchaser the option of buying the computer without the proprietary software and without paying the license fee. The imposed payment is a secondary wrong, and should not distract us from the essential injustice of proprietary software, the loss of freedom which results from using it. Nonetheless, the abuse of forcing users to pay for it gives certain proprietary software developers an additional unfair advantage, detrimental to users' freedom. It is proper for the state to prevent this abuse.

Computational Sovereignty

Several policies affect the computational sovereignty of the state. State entities must maintain control over their computing, not cede control to private hands. These points apply to all computers, including smartphones.

---

[2] See both our anti-DRM campaigns page, at `http://defectivebydesign.org/what_is_drm`, and p. 95 for more on this issue.

- **Migrate to free software**
  State entities must migrate to free software, and must not install, or continue using, any nonfree software except under a temporary exception. Only one agency should have the authority to grant these temporary exceptions, and only when shown compelling reasons. This agency's goal should be to reduce the number of exceptions to zero.
- **Develop free IT solutions**
  When a state entity pays for development of a computing solution, the contract must require it be delivered as free software, and that it be designed such that one can both run it and develop it on a 100-percent-free environment. All contracts must require this, so that if the developer does not comply with these requirements, the work cannot be paid for.
- **Choose computers for free software**
  When a state entity buys or leases computers, it must choose among the models that come closest, in their class, to being capable of running without any proprietary software. The state should maintain, for each class of computers, a list of the models authorized based on this criterion. Models available to both the public and the state should be preferred to models available only to the state.
- **Negotiate with manufacturers**
  The state should negotiate actively with manufacturers to bring about the availability in the market (to the state and the public) of suitable hardware products, in all pertinent product areas, that require no proprietary software.
- **Unite with other states**
  The state should invite other states to negotiate collectively with manufacturers about suitable hardware products. Together they will have more clout.

Computational Sovereignty II

The computational sovereignty (and security) of the state includes control over the computers that do the state's work. This requires avoiding Service as a Software Substitute,[3] unless the service is run by a state agency under the same branch of government, as well as other practices that diminish the state control over its computing. Therefore,

- **State must control its computers**
  Every computer that the state uses must belong to or be leased by the same branch of government that uses it, and that branch must not cede to outsiders the right to decide who has physical access to the computer, who can do maintenance (hardware or software) on it, or what software should be installed in it. If the computer is not portable, then while in use it must be in a physical space of which the state is the occupant (either as owner or as tenant).

---

[3] See "Who Does That Server Really Serve?" (p. 243) for more on SaaSS.

Influence Development

State policy affects free and nonfree software development:

- **Encourage free**
  The state should encourage developers to create or enhance free software and make it available to the public, e.g. by tax breaks and other financial incentive. Contrariwise, no such incentives should be granted for development, distribution or use of nonfree software.
- **Don't encourage nonfree**
  In particular, proprietary software developers should not be able to "donate" copies to schools and claim a tax write-off for the nominal value of the software. Proprietary software is not legitimate in a school.

E-Waste

Freedom should not imply e-waste:

- **Replaceable software**
  Many modern computers are designed to make it impossible to replace their preloaded software with free software. Thus, the only way to free them is to junk them. This practice is harmful to society.

  Therefore, it should be illegal, or at least substantially discouraged through heavy taxation, to sell, import or distribute in quantity a new computer (that is, not second-hand) or computer-based product for which secrecy about hardware interfaces or intentional restrictions prevent users from developing, installing and using replacements for any and all of the installed software that the manufacturer could upgrade. This would apply, in particular, to any device on which "jailbreaking" is needed to install a different operating system, or in which the interfaces for some peripherals are secret.

Technological Neutrality

With the measures in this article, the state can recover control over its computing, and lead the country's citizens, businesses and organizations towards control over their computing. However, some object on the grounds that this would violate the "principle" of technological neutrality.

The idea of technological neutrality is that the state should not impose arbitrary preferences on technical choices. Whether that is a valid principle is disputable, but it is limited in any case to issues that are merely technical. The measures advocated here address issues of ethical, social and political importance, so they are outside the scope of *technological* neutrality.[4] Only those who wish to subjugate a country would suggest that its government be "neutral" about its sovereignty or its citizens' freedom.

[4] See my article "Technological Neutrality and Free Software," at `http://www.gnu.org/philosophy/technological-neutrality.html`, for more on this issue.

7 Why Free Software Needs Free Documentation

The biggest deficiency in free operating systems is not in the software—it is the lack of good free manuals that we can include in these systems. Many of our most important programs do not come with full manuals. Documentation is an essential part of any software package; when an important free software package does not come with a free manual, that is a major gap. We have many such gaps today.

Once upon a time, many years ago, I thought I would learn Perl. I got a copy of a free manual, but I found it hard to read. When I asked Perl users about alternatives, they told me that there were better introductory manuals—but those were not free.

Why was this? The authors of the good manuals had written them for O'Reilly Associates, which published them with restrictive terms—no copying, no modification, source files not available—which exclude them from the free software community.

That wasn't the first time this sort of thing has happened, and (to our community's great loss) it was far from the last. Proprietary manual publishers have enticed a great many authors to restrict their manuals since then. Many times I have heard a GNU user eagerly tell me about a manual that he is writing, with which he expects to help the GNU Project—and then had my hopes dashed, as he proceeded to explain that he had signed a contract with a publisher that would restrict it so that we cannot use it.

Given that writing good English is a rare skill among programmers, we can ill afford to lose manuals this way.

Free documentation, like free software, is a matter of freedom, not price. The problem with these manuals was not that O'Reilly Associates charged a price for printed copies—that in itself is fine. (The Free Software Foundation sells printed copies of free GNU manuals, too.[1]) But GNU manuals are available in source code form, while these manuals are available only on paper. GNU manuals come with permission to copy and modify; the Perl manuals do not. These restrictions are the problems.

The criterion for a free manual is pretty much the same as for free software: it is a matter of giving all users certain freedoms. Redistribution (including commercial redistribution) must be permitted, so that the manual can accompany

[1] See `http://shop.fsf.org/category/books/` and `http://gnu.org/doc/doc.html`.

This essay was originally published on `http://gnu.org`, in 1996. This version is part of *Free Software, Free Society: Selected Essays of Richard M. Stallman*, 3rd ed. (Boston: GNU Press, 2015).

every copy of the program, on line or on paper. Permission for modification is crucial too.

As a general rule, I don't believe that it is essential for people to have permission to modify all sorts of articles and books. The issues for writings are not necessarily the same as those for software. For example, I don't think you or I are obliged to give permission to modify articles like this one, which describe our actions and our views.

But there is a particular reason why the freedom to modify is crucial for documentation for free software. When people exercise their right to modify the software, and add or change its features, if they are conscientious they will change the manual too—so they can provide accurate and usable documentation with the modified program. A manual which forbids programmers from being conscientious and finishing the job, or more precisely requires them to write a new manual from scratch if they change the program, does not fill our community's needs.

While a blanket prohibition on modification is unacceptable, some kinds of limits on the method of modification pose no problem. For example, requirements to preserve the original author's copyright notice, the distribution terms, or the list of authors, are OK. It is also no problem to require modified versions to include notice that they were modified, even to have entire sections that may not be deleted or changed, as long as these sections deal with nontechnical topics. (Some GNU manuals have them.)

These kinds of restrictions are not a problem because, as a practical matter, they don't stop the conscientious programmer from adapting the manual to fit the modified program. In other words, they don't block the free software community from making full use of the manual.

However, it must be possible to modify all the *technical* content of the manual, and then distribute the result through all the usual media, through all the usual channels; otherwise, the restrictions do block the community, the manual is not free, and so we need another manual.

Unfortunately, it is often hard to find someone to write another manual when a proprietary manual exists. The obstacle is that many users think that a proprietary manual is good enough—so they don't see the need to write a free manual. They do not see that the free operating system has a gap that needs filling.

Why do users think that proprietary manuals are good enough? Some have not considered the issue. I hope this article will do something to change that.

Other users consider proprietary manuals acceptable for the same reason so many people consider proprietary software acceptable: they judge in purely practical terms, not using freedom as a criterion. These people are entitled to their opinions, but since those opinions spring from values which do not include freedom, they are no guide for those of us who do value freedom.

Please spread the word about this issue. We continue to lose manuals to proprietary publishing. If we spread the word that proprietary manuals are not sufficient, perhaps the next person who wants to help GNU by writing documentation will realize, before it is too late, that he must above all make it free.

We can also encourage commercial publishers to sell free, copylefted manuals instead of proprietary ones.[2] One way you can help this is to check the distribution terms of a manual before you buy it, and prefer copylefted manuals to noncopylefted ones.

[2] See `http://gnu.org/doc/other-free-books.html` for a list of free books available from other publishers.

8 Selling Free Software

Many people believe that the spirit of the GNU Project is that you should not charge money for distributing copies of software, or that you should charge as little as possible—just enough to cover the cost. This is a misunderstanding.

Actually, we encourage people who redistribute free software[1] to charge as much as they wish or can. If a license does not permit users to make copies and sell them, it is a nonfree license. If this seems surprising to you, please read on.

The word "free" has two legitimate general meanings; it can refer either to freedom or to price. When we speak of "free software", we're talking about freedom, not price. (Think of "free speech", not "free beer".) Specifically, it means that a user is free to run the program, change the program, and redistribute the program with or without changes.

Free programs are sometimes distributed gratis, and sometimes for a substantial price. Often the same program is available in both ways from different places. The program is free regardless of the price, because users have freedom in using it.

Nonfree programs[2] are usually sold for a high price, but sometimes a store will give you a copy at no charge. That doesn't make it free software, though. Price or no price, the program is nonfree because its users are denied freedom.

Since free software is not a matter of price, a low price doesn't make the software free, or even closer to free. So if you are redistributing copies of free software, you might as well charge a substantial fee and *make some money.* Redistributing free software is a good and legitimate activity; if you do it, you might as well make a profit from it.

Free software is a community project, and everyone who depends on it ought to look for ways to contribute to building the community. For a distributor, the way to do this is to give a part of the profit to free software development projects or to the Free Software Foundation. This way you can advance the world of free software.

Distributing free software is an opportunity to raise funds for development. Don't waste it!

In order to contribute funds, you need to have some extra. If you charge too low a fee, you won't have anything to spare to support development.

---

[1] See p. 3 for the full definition of free software.

[2] Also known as "proprietary software." See p. 73 for more on this category of software.

For some views on the ideas of selling exceptions to free software licenses, such as the GNU GPL, see p. 219.

This essay was originally published on `http://gnu.org`, in 1996. This version is part of *Free Software, Free Society: Selected Essays of Richard M. Stallman*, 3rd ed. (Boston: GNU Press, 2015).

Will a Higher Distribution Price Hurt Some Users?

People sometimes worry that a high distribution fee will put free software out of range for users who don't have a lot of money. With proprietary software, a high price does exactly that—but free software is different.

The difference is that free software naturally tends to spread around, and there are many ways to get it.

Software hoarders try their damnedest to stop you from running a proprietary program without paying the standard price. If this price is high, that does make it hard for some users to use the program.

With free software, users don't *have* to pay the distribution fee in order to use the software. They can copy the program from a friend who has a copy, or with the help of a friend who has network access. Or several users can join together, split the price of one CD-ROM, then each in turn can install the software. A high CD-ROM price is not a major obstacle when the software is free.

Will a Higher Distribution Price Discourage Use of Free Software?

Another common concern is for the popularity of free software. People think that a high price for distribution would reduce the number of users, or that a low price is likely to encourage users.

This is true for proprietary software—but free software is different. With so many ways to get copies, the price of distribution service has less effect on popularity.

In the long run, how many people use free software is determined mainly by *how much free software can do,* and how easy it is to use. Many users do not make freedom their priority; they may continue to use proprietary software if free software can't do all the jobs they want done. Thus, if we want to increase the number of users in the long run, we should above all *develop more free software.*

The most direct way to do this is by writing needed free software[3] or manuals[4] yourself. But if you do distribution rather than writing, the best way you can help is by raising funds for others to write them.

The Term "Selling Software" Can Be Confusing Too

Strictly speaking, "selling" means trading goods for money. Selling a copy of a free program is legitimate, and we encourage it.

However, when people think of "selling software,"[5] they usually imagine doing it the way most companies do it: making the software proprietary rather than free.

So unless you're going to draw distinctions carefully, the way this article does, we suggest it is better to avoid using the term "selling software" and choose some other wording instead. For example, you could say "distributing free software for a fee"—that is unambiguous.

---

[3] See the Savannah Task List, at `http://savannah.gnu.org/projects/tasklist`.
[4] See `http://gnu.org/doc/doc.html`.
[5] See p. 101 for more on how the expression "sell software" is ambiguous.

High or Low Fees, and the GNU GPL

Except for one special situation, the GNU General Public License (GNU GPL) has no requirements about how much you can charge for distributing a copy of free software. You can charge nothing, a penny, a dollar, or a billion dollars. It's up to you, and the marketplace, so don't complain to us if nobody wants to pay a billion dollars for a copy.

The one exception is in the case where binaries are distributed without the corresponding complete source code. Those who do this are required by the GNU GPL to provide source code on subsequent request. Without a limit on the fee[6] for the source code, they would be able set a fee too large for anyone to pay—such as a billion dollars—and thus pretend to release source code while in truth concealing it. So in this case we have to limit the fee for source in order to ensure the user's freedom. In ordinary situations, however, there is no such justification for limiting distribution fees, so we do not limit them.

Sometimes companies whose activities cross the line stated in the GNU GPL plead for permission, saying that they "won't charge money for the GNU software" or such like. That won't get them anywhere with us. Free software is about freedom, and enforcing the GPL is defending freedom. When we defend users' freedom, we are not distracted by side issues such as how much of a distribution fee is charged. Freedom is the issue, the whole issue, and the only issue.

---

[6] See section 6 of the GNU GPL (p. 195).

9 Free Hardware and Free Hardware Designs

To what extent do the ideas of free software extend to hardware? Is it a moral obligation to make our hardware designs free, just as it is to make our software free? Does maintaining our freedom require rejecting hardware made from nonfree designs?

Definitions

Free software is a matter of freedom, not price; broadly speaking, it means that users are free to use the software and to copy and redistribute the software, with or without changes. More precisely, the definition is formulated in terms of the four essential freedoms.[1] To emphasize that "free" refers to freedom, not price, we often use the French or Spanish word "libre" along with "free."

Applying the same concept directly to hardware, *free hardware* means hardware that users are free to use and to copy and redistribute with or without changes. However, there are no copiers for hardware, aside from keys, DNA, and plastic objects' exterior shapes. Most hardware is made by fabrication from some sort of design. The design comes before the hardware.

Thus, the concept we really need is that of a *free hardware design.* That's simple: it means a design that permits users to use the design (i.e., fabricate hardware from it) and to copy and redistribute it, with or without changes. The design must provide the same four freedoms that define free software.

Then we can refer to hardware made from a free design as "free hardware," or "free-design hardware" to avoid possible misunderstanding.

People first encountering the idea of free software often think it means you can get a copy gratis. Many free programs are available for zero price, since it costs you nothing to download your own copy, but that's not what "free" means here. (In fact, some spyware programs such as Flash Player and Angry Birds are gratis although they are not free.) Saying "libre" along with "free" helps clarify the point.[2]

---

[1] See p. 3 for the list of the four freedoms.
[2] For a growing list of the ways in which surveillance has spread across industries, see `http://gnu.org/philosophy/proprietary/proprietary-surveillance.html`.

Most of this article was published in two parts on the `Wired` web site, as "Why We Need Free Digital Hardware Designs" (*Wired,* 11 March 2015, `http://wired.com/2015/03/need-free-digital-hardware-designs`) and "Hardware Designs Should Be Free. Here's How to Do It." (*Wired,* 18 March 2015, `http://wired.com/2015/03/richard-stallman-how-to-make-hardware-designs-free`).

It was published on `http://gnu.org` in 2015. This version is part of *Free Software, Free Society: Selected Essays of Richard M. Stallman,* 3rd ed. (Boston: GNU Press, 2015).

For hardware, this confusion tends to go in the other direction; hardware costs money to produce, so commercially made hardware won't be gratis (unless it is a loss-leader or a tie-in), but that does not prevent its design from being free/libre. Things you make in your own 3D printer can be quite cheap, but not exactly gratis since you will have to pay for the raw materials. In ethical terms, the freedom issue trumps the price issue totally, since a device that denies freedom to its users is worth less than nothing.

The terms "open hardware" and "open source hardware" are used by some with the same concrete meaning as "free hardware," but those terms downplay freedom as an issue. They were derived from the term "open source software," which refers more or less to free software but without talking about freedom or presenting the issue as a matter of right or wrong.[3] To underline the importance of freedom, we make a point of referring to freedom whenever it is pertinent; since "open" fails to do that, let's not substitute it for "free."

Hardware and Software

Hardware and software are fundamentally different. A program, even in compiled executable form, is a collection of data which can be interpreted as instruction for a computer. Like any other digital work, it can be copied and changed using a computer. A copy of a program has no inherent physical form or embodiment.

By contrast, hardware is a physical structure and its physicality is crucial. While the hardware's design might be represented as data, in some cases even as a program, the design is not the hardware. A design for a CPU can't execute a program. You won't get very far trying to type on a design for a keyboard or display pixels on a design for a screen.

Furthermore, while you can use a computer to modify or copy the hardware design, a computer can't convert the design into the physical structure it describes. That requires fabrication equipment.

The Boundary between Hardware and Software

What is the boundary, in digital devices, between hardware and software? It follows from the definitions. Software is the operational part of a device that can be copied and changed in a computer; hardware is the operational part that can't be. This is the right way to make the distinction because it relates to the practical consequences.

There is a gray area between hardware and software that contains firmware that *can* be upgraded or replaced, but is not meant ever to be upgraded or replaced once the product is sold. In conceptual terms, the gray area is rather narrow. In practice, it is important because many products fall in it. We can treat that firmware as hardware with a small stretch.

---

[3] See "Why Open Source Misses the Point of Free Software" (p. 75) for more on this issue.

Some have said that preinstalled firmware programs and Field-Programmable Gate Array chips (FPGAs) "blur the boundary between hardware and software," but I think that is a misinterpretation of the facts. Firmware that is installed during use is software; firmware that is delivered inside the device and can't be changed is software by nature, but we can treat it as if it were a circuit. As for FPGAs, the FPGA itself is hardware, but the gate pattern that is loaded into the FPGA is a kind of firmware.

Running free gate patterns on FPGAs could potentially be a useful method for making digital devices that are free at the circuit level. However, to make FPGAs usable in the free world, we need free development tools for them. The obstacle is that the format of the gate pattern file that gets loaded into the FPGA is secret. For many years there was no model of FPGA for which those files could be produced without nonfree (proprietary) tools.

As of 2015, free software tools are available for programming the Lattice iCE40,[4] a common model of FPGA, from input written in a hardware description language (HDL). It is also possible to compile C programs and run them on the Xilinx Spartan 6 LX9 FPGA with free tools,[5] but those do not support HDL input. We recommend that you reject other FPGA models until they too are supported by free tools.

As for the HDL code itself, it can act as software (when it is run on an emulator or loaded into an FPGA) or as a hardware design (when it is realized in immutable silicon or a circuit board).

The Ethical Question for 3D Printers

Ethically, software must be free;[6] a nonfree program is an injustice. Should we take the same view for hardware designs?

We certainly should, in the fields that 3D printing (or, more generally, any sort of personal fabrication) can handle. Printer patterns to make a useful, practical object (i.e., functional rather than decorative) *must* be free because they are works made for practical use. Users deserve control over these works, just as they deserve control over the software they use. Distributing a nonfree functional object design is as wrong as distributing a nonfree program.

Be careful to choose 3D printers that work with exclusively free software; the Free Software Foundation endorses such printers.[7] Some 3D printers are made from free hardware designs, but MakerBot's hardware designs are nonfree.[8]

---

[4] See `http://clifford.at/icestorm/`.
[5] See `https://github.com/Wolfgang-Spraul/fpgatools`.
[6] See "Free Software Is Even More Important Now" (p. 28).
[7] See `http://fsf.org/resources/hw/endorsement`.
[8] Rich Brown, "Pulling Back from Open Source Hardware, MakerBot Angers Some Adherents," 27 September 2012, `http://cnet.com/news/pulling-back-from-open-source-hardware-makerbot-angers-some-adherents/`.

Must We Reject Nonfree Digital Hardware?

Is a nonfree digital[9] hardware design an injustice? Must we, for our freedom's sake, reject all digital hardware made from nonfree designs, as we must reject nonfree software?

Due to the conceptual parallel between hardware designs and software source code, many hardware hackers are quick to condemn nonfree hardware designs just like nonfree software. I disagree because the circumstances for hardware and software are different.

Present-day chip and board fabrication technology resembles the printing press: it lends itself to mass production in a factory. It is more like copying books in 1950 than like copying software today.

Freedom to copy and change software is an ethical imperative because those activities are feasible for those who use software: the equipment that enables you to use the software (a computer) is also sufficient to copy and change it. Today's mobile computers are too weak to be good for this, but anyone can find a computer that's powerful enough.

Moreover, a computer suffices to download and run a version changed by someone else who knows how, even if you are not a programmer. Indeed, nonprogrammers download software and run it every day. This is why free software makes a real difference to nonprogrammers.

How much of this applies to hardware? Not everyone who can use digital hardware knows how to change a circuit design, or a chip design, but anyone who has a PC has the equipment needed to do so. Thus far, hardware is parallel to software, but next comes the big difference.

You can't build and run a circuit design or a chip design in your computer. Constructing a big circuit is a lot of painstaking work, and that's once you have the circuit board. Fabricating a chip is not feasible for individuals today; only mass production can make them cheap enough. With today's hardware technology, users can't download and run John H Hacker's modified version of a digital hardware design, as they could run John S Hacker's modified version of a program. Thus, the four freedoms don't give users today collective control over a hardware design as they give users collective control over a program. That's where the reasoning showing that all software must be free fails to apply to today's hardware technology.

In 1983 there was no free operating system, but it was clear that if we had one, we could immediately use it and get software freedom. All that was missing was the code for one.

In 2014, if we had a free design for a CPU chip suitable for a PC, mass-produced chips made from that design would not give us the same freedom in the hardware domain. If we're going to buy a product mass produced in a factory, this dependence on the factory causes most of the same problems as a

[9] As used here, "digital hardware" includes hardware with some analog circuits and components in addition to digital ones.

nonfree design. For free designs to give us hardware freedom, we need future fabrication technology.

We can envision a future in which our personal fabricators can make chips, and our robots can assemble and solder them together with transformers, switches, keys, displays, fans and so on. In that future we will all make our own computers (and fabricators and robots), and we will all be able to take advantage of modified designs made by those who know hardware. The arguments for rejecting nonfree software will then apply to nonfree hardware designs too.

That future is years away, at least. In the meantime, there is no need to reject hardware with nonfree designs on principle.

We Need Free Digital Hardware Designs

Although we need not reject digital hardware made from nonfree designs in today's circumstances, we need to develop free designs and should use them when feasible. They provide advantages today, and in the future they may be the only way to use free software.

Free hardware designs offer practical advantages. Multiple companies can fabricate one, which reduces dependence on a single vendor. Groups can arrange to fabricate them in quantity. Having circuit diagrams or HDL code makes it possible to study the design to look for errors or malicious functionalities (it is known that the NSA has procured malicious weaknesses in some computing hardware). Furthermore, free designs can serve as building blocks to design computers and other complex devices, whose specs will be published and which will have fewer parts that could be used against us.

Free hardware designs may become usable for some parts of our computers and networks, and for embedded systems, before we are able to make entire computers this way.

Free hardware designs may become essential even before we can fabricate the hardware personally, if they become the only way to avoid nonfree software. As common commercial hardware is increasingly designed to subjugate users, it becomes increasingly incompatible with free software, because of secret specifications and requirements for code to be signed by someone other than you. Cell phone modem chips and even some graphics accelerators already require firmware to be signed by the manufacturer. Any program in your computer, that someone else is allowed to change but you're not, is an instrument of unjust power over you; hardware that imposes that requirement is malicious hardware. In the case of cell phone modem chips, all the models now available are malicious.

Some day, free-design digital hardware may be the only platform that permits running a free system at all. Let us aim to have the necessary free digital designs before then, and hope that we have the means to fabricate them cheaply enough for all users.

If you design hardware, please make your designs free. If you use hardware, please join in urging and pressuring companies to make hardware designs free.

Levels of Design

Software has levels of implementation; a package might include libraries, commands and scripts, for instance. But these levels don't make a significant difference for software freedom because it is feasible to make all the levels free. Designing components of a program is the same sort of work as designing the code that combines them; likewise, building the components from source is the same sort of operation as building the combined program from source. To make the whole thing free simply requires continuing the work until we have done the whole job.

Therefore, we insist that a program be free at all levels. For a program to qualify as free, every line of the source code that composes it must be free, so that you can rebuild the program out of free source code alone.

Physical objects, by contrast, are often built out of components that are designed and build in a different kind of factory. For instance, a computer is made from chips, but designing (or fabricating) chips is very different from designing (or fabricating) the computer out of chips.

Thus, we need to distinguish *levels* in the design of a digital product (and maybe some other kinds of products). The circuit that connects the chips is one level; each chip's design is another level. In an FPGA, the interconnection of primitive cells is one level, while the primitive cells themselves are another level. In the ideal future we will want the design be free at all levels. Under present circumstances, just making one level free is a significant advance.

However, if a design at one level combines free and nonfree parts—for example, a "free" HDL circuit that incorporates proprietary "soft cores"—we must conclude that the design as a whole is nonfree at that level. Likewise for nonfree "wizards" or "macros," if they specify part of the interconnections of chips or programmably connected parts of chips. The free parts may be a step towards the future goal of a free design, but reaching that goal entails replacing the nonfree parts. They can never be admissible in the free world.

Licenses and Copyright for Free Hardware Designs

You make a hardware design free by releasing it under a free license. We recommend using the GNU General Public License, version 3 or later. We designed GPL version 3 with a view to such use.

Copyleft on circuits, and on nondecorative object shapes, doesn't go as far as one might suppose. The copyright on these designs only applies to the way the design is drawn or written. Copyleft is a way of using copyright law, so its effect carries only as far as copyright law carries.

For instance, a circuit, as a topology, cannot be copyrighted (and therefore cannot be copylefted). Definitions of circuits written in HDL can be copyrighted (and therefore copylefted), but the copyleft covers only the details of expression of the HDL code, not the circuit topology it generates. Likewise, a drawing or layout of a circuit can be copyrighted, so it can be copylefted, but this only covers the drawing or layout, not the circuit topology. Anyone can legally draw the same circuit topology in a different-looking way, or write a different HDL definition that produces the same circuit.

Copyright doesn't cover physical circuits, so when people build instances of the circuit, the design's license will have no legal effect on what they do with the devices they have built.

For drawings of objects, and 3D printer models, copyright doesn't cover making a different drawing of the same purely functional object shape. It also doesn't cover the functional physical objects made from the drawing. As far as copyright is concerned, everyone is free to make them and use them (and that's a freedom we need very much). In the US, copyright does not cover the functional aspects that the design describes,[10] but does cover decorative aspects. When one object has decorative aspects and functional aspects, you get into tricky ground.[11] All this may be true in your country as well, or it may not. Before producing objects commercially or in quantity, you should consult a local lawyer. Copyright is not the only issue you need to be concerned with. You might be attacked using patents, most likely held by entities that had nothing to do with making the design you're using, and there may be other legal issues as well.

Keep in mind that copyright law and patent law are totally different. It is a mistake to suppose that they have anything in common. This is why the term "intellectual property" is pure confusion and should be totally rejected.[12]

Promoting Free Hardware through Repositories

The most effective way to push for published hardware designs to be free is through rules in the repositories where they are published. Repository operators should place the freedom of the people who will use the designs above the preferences of people who make the designs. This means requiring designs of useful objects to be free, as a condition for posting them.

For decorative objects, that argument does not apply, so we don't have to insist they must be free. However, we should insist that they be sharable. Thus, a repository that handles both decorative object models and functional ones should have an appropriate license policy for each category.

For digital designs, I suggest that the repository insist on GNU GPL v3-or-later, Apache 2.0, or CC-0. For functional 3D designs, the repository should ask the design's author to choose one of four licenses: GNU GPL v3-or-later, Apache 2.0, CC-SA, CC-BY or CC-0. For decorative designs, it should GNU GPL v3-or-later, Apache 2.0, CC-0, or any of the CC licenses.

---

[10] See the US Copyright Office definition of "useful article," at `http://copyright.gov/register/va-useful.html`.

[11] An article by Public Knowledge ("3 Steps for Licensing Your 3D Printed Stuff," 6 March 2015, `https://publicknowledge.org/assets/uploads/documents/3_Steps_for_Licensing_Your_3D_Printed_Stuff.pdf`) gives useful information about this complexity, for the US, though it falls into the common mistake of using the bogus concept of "intellectual property" and the propaganda term "protection," which should not be used in connection with copyright. See p. 100 for the reason why.

[12] See "Did You Say 'Intellectual Property'? It's a Seductive Mirage" (p. 83).

The repository should require all designs to be published as source code, and source code in secret formats usable only by proprietary design programs is not really adequate. For a 3D model, the STL format is not the preferred format for changing the design and thus is not source code, so the repository should not accept it, except perhaps accompanying real source code.

There is no reason to choose one single format for the source code of hardware designs, but source formats that cannot yet be handled with free software should be accepted reluctantly at best.

Free Hardware and Warranties

In general, the authors of free hardware designs have no moral obligation to offer a warranty to those that fabricate the design. This is a different issue from the sale of physical hardware, which ought to come with a warranty from the seller and/or the manufacturer.

Conclusion

We already have suitable licenses to make our hardware designs free. What we need is to recognize as a community that this is what we should do and to insist on free designs when we fabricate objects ourselves.

10 Applying the Free Software Criteria

The four essential freedoms provide the criteria for whether a particular piece of code is free/libre (i.e., respects its users' freedom).[1] How should we apply them to judge whether a software package, an operating system, a computer, or a web page is fit to recommend?

Whether a program is free affects first of all our decisions about our private activities: to maintain our freedom, we need to reject the programs that would take it away. However, it also affects what we should say to others and do with others.

A nonfree program is an injustice. To distribute a nonfree program, to recommend a nonfree program to other people, or more generally steer them into a course that leads to using nonfree software, means leading them to give up their freedom. To be sure, leading people to use nonfree software is not the same as installing nonfree software in their computers, but we should not lead people in the wrong direction.

At a deeper level, we must not present a nonfree program as a solution because that would grant it legitimacy. Non-free software is a problem; to present it as a solution denies the existence of the problem.[2]

This article explains how we apply the basic free software criteria to judging various kinds of things, so we can decide whether to recommend them or not.

Software Packages

For a software package to be free, all the code in it must be free. But not only the code. Since documentation files including manuals, README, change log, and so on are essential technical parts of a software package, they must be free as well.[3] A software package is typically used alongside many other packages, and interacts with some of them. Which kinds of interaction with nonfree programs are ethically acceptable?

We developed GNU so that there would be a free operating system, because in 1983 none existed. As we developed the initial components of GNU, in the 1980s, it was inevitable that each component depended on nonfree software. For instance, no C program could run without a nonfree C compiler until GCC was working, and none could run without Unix libc until glibc was working. Each component could run only on nonfree systems, because all systems were nonfree.

---

[1] See p. 3 for the full definition of free software.

[2] My article "Avoiding Ruinous Compromises" (p. 253) elaborates on this issue.

[3] See "Free Software Needs Free Documentation" (p. 40) for more on this issue.

After we released a component that could run on some nonfree systems, users ported it to other nonfree systems; those ports were no worse, ethically, than the platform-specific code we needed to develop these components, so we incorporated their patches.

When the kernel, Linux, was freed in 1992, it filled the last gap in the GNU system. (Initially, in 1991, Linux had been distributed under a nonfree license.) The combination of GNU and Linux made a complete free operating system—GNU/Linux.[4]

At that point, we could have deleted the support for nonfree platforms, but we decided not to. A nonfree system is an injustice, but it's not our fault a user runs one. Supporting a free program on that system does not compound the injustice. And it's useful, not only for users of those systems, but also for attracting more people to contribute to developing the free program.

However, a nonfree program that runs on top of a free program is a completely different issue, because it leads users to take a step away from freedom. In some cases we disallow this: for instance, GCC prohibits nonfree plug-ins.[5] When a program permits nonfree add-ons, it should at least not steer people towards using them. For instance, we choose LibreOffice over OpenOffice because OpenOffice suggests use of nonfree add-ons, while LibreOffice shuns them. We developed IceCat[6] initially to avoid proposing the nonfree add-ons suggested by Firefox.

In practice, if the IceCat package explains how to run IceCat on MacOS, that will not lead people to run MacOS. But if it talked about some nonfree add-on, that would encourage IceCat users to install the add-on. Therefore, the IceCat package, including manuals and web site, shouldn't talk about such things.

Sometimes a free program and a nonfree program interoperate but neither is based on the other. Our rule for such cases is that if the nonfree program is very well known, we should tell people how to use our free program with it; but if the proprietary program is obscure, we should not hint that it exists. Sometimes we support interoperation with the nonfree program if that is installed, but avoid telling users about the possibility of doing so.

We reject "enhancements" that would work only on a nonfree system. Those would encourage people to use the nonfree system instead of GNU, scoring an own-goal.

---

[4] See "Linux and the GNU System" (p. 64) for information.

[5] For the reason why GCC prohibits nonfree plug-ins, see my response on the GCC mailing list, at `https://gcc.gnu.org/ml/gcc/2014-01/msg00247.html`.

[6] See `http://directory.fsf.org/wiki/IceCat`.

GNU/Linux Distros

After the liberation of Linux in 1992, people began developing GNU/Linux distributions ("distros"). Only a few distros are entirely free software.

The rules for a software package apply to a distro too: an ethical distro must contain only free software and steer users only towards free software. But what does it mean for a distro to "contain" a particular software package?

Some distros install programs from binary packages that are part of the distro; others build each program from upstream source, and literally *contain* only the recipes to download and build it. For issues of freedom, how a distro installs a given package is not significant; if it presents that package as an option, or its web site does, we say it "contains" that package.

The users of a free system have control over it, so they can install whatever they wish. Free distros provide general facilities with which users can install their own programs and their modified versions of free programs; they can also install nonfree programs. Providing these general facilities is not an ethical flaw in the distro, because the distro's developers are not responsible for what users get and install on their own initiative.

The developers become responsible for installation of nonfree software when they steer the users toward a nonfree program—for instance, by putting it in the distro's list of packages, or distributing it from their server, or presenting it as a solution rather than a problem. This is the point where most GNU/Linux distros have an ethical flaw.

People who install software packages on their own have a certain level of sophistication: if we tell them "Baby contains nonfree code, but Gbaby is free," we can expect them to take care to remember which is which. But distros are recommended to ordinary users who would forget such details. They would think, "What name did they say I should use? I think it was Baby."

Therefore, to recommend a distro to the general public, we insist that its name not be similar to a distro we reject, so our message recommending only the free distro can be reliably transmitted.

Another difference between a distro and a software package is how likely it is for nonfree code to be added. The developers of a program carefully check the code they add. If they have decided to make the program free, they are unlikely to add nonfree code. There have been exceptions, including the very harmful case of the "binary blobs" that were added to Linux, but they are a small fraction of the free programs that exist.

By contrast, a GNU/Linux distro typically contains thousands of packages, and the distro's developers may add hundreds of packages a year. Without a careful effort to avoid packages that contain some nonfree software, some will surely creep in. Since the free distros are few in number, as a condition for listing that distro, we ask the developers of each free distro to make a commitment to keep the distro free software by removing any nonfree code or malware. See the GNU free system distribution guidelines, at `http://gnu.org/distros/free-system-distribution-guidelines.html`.

We don't ask for such promises for free software packages: it's not feasible, and fortunately not necessary. To get promises from the developers of 30,000 free programs to keep them free would avoid a few problems, at the cost of much work for the FSF staff; in addition, most of those developers have no relationship with the GNU Project and might have no interest in making us any promises. So we deal with the rare cases that change from free to nonfree, when we find out about them.

Peripherals

A computer peripheral needs software in the computer—perhaps a driver, perhaps firmware to be loaded by the system into the peripheral to make it run. Thus, a peripheral is acceptable to use and recommend if it can be used from a computer that has no nonfree software installed—if the peripheral's driver, and any firmware that the system needs to load into it, are free.

It is simple to check this: connect the peripheral to a computer running a totally free GNU/Linux distro and see if it works. But most users would like to know *before* they buy the peripheral, so we list information about many peripherals in `h-node.org`, a hardware database for fully free operating systems.

Computers

A computer contains software at various levels. On what criterion should we certify that a computer "Respects Your Freedom"?

Obviously the operating system and everything above it must be free. In the 90s, the startup software (BIOS, then) became replaceable, and since it runs on the CPU, it is the same sort of issue as the operating system. Thus, programs such as firmware and drivers that are installed in or with the system or the startup software must be free.

If a computer has hardware features that require nonfree drivers or firmware installed with the system, we may be able to endorse it. If it is usable without those features, and if we think most people won't be led to install the nonfree software to make them function, then we can endorse it. Otherwise, we can't. This will be a judgment call.

A computer can have modifiable preinstalled firmware and microcode at lower levels. It can also have code in true read-only memory. We decided to ignore these programs in our certification criteria today, because otherwise no computer could comply, and because firmware that is not normally changed is ethically equivalent to circuits. So our certification criteria cover only the code that runs on the computer's main processor and is not in true read-only memory. When and as free software becomes possible for other levels of processing, we will require free software at those levels too.

Since certifying a product is active promotion of it, we insist that the seller support us in return, by talking about free software rather than open source[7] and referring to the combination of GNU and Linux as "GNU/Linux."[8] We have no obligation to actively promote projects that won't recognize our work and support our movement.

See `http://www.fsf.org/resources/hw/endorsement/criteria` for our certification criteria.

Web Pages

Nowadays many web pages contain complex JavaScript programs and won't work without them. This is a harmful practice since it hampers users' control over their computing. Furthermore, most of these programs are nonfree, an injustice. Often the JavaScript code spies on the user.[9] JavaScript has morphed into a attack on users' freedom.

To address this problem, we have developed LibreJS, an add-on for Firefox that blocks nontrivial nonfree JavaScript code. (There is no need to block the simple scripts that implement minor user interface hacks.) We ask sites to please free their JavaScript programs and mark their licenses for LibreJS to recognize.

Meanwhile, is it ethical to link to a web page that contains a nonfree JavaScript program? If we were totally unyielding, we would link only to free JavaScript code. However, many pages do work even when their JavaScript code is not run. Also, you will most often encounter nonfree JavaScript in other ways besides following our links; to avoid it, you must use LibreJS or disable JavaScript. So we have decided to go ahead and link to pages that work without nonfree JavaScript, while urging users to protect themselves from nonfree JavaScript in general.

However, if a page can't do its job without running the nonfree JavaScript code, linking to it undeniably asks people to run that nonfree code. On principle, we do not link to such pages.

Conclusion

Applying the basic idea that *software should be free* to different situations leads to different practical policies. As new situations arise, the GNU Project and the Free Software Foundation will adapt our freedom criteria so as to lead computer users towards freedom, in practice and in principle. By recommending only freedom-respecting programs, distros, and hardware products, and stating your policy, you can give much-needed support to the free software movement.

---

[7] See "Free Software Is Even More Important Now" (p. 28) and "Why Open Source Misses the Point of Free Software" (p. 75).

[8] See "What's in a Name" (p. 61).

[9] See "The JavaScript Trap" (p. 230).

Part II:
What's in a Name?

11 What's in a Name?

Names convey meanings; our choice of names determines the meaning of what we say. An inappropriate name gives people the wrong idea. A rose by any other name would smell as sweet—but if you call it a pen, people will be rather disappointed when they try to write with it. And if you call pens "roses," people may not realize what they are good for. If you call our operating system Linux, that conveys a mistaken idea of the system's origin, history, and purpose. If you call it GNU/Linux, that conveys (though not in detail) an accurate idea.

Does this really matter for our community? Is it important whether people know the system's origin, history, and purpose? Yes—because people who forget history are often condemned to repeat it. The Free World that has developed around GNU/Linux is not guaranteed to survive; the problems that led us to develop GNU are not completely eradicated, and they threaten to come back.

When I explain why it's appropriate to call the operating system GNU/Linux rather than Linux, people sometimes respond this way:

> Granted that the GNU Project deserves credit for this work, is it really worth a fuss when people don't give credit? Isn't the important thing that the job was done, not who did it? You ought to relax, take pride in the job well done, and not worry about the credit.

This would be wise advice, if only the situation were like that—if the job were done and it were time to relax. If only that were true! But challenges abound, and this is no time to take the future for granted. Our community's strength rests on commitment to freedom and cooperation. Using the name GNU/Linux is a way for people to remind themselves and inform others of these goals.

It is possible to write good free software without thinking of GNU; much good work has been done in the name of Linux also. But the term "Linux" has been associated ever since it was first coined with a philosophy that does not make a commitment to the freedom to cooperate. As the name is increasingly used by business, we will have even more trouble making it connect with community spirit.

A great challenge to the future of free software comes from the tendency of the "Linux" distribution companies to add nonfree software to GNU/Linux

---

To learn more about this issue, you can read our GNU/Linux FAQ, at `http://gnu.org/gnu/gnu-linux-faq.html`, the essay "Linux and the GNU System" (p. 64), which gives a history of the GNU/Linux system as it relates to this issue of naming, and the article "GNU Users Who Have Never Heard of GNU," at `http://gnu.org/gnu/gnu-users-never-heard-of-gnu.html`.

This essay was originally published on `http://gnu.org`, in 2000. This version is part of *Free Software, Free Society: Selected Essays of Richard M. Stallman*, 3rd ed. (Boston: GNU Press, 2015).

in the name of convenience and power. All the major commercial distribution developers do this; none limits itself to free software. Most of them do not clearly identify the nonfree packages in their distributions. Many even develop nonfree software and add it to the system. Some outrageously advertise "Linux" systems that are "licensed per seat," which give the user as much freedom as Microsoft Windows.

People try to justify adding nonfree software in the name of the "popularity of Linux"—in effect, valuing popularity above freedom. Sometimes this is openly admitted. For instance, *Wired* magazine said that Robert McMillan, editor of *Linux Magazine*, "feels that the move toward open source software should be fueled by technical, rather than political, decisions."And Caldera's CEO openly urged users to drop the goal of freedom and work instead for the "popularity of Linux."[1]

Adding nonfree software to the GNU/Linux system may increase the popularity, if by popularity we mean the number of people using some of GNU/Linux in combination with nonfree software. But at the same time, it implicitly encourages the community to accept nonfree software as a good thing, and forget the goal of freedom. It is not good to drive faster if you can't stay on the road.

When the nonfree "add-on" is a library or programming tool, it can become a trap for free software developers. When they write free software that depends on the nonfree package, their software cannot be part of a completely free system. Motif and Qt trapped large amounts of free software in this way in the past, creating problems whose solutions took years. Motif remained somewhat of a problem until it became obsolete and was no longer used. Later, Sun's nonfree

Java implementation had a similar effect: the Java Trap,[2] fortunately now mostly corrected. If our community keeps moving in this direction, it could redirect the future of GNU/Linux into a mosaic of free and nonfree components. Five years from now, we will surely still have plenty of free software; but if we are not careful, it will hardly be usable without the nonfree software that users expect to find with it. If this happens, our campaign for freedom will have failed.

If releasing free alternatives were simply a matter of programming, solving future problems might become easier as our community's development resources increase. But we face obstacles that threaten to make this harder: laws that prohibit free software. As software patents mount up, and as laws like the Digital Millennium Copyright Act are used to prohibit the development of free software for important jobs such as viewing a DVD or listening to a RealAudio stream, we will find ourselves with no clear way to fight the patented and secret data formats except to *reject the nonfree programs that use them.*

Meeting these challenges will require many different kinds of effort. But what we need above all, to confront any kind of challenge, is to remember the

---

[1] Dietmar Muller, "Stallman: Love Is Not Free," 10 July 2001, `http://zdnet.com/article/stallman-love-is-not-free/`.

[2] See "Free but Shackled—The Java Trap," at `http://gnu.org/philosophy/java-trap.html`, for more on this issue.

goal of freedom to cooperate. We can't expect a mere desire for powerful, reliable software to motivate people to make great efforts. We need the kind of determination that people have when they fight for their freedom and their community—determination to keep on for years and not give up.

In our community, this goal and this determination emanate mainly from the GNU Project. We're the ones who talk about freedom and community as something to stand firm for; the organizations that speak of "Linux" normally don't say this. The magazines about "Linux" are typically full of ads for nonfree software; the companies that package "Linux" add nonfree software to the system; other companies "support Linux" by developing nonfree applications to run on GNU/Linux; the user groups for "Linux" typically invite salesmen to present those applications. The main place people in our community are likely to come across the idea of freedom and determination is in the GNU Project.

But when people come across it, will they feel it relates to them?

People who know they are using a system that came out of the GNU Project can see a direct relationship between themselves and GNU. They won't automatically agree with our philosophy, but at least they will see a reason to think seriously about it. In contrast, people who consider themselves "Linux users," and believe that the GNU Project "developed tools which proved to be useful in Linux," typically perceive only an indirect relationship between GNU and themselves. They may just ignore the GNU philosophy when they come across it.

The GNU Project is idealistic, and anyone encouraging idealism today faces a great obstacle: the prevailing ideology encourages people to dismiss idealism as "impractical." Our idealism has been extremely practical: it is the reason we have a free GNU/Linux operating system. People who love this system ought to know that it is our idealism made real.

If "the job" really were done, if there were nothing at stake except credit, perhaps it would be wiser to let the matter drop. But we are not in that position. To inspire people to do the work that needs to be done, we need to be recognized for what we have already done. Please help us, by calling the operating system GNU/Linux.

12 Linux and the GNU System

Many computer users run a modified version of the GNU system[1] every day, without realizing it. Through a peculiar turn of events, the version of GNU which is widely used today is often called "Linux," and many of its users are not aware that it is basically the GNU system, developed by the GNU Project.[2]

There really is a Linux, and these people are using it, but it is just a part of the system they use. Linux is the kernel: the program in the system that allocates the machine's resources to the other programs that you run. The kernel is an essential part of an operating system, but useless by itself; it can only function in the context of a complete operating system. Linux is normally used in combination with the GNU operating system: the whole system is basically GNU with Linux added, or GNU/Linux. All the so-called "Linux" distributions are really distributions of GNU/Linux.

Many users do not understand the difference between the kernel, which is Linux, and the whole system, which they also call "Linux." The ambiguous use of the name doesn't help people understand. These users often think that Linus Torvalds developed the whole operating system in 1991, with a bit of help.

Programmers generally know that Linux is a kernel. But since they have generally heard the whole system called "Linux" as well, they often envisage a history that would justify naming the whole system after the kernel. For example, many believe that once Linus Torvalds finished writing Linux, the kernel, its users looked around for other free software to go with it, and found that (for no particular reason) most everything necessary to make a Unix-like system was already available.

What they found was no accident—it was the not-quite-complete GNU system. The available free software[3] added up to a complete system because the GNU Project had been working since 1984 to make one. In the GNU Manifesto[4] we set forth the goal of developing a free Unix-like system, called GNU. The Initial Announcement[5] of the GNU Project also outlines some of the original plans for the GNU system. By the time Linux was started, GNU was almost finished.

---

[1] See p. 71 for information on GNU system.

[2] For more information, see both "GNU Users Who Have Never Heard of GNU," at `http://gnu.org/gnu/gnu-users-never-heard-of-gnu.html`, and "Overview of the GNU System," at `http://gnu.org/gnu/gnu-history.html`.

[3] See p. 3 for the full definition of free software.

[4] See `http://gnu.org/gnu/manifesto.html` for the "GNU Manifesto."

[5] See p. 26 for the "Initial Announcement."

This essay was originally published on `http://gnu.org`, in 1997. This version is part of *Free Software, Free Society: Selected Essays of Richard M. Stallman*, 3rd ed. (Boston: GNU Press, 2015).

Most free software projects have the goal of developing a particular program for a particular job. For example, Linus Torvalds set out to write a Unix-like kernel (Linux); Donald Knuth set out to write a text formatter (TeX); Bob Scheifler set out to develop a window system (the X Window System). It's natural to measure the contribution of this kind of project by specific programs that came from the project.

If we tried to measure the GNU Project's contribution in this way, what would we conclude? One CD-ROM vendor found that in their "Linux distribution," GNU software[6] was the largest single contingent, around 28 percent of the total source code, and this included some of the essential major components without which there could be no system. Linux itself was about 3 percent. (The proportions in 2008 are similar: in the "main" repository of gNewSense, Linux is 1.5 percent and GNU packages are 15 percent.) So if you were going to pick a name for the system based on who wrote the programs in the system, the most appropriate single choice would be "GNU."

But that is not the deepest way to consider the question. The GNU Project was not, is not, a project to develop specific software packages. It was not a project to develop a C compiler,[7] although we did that. It was not a project to develop a text editor, although we developed one. The GNU Project set out to develop *a complete free Unix-like system:* GNU.

Many people have made major contributions to the free software in the system, and they all deserve credit for their software. But the reason it is *an integrated system*—and not just a collection of useful programs—is because the GNU Project set out to make it one. We made a list of the programs needed to make a *complete* free system, and we systematically found, wrote, or found people to write everything on the list. We wrote essential but unexciting[8] components because you can't have a system without them. Some of our system components, the programming tools, became popular on their own among programmers, but we wrote many components that are not tools.[9] We even developed a chess game, GNU Chess, because a complete system needs games too.

By the early 90s we had put together the whole system aside from the kernel. We had also started a kernel, the GNU Hurd (`http://gnu.org/software/hurd/hurd.html`), which runs on top of Mach. Developing this kernel has been

---

[6] See p. 72 for more information on GNU software.

[7] See `http://gnu.org/software/gcc/` for the GCC homepage.

[8] These unexciting but essential components include the GNU assembler (GAS) and the linker (GNU ld), both are now part of the GNU Binutils package (`http://gnu.org/software/binutils/`), GNU tar (`http://gnu.org/software/tar/`), and many more.

[9] For instance, The Bourne Again Shell (BASH), the PostScript interpreter Ghostscript (`http://gnu.org/software/ghostscript/ghostscript.html`), and the GNU C Library (`http://gnu.org/software/libc/libc.html`) are not programming tools. Neither are GNUCash, GNOME, and GNU Chess.

a lot harder than we expected; the GNU Hurd started working reliably in 2001, but it is a long way from being ready for people to use in general.[10]

Fortunately, we didn't have to wait for the Hurd, because of Linux. Once Torvalds freed Linux in 1992, it fit into the last major gap in the GNU system. People could then combine Linux with the GNU system[11] to make a complete free system—a version of the GNU system which also contained Linux. The GNU/Linux system, in other words.

Making them work well together was not a trivial job. Some GNU components[12] needed substantial change to work with Linux. Integrating a complete system as a distribution that would work "out of the box" was a big job, too. It required addressing the issue of how to install and boot the system—a problem we had not tackled, because we hadn't yet reached that point. Thus, the people who developed the various system distributions did a lot of essential work. But it was work that, in the nature of things, was surely going to be done by someone.

The GNU Project supports GNU/Linux systems as well as *the* GNU system. The FSF funded the rewriting of the Linux-related extensions to the GNU C Library, so that now they are well integrated, and the newest GNU/Linux systems use the current library release with no changes. The FSF also funded an early stage of the development of Debian GNU/Linux.

Today there are many different variants of the GNU/Linux system (often called "distros"). Most of them include nonfree software—their developers follow the philosophy associated with Linux rather than that of GNU. But there are also completely free GNU/Linux distros.[13] The FSF supports computer facilities for gNewSense (`http://gnewsense.org`).

Making a free GNU/Linux distribution is not just a matter of eliminating various nonfree programs. Nowadays, the usual version of Linux contains nonfree programs too. These programs are intended to be loaded into I/O devices when the system starts, and they are included, as long series of numbers, in the "source code" of Linux. Thus, maintaining free GNU/Linux distributions now entails maintaining a free version of Linux (`http://directory.fsf.org/project/linux`) too.

Whether you use GNU/Linux or not, please don't confuse the public by using the name "Linux" ambiguously. Linux is the kernel, one of the essential major components of the system. The system as a whole is basically the GNU system, with Linux added. When you're talking about this combination, please call it "GNU/Linux."

---

[10] See `http://gnu.org/software/hurd/hurd-and-linux.html` for why the FSF developed the GNU Hurd kernel.

[11] See "Notes for Linux Release 0.01," at `http://ftp.funet.fi/pub/linux/historical/kernel/old-versions/RELNOTES-0.01`.

[12] For instance, the GNU C Library (`http://gnu.org/software/libc/libc.html`).

[13] See `http://gnu.org/distros/` for a list of all the completely free distributions we know about.

This article and "The GNU Project" (p. 9) are good choices for promoting "GNU/Linux." If you mention Linux, the kernel, and want to add a further reference, the FOLDOC (the Free On-Line Dictionary of Computing) web address, `http://foldoc.org/linux`, is a good URL to use.

Postscripts

Aside from GNU, one other project has independently produced a free Unix-like operating system. This system is known as BSD, and it was developed at UC Berkeley. It was nonfree in the 80s, but became free in the early 90s. A free operating system that exists today is almost certainly either a variant of the GNU system, or a kind of BSD system.[14]

People sometimes ask whether BSD too is a version of GNU, like GNU/Linux. The BSD developers were inspired to make their code free software by the example of the GNU Project, and explicit appeals from GNU activists helped persuade them, but the code had little overlap with GNU. BSD systems today use some GNU programs, just as the GNU system and its variants use some BSD programs; however, taken as wholes, they are two different systems that evolved separately. The BSD developers did not write a kernel and add it to the GNU system, and a name like GNU/BSD would not fit the situation.[15]

---

[14] Since that was written, a nearly-all-free Windows-like system has been developed, but technically it is not at all like GNU or Unix, so it doesn't really affect this issue. Most of the kernel of Solaris has been made free, but if you wanted to make a free system out of that, aside from replacing the missing parts of the kernel, you would also need to put it into GNU or BSD.

[15] On the other hand, in the years since this article was written, the GNU C Library has been ported to several versions of the BSD kernel, which made it straightforward to combine the GNU system with that kernel. Just as with GNU/Linux, these are indeed variants of GNU, and are therefore called, for instance, GNU/kFreeBSD and GNU/kNetBSD depending on the kernel of the system. Ordinary users on typical desktops can hardly distinguish between GNU/Linux and GNU/*BSD.

13 Categories of Free and Nonfree Software

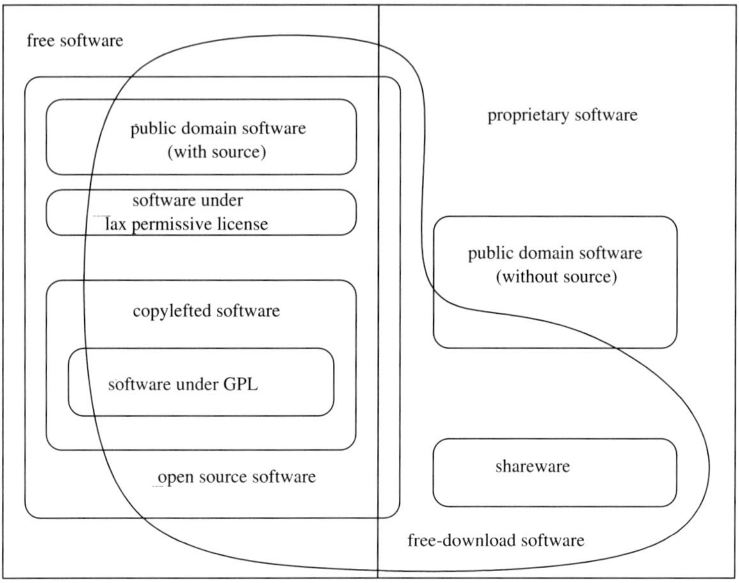

This diagram, originally by Chao-Kuei and updated by several others since, explains the different categories of software. It's available as a Scalable Vector Graphic, at `http://gnu.org/philosophy/category.svg`*, and as an XFig document, at* `http://gnu.org/philosophy/category.fig`*, under the terms of any of the GNU GPL v2-or-later, the GNU FDL v1.2-or-later, or the Creative Commons Attribution-Share Alike v2.0-or-later.*

See also "Words to Avoid (or Use with Care) Because They Are Loaded or Confusing" (p. 89).

This list was originally published on `http://gnu.org`, in 1996. This version is part of *Free Software, Free Society: Selected Essays of Richard M. Stallman*, 3rd ed. (Boston: GNU Press, 2015).

Free Software

Free software is software that comes with permission for anyone to use, copy, and/or distribute, either verbatim or with modifications, either gratis or for a fee. In particular, this means that source code must be available. "If it's not source, it's not software." This is a simplified description; see also the full definition, on p. 3.

If a program is free, then it can potentially be included in a free operating system such as GNU, or free versions of the GNU/Linux system.[1]

There are many different ways to make a program free—many questions of detail, which could be decided in more than one way and still make the program free. Some of the possible variations are described below. For information on specific free software licenses, see the license list page, at `http://gnu.org/licenses/license-list.html`.

Free software is a matter of freedom, not price. But proprietary software companies typically use the term "free software" to refer to price. Sometimes they mean that you can obtain a binary copy at no charge; sometimes they mean that a copy is bundled with a computer that you are buying, and the price includes both. Either way, it has nothing to do with what we mean by free software in the GNU Project.

Because of this potential confusion, when a software company says its product is free software, always check the actual distribution terms to see whether users really have all the freedoms that free software implies. Sometimes it really is free software; sometimes it isn't.

Many languages have two separate words for "free" as in freedom and "free" as in zero price. For example, French has "libre" and "gratuit." Not so English; there is a word "gratis" that refers unambiguously to price, but no common adjective that refers unambiguously to freedom. So if you are speaking another language, we suggest you translate "free" into your language to make it clearer. See our list of translations of the term "free software" into various other languages (p. 274).

Free software is often more reliable than nonfree software.[2]

Open Source Software

The term "open source" software is used by some people to mean more or less the same category as free software. It is not exactly the same class of software: they accept some licenses that we consider too restrictive, and there are free software licenses they have not accepted. However, the differences in extension of the category are small: nearly all free software is open source, and nearly all open source software is free.

We prefer the term "free software" because it refers to freedom—something that the term "open source" does not do.[3]

---

[1] See "Linux and the GNU System" (p. 64) for more information.

[2] See "Free Software Is More Reliable!" at `http://gnu.org/software/reliability.html`.

[3] See "Why Open Source Misses the Point of Free Software" (p. 75).

Public Domain Software

Public domain software is software that is not copyrighted. If the source code is in the public domain, that is a special case of noncopylefted free software, which means that some copies or modified versions may not be free at all.

In some cases, an executable program can be in the public domain but the source code is not available. This is not free software, because free software requires accessibility of source code. Meanwhile, most free software is not in the public domain; it is copyrighted, and the copyright holders have legally given permission for everyone to use it in freedom, using a free software license.

Sometimes people use the term "public domain" in a loose fashion to mean "free" or "available gratis." However, "public domain" is a legal term and means, precisely, "not copyrighted." For clarity, we recommend using "public domain" for that meaning only, and using other terms to convey the other meanings.

Under the Berne Convention, which most countries have signed, anything written down is automatically copyrighted. This includes programs. Therefore, if you want a program you have written to be in the public domain, you must take some legal steps to disclaim the copyright on it; otherwise, the program is copyrighted.

Copylefted Software

Copylefted software is free software whose distribution terms ensure that all copies of all versions carry more or less the same distribution terms. This means, for instance, that copyleft licenses generally disallow others to add additional requirements to the software (though a limited set of safe added requirements can be allowed) and require making source code available. This shields the program, and its modified versions, from some of the common ways of making a program proprietary.

Some copyleft licenses, such as GPL version 3, block other means of turning software proprietary, such as tivoization.[4]

In the GNU Project, we copyleft almost all the software we write, because our goal is to give *every* user the freedoms implied by the term "free software." See our copyleft article (p. 184) for more explanation of how copyleft works and why we use it.

Copyleft is a general concept; to copyleft an actual program, you need to use a specific set of distribution terms. There are many possible ways to write copyleft distribution terms, so in principle there can be many copyleft free software licenses. However, in actual practice nearly all copylefted software uses the GNU General Public License. Two different copyleft licenses are usually "incompatible," which means it is illegal to merge the code using one license with the code using the other license; therefore, it is good for the community if people use a single copyleft license.

---

[4] See "Why Upgrade to GPLv3" (p. 204) for more on this.

Noncopylefted Free Software

Noncopylefted free software comes from the author with permission to redistribute and modify, and also to add additional restrictions to it.

If a program is free but not copylefted, then some copies or modified versions may not be free at all. A software company can compile the program, with or without modifications, and distribute the executable file as a proprietary software product.

The X Window System illustrates this. The X Consortium released X11 with distribution terms that made it noncopylefted free software, and subsequent developers have mostly followed the same practice. A copy which has those distribution terms is free software. However, there are nonfree versions as well, and there are (or at least were) popular workstations and PC graphics boards for which nonfree versions are the only ones that work. If you are using this hardware, X11 is not free software for you. The developers of X11 even made X11 nonfree for a while;[5] they were able to do this because others had contributed their code under the same noncopyleft license.

Lax Permissive Licensed Software

Lax permissive licenses include the X11 license and the two BSD licenses.[6] These licenses permit almost any use of the code, including distributing proprietary binaries with or without changing the source code.

GPL-Covered Software

The GNU GPL (General Public License) is one specific set of distribution terms for copylefting a program. The GNU Project uses it as the distribution terms for most GNU software.

To equate free software with GPL-covered software is therefore an error.

The GNU Operating System

The GNU operating system is the Unix-like operating system, which is entirely free software, that we in the GNU Project have developed since 1984.[7]

A Unix-like operating system consists of many programs. The GNU system includes all of the official GNU packages. It also includes many other packages, such as the X Window System and TeX, which are not GNU software.

The first test release of the complete GNU system was in 1996. This includes the GNU Hurd, our kernel, developed since 1990. In 2001 the GNU system (including the GNU Hurd) began working fairly reliably, but the Hurd still lacks some important features, so it is not widely used. Meanwhile, the GNU/Linux system, an offshoot of the GNU operating system which uses Linux as the kernel

---

[5] See "The X Window System Trap" (p. 178).

[6] See "The BSD License Problem," at http://gnu.org/philosophy/bsd.html.

[7] See "Overview of the GNU System," at http://gnu.org/gnu/gnu-history.html, for more historical background.

instead of the GNU Hurd, has been a great success since the 90s.[8] As this shows, the GNU system is not a single static set of programs; users and distributors may select different packages according to their needs and desires. The result is still a variant of the GNU system.

Since the purpose of GNU is to be free, every single component in the GNU operating system is free software. They don't all have to be copylefted, however; any kind of free software is legally suitable to include if it helps meet technical goals.

GNU Programs

"GNU programs" is equivalent to GNU software. A program Foo is a GNU program if it is GNU software. We also sometimes say it is a "GNU package."

GNU Software

"GNU software" is software that is released under the auspices of the GNU Project.[9] If a program is GNU software, we also say that it is a GNU program or a GNU package. The README or manual of a GNU package should say it is one; also, the Free Software Directory[10] identifies all GNU packages.

Most GNU software is copylefted, but not all; however, all GNU software must be free software.

Some GNU software was written by staff of the Free Software Foundation, but most GNU software comes from many volunteers.[11] (Some of these volunteers are paid by companies or universities, but they are volunteers for us.) Some contributed software is copyrighted by the Free Software Foundation; some is copyrighted by the contributors who wrote it.

FSF-Copyrighted GNU Software

The developers of GNU packages can transfer the copyright to the FSF, or they can keep it. The choice is theirs.

If they have transferred the copyright to the FSF, the program is FSF-copyrighted GNU software, and the FSF can enforce its license. If they have kept the copyright, enforcing the license is their responsibility.

The FSF does not accept copyright assignments of software that is not an official GNU package, as a rule.

Nonfree Software

Nonfree software is any software that is not free. Its use, redistribution or modification is prohibited, or requires you to ask for permission, or is restricted so much that you effectively can't do it freely.

---

[8] See "Linux and the GNU System" (p. 64) for more information.

[9] See "Overview of the GNU System," at `http://gnu.org/gnu/gnu-history.html`, for more historical background.

[10] See `http://directory.fsf.org`.

[11] See `http://gnu.org/people/people.html`.

Proprietary Software

Proprietary software is another name for nonfree software. In the past we subdivided nonfree software into "semifree software," which could be modified and redistributed noncommercially, and "proprietary software," which could not be. But we have dropped that distinction and now use "proprietary software" as synonymous with nonfree software.

The Free Software Foundation follows the rule that we cannot install any proprietary program on our computers except temporarily for the specific purpose of writing a free replacement for that very program. Aside from that, we feel there is no possible excuse for installing a proprietary program.

For example, we felt justified in installing Unix on our computer in the 1980s, because we were using it to write a free replacement for Unix. Nowadays, since free operating systems are available, the excuse is no longer applicable; we do not use any nonfree operating systems, and any new computer we install must run a completely free operating system.

We don't insist that users of GNU, or contributors to GNU, have to live by this rule. It is a rule we made for ourselves. But we hope you will follow it too, for your freedom's sake.

Freeware

The term "freeware" has no clear accepted definition, but it is commonly used for packages which permit redistribution but not modification (and their source code is not available). These packages are *not* free software, so please don't use "freeware" to refer to free software.

Shareware

Shareware is software which comes with permission for people to redistribute copies, but says that anyone who continues to use a copy is *required* to pay a license fee.

Shareware is not free software, or even semifree. There are two reasons it is not:

- For most shareware, source code is not available; thus, you cannot modify the program at all.
- Shareware does not come with permission to make a copy and install it without paying a license fee, not even for individuals engaging in nonprofit activity. (In practice, people often disregard the distribution terms and do this anyway, but the terms don't permit it.)

Private software

Private or custom software is software developed for one user (typically an organization or company). That user keeps it and uses it, and does not release it to the public either as source code or as binaries.

A private program is free software (in a somewhat trivial sense) if its sole user has the four freedoms. In particular, if the user has full rights to the private program, the program is free. However, if the user distributes copies to others and does not provide the four freedoms with those copies, those copies are not free software.

Free software is a matter of freedom, not access. In general we do not believe it is wrong to develop a program and not release it. There are occasions when a program is so important that one might argue that withholding it from the public is doing wrong to humanity. However, such cases are rare. Most programs are not that important, and declining to release them is not particularly wrong. Thus, there is no conflict between the development of private or custom software and the principles of the free software movement.

Nearly all employment for programmers is in development of custom software; therefore most programming jobs are, or could be, done in a way compatible with the free software movement.

Commercial Software

"Commercial" and "proprietary" are not the same! Commercial software is software developed by a business as part of its business. Most commercial software is proprietary, but there is commercial free software, and there is noncommercial nonfree software.

For example, GNU Ada is developed by a company. It is always distributed under the terms of the GNU GPL, and every copy is free software; but its developers sell support contracts. When their salesmen speak to prospective customers, sometimes the customers say, "We would feel safer with a commercial compiler." The salesmen reply, "GNU Ada *is* a commercial compiler; it happens to be free software." For the GNU Project, the priorities are in the other order: the important thing is that GNU Ada is free software; that it is commercial is just a detail. However, the additional development of GNU Ada that results from its being commercial is definitely beneficial. Please help spread the awareness that free commercial software is possible. You can do this by making an effort not to say "commercial" when you mean "proprietary."

14 Why Open Source Misses the Point of Free Software

When we call software "free," we mean that it respects the users' essential freedoms: the freedom to run it, to study and change it, and to redistribute copies with or without changes.[1] This is a matter of freedom, not price, so think of "free speech," not "free beer."

These freedoms are vitally important. They are essential, not just for the individual users' sake, but for society as a whole because they promote social solidarity—that is, sharing and cooperation. They become even more important as our culture and life activities are increasingly digitized. In a world of digital sounds, images, and words, free software becomes increasingly essential for freedom in general.

Tens of millions of people around the world now use free software; the public schools of some regions of India and Spain now teach all students to use the free GNU/Linux operating system.[2] Most of these users, however, have never heard of the ethical reasons for which we developed this system and built the free software community, because nowadays this system and community are more often spoken of as "open source," attributing them to a different philosophy in which these freedoms are hardly mentioned.

The free software movement has campaigned for computer users' freedom since 1983. In 1984 we launched the development of the free operating system GNU, so that we could avoid the nonfree operating systems that deny freedom to their users. During the 1980s, we developed most of the essential components of the system and designed the GNU General Public License (GNU GPL) to release them under—a license designed specifically to protect freedom for all users of a program.

Not all of the users and developers of free software agreed with the goals of the free software movement. In 1998, a part of the free software community splintered off and began campaigning in the name of "open source." The term was originally proposed to avoid a possible misunderstanding of the term "free software," but it soon became associated with philosophical views quite different from those of the free software movement.

Some of the supporters of open source considered the term a "marketing campaign for free software," which would appeal to business executives by highlighting the software's practical benefits, while not raising issues of right and

---

[1] See p. 3 for the full definition of free software.

[2] See "Linux and the GNU System" (p. 64) for more on the operating system.

This essay was originally published on `http://gnu.org`, in 2007. This version is part of *Free Software, Free Society: Selected Essays of Richard M. Stallman*, 3rd ed. (Boston: GNU Press, 2015).

wrong that they might not like to hear. Other supporters flatly rejected the free software movement's ethical and social values. Whichever their views, when campaigning for open source, they neither cited nor advocated those values. The term "open source" quickly became associated with ideas and arguments based only on practical values, such as making or having powerful, reliable software. Most of the supporters of open source have come to it since then, and they make the same association.

The two terms describe almost the same category of software, but they stand for views based on fundamentally different values. Open source is a development methodology; free software is a social movement. For the free software movement, free software is an ethical imperative, essential respect for the users' freedom. By contrast, the philosophy of open source considers issues in terms of how to make software "better"—in a practical sense only. It says that nonfree software is an inferior solution to the practical problem at hand. Most discussion of "open source" pays no attention to right and wrong, only to popularity and success.[3]

For the free software movement, however, nonfree software is a social problem, and the solution is to stop using it and move to free software.

"Free software." "Open source." If it's the same software (or nearly so[4]), does it matter which name you use? Yes, because different words convey different ideas. While a free program by any other name would give you the same freedom today, establishing freedom in a lasting way depends above all on teaching people to value freedom. If you want to help do this, it is essential to speak of "free software."

We in the free software movement don't think of the open source camp as an enemy; the enemy is proprietary (nonfree) software. But we want people to know we stand for freedom, so we do not accept being mislabeled as open source supporters.

Practical Differences between Free Software and Open Source

In practice, open source stands for criteria a little weaker than those of free software. As far as we know, all existing free software would qualify as open source. Nearly all open source software is free software, but there are exceptions. First, some open source licenses are too restrictive, so they do not qualify as free licenses. For example, "Open Watcom" is nonfree because its license does not allow making a modified version and using it privately. Fortunately, few programs use such licenses.

Second, and more important in practice, many products containing computers check signatures on their executable programs to block users from installing

---

[3] For a typical example, see, for instance, Jay Lyman's article "Open Source Is Woven Into the Latest, Hottest Trends" (12 September 2013, `http://www.linuxinsider.com/story/Open-Source-Is-Woven-Into-the-Latest-Hottest-Trends-78937.html`).

[4] See "How Free Software and Open Source Relate as Categories of Programs," at `http://gnu.org/philosophy/free-open-overlap.html`.

different executables; only one privileged company can make executables that can run in the device or can access its full capabilities. We call these devices "tyrants," and the practice is called "tivoization" after the product (Tivo) where we first saw it. Even if the executable is made from free source code, the users cannot run modified versions of it, so the executable is nonfree.

The criteria for open source do not recognize this issue; they are concerned solely with the licensing of the source code. Thus, these unmodifiable executables, when made from source code such as Linux that is open source and free, are open source but not free. Many Android products contain nonfree tivoized executables of Linux.

Common Misunderstandings of "Free Software" and "Open Source"

The term "free software" is prone to misinterpretation: an unintended meaning, "software you can get for zero price," fits the term just as well as the intended meaning, "software which gives the user certain freedoms." We address this problem by publishing the definition of free software, and by saying "Think of 'free speech,' not 'free beer.'" This is not a perfect solution; it cannot completely eliminate the problem. An unambiguous and correct term would be better, if it didn't present other problems.

Unfortunately, all the alternatives in English have problems of their own. We've looked at many that people have suggested, but none is so clearly "right" that switching to it would be a good idea. (For instance, in some contexts the French and Spanish word "libre" works well, but people in India do not recognize it at all.) Every proposed replacement for "free software" has some kind of semantic problem—and this includes "open source software."

The official definition of "open source software" (which is published by the Open Source Initiative and is too long to include here[5]) was derived indirectly from our criteria for free software. It is not the same; it is a little looser in some respects. Nonetheless, their definition agrees with our definition in most cases.

However, the obvious meaning for the expression "open source software"—and the one most people seem to think it means—is "You can look at the source code." That criterion is much weaker than the free software definition, much weaker also than the official definition of open source. It includes many programs that are neither free nor open source.

Since that obvious meaning for "open source" is not the meaning that its advocates intend, the result is that most people misunderstand the term. According to writer Neal Stephenson, "Linux is 'open source' software meaning, simply that anyone can get copies of its source code files."[6] I don't think he deliberately sought to reject or dispute the official definition. I think he simply applied the conventions of the English language to come up with a meaning for the term. The state of Kansas published a similar definition: "Make use of open-source software (OSS). OSS is software for which the source code is freely

[5] See `http://opensource.org/docs/osd` for the full definition.

[6] Neal Stephenson, *In the Beginning...Was the Command Line* (New York: HarperCollins Publishers, 1999), p. 94.

and publicly available, though the specific licensing agreements vary as to what one is allowed to do with that code."[7]

The New York Times ran an article that stretched the meaning of the term to refer to user beta testing[8]—letting a few users try an early version and give confidential feedback—which proprietary software developers have practiced for decades.

The term has even been stretched to include designs for equipment that are published without a patent.[9] Patent-free equipment designs can be laudable contributions to society, but the term "source code" does not pertain to them.

Open source supporters try to deal with this by pointing to their official definition, but that corrective approach is less effective for them than it is for us. The term "free software" has two natural meanings, one of which is the intended meaning, so a person who has grasped the idea of "free speech, not free beer" will not get it wrong again. But the term "open source" has only one natural meaning, which is different from the meaning its supporters intend. So there is no succinct way to explain and justify its official definition. That makes for worse confusion.

Another misunderstanding of "open source" is the idea that it means "not using the GNU GPL." This tends to accompany another misunderstanding that "free software" means "GPL-covered software." These are both mistaken, since the GNU GPL qualifies as an open source license and most of the open source licenses qualify as free software licenses. There are many free software licenses aside from the GNU GPL.[10]

The term "open source" has been further stretched by its application to other activities, such as government, education, and science, where there is no such thing as source code, and where criteria for software licensing are simply not pertinent. The only thing these activities have in common is that they somehow invite people to participate. They stretch the term so far that it only means "participatory" or "transparent", or less than that. At worst, it has become a vacuous buzzword.[11]

---

[7] Kansas Statewide Technology Architecture, "Information Architecture," version 8.0, 20.3.8, accessed 11 October 2001, `https://web.archive.org/web/20001011193422/http://da.state.ks.us/ITEC/TechArchPt6ver80.pdf`.

[8] Mary Jane Irwin, "The Brave New World of Open-Source Game Design," *New York Times*, online ed., 7 February 2009, `http://www.nytimes.com/external/gigaom/2009/02/07/07gigaom-the-brave-new-world-of-open-source-game-design-37415.html`.

[9] Karl Mathiesen and Tess Riley, "Texas Teenager Creates $20 Water Purifier to Tackle Toxic E-Waste Pollution," 27 August 2015, `http://theguardian.com/sustainable-business/2015/aug/27/texas-teenager-water-purifier-toxic-e-waste-pollution`.

[10] See "Various Licenses and Comments about Them," at `http://gnu.org/licenses/license-list.html`.

[11] Evgeny Morozov, "Open and Closed," 16 March 2013, `http://www.nytimes.com/2013/03/17/opinion/sunday/morozov-open-and-closed.html`.

Different Values Can Lead to Similar Conclusions. . . but Not Always

Radical groups in the 1960s had a reputation for factionalism: some organizations split because of disagreements on details of strategy, and the two daughter groups treated each other as enemies despite having similar basic goals and values. The right wing made much of this and used it to criticize the entire left.

Some try to disparage the free software movement by comparing our disagreement with open source to the disagreements of those radical groups. They have it backwards. We disagree with the open source camp on the basic goals and values, but their views and ours lead in many cases to the same practical behavior—such as developing free software.

As a result, people from the free software movement and the open source camp often work together on practical projects such as software development. It is remarkable that such different philosophical views can so often motivate different people to participate in the same projects. Nonetheless, there are situations where these fundamentally different views lead to very different actions.

The idea of open source is that allowing users to change and redistribute the software will make it more powerful and reliable. But this is not guaranteed. Developers of proprietary software are not necessarily incompetent. Sometimes they produce a program that is powerful and reliable, even though it does not respect the users' freedom. Free software activists and open source enthusiasts will react very differently to that.

A pure open source enthusiast, one that is not at all influenced by the ideals of free software, will say, "I am surprised you were able to make the program work so well without using our development model, but you did. How can I get a copy?" This attitude will reward schemes that take away our freedom, leading to its loss.

The free software activist will say, "Your program is very attractive, but I value my freedom more. So I reject your program. I will get my work done some other way, and support a project to develop a free replacement." If we value our freedom, we can act to maintain and defend it.

Powerful, Reliable Software Can Be Bad

The idea that we want software to be powerful and reliable comes from the supposition that the software is designed to serve its users. If it is powerful and reliable, that means it serves them better.

But software can be said to serve its users only if it respects their freedom. What if the software is designed to put chains on its users? Then powerfulness means the chains are more constricting, and reliability that they are harder to remove. Malicious features, such as spying on the users, restricting the users, back doors, and imposed upgrades are common in proprietary software, and some open source supporters want to implement them in open source programs.

Under pressure from the movie and record companies, software for individuals to use is increasingly designed specifically to restrict them. This malicious feature is known as Digital Restrictions Management (DRM) (see our campaign against it, at `DefectiveByDesign.org`) and is the antithesis in spirit of the freedom that free software aims to provide. And not just in spirit: since the goal of DRM is to trample your freedom, DRM developers try to make it hard, impossible, or even illegal for you to change the software that implements the DRM.

Yet some open source supporters have proposed "open source DRM" software. Their idea is that, by publishing the source code of programs designed to restrict your access to encrypted media and by allowing others to change it, they will produce more powerful and reliable software for restricting users like you. The software would then be delivered to you in devices that do not allow you to change it.

This software might be open source and use the open source development model, but it won't be free software since it won't respect the freedom of the users that actually run it. If the open source development model succeeds in making this software more powerful and reliable for restricting you, that will make it even worse.

Fear of Freedom

The main initial motivation of those who split off the open source camp from the free software movement was that the ethical ideas of "free software" made some people uneasy. That's true: raising ethical issues such as freedom, talking about responsibilities as well as convenience, is asking people to think about things they might prefer to ignore, such as whether their conduct is ethical. This can trigger discomfort, and some people may simply close their minds to it. It does not follow that we ought to stop talking about these issues.

That is, however, what the leaders of open source decided to do. They figured that by keeping quiet about ethics and freedom, and talking only about the immediate practical benefits of certain free software, they might be able to "sell" the software more effectively to certain users, especially business.

This approach has proved effective, in its own terms. The rhetoric of open source has convinced many businesses and individuals to use, and even develop, free software, which has extended our community—but only at the superficial, practical level. The philosophy of open source, with its purely practical values, impedes understanding of the deeper ideas of free software; it brings many people into our community, but does not teach them to defend it. That is good, as far as it goes, but it is not enough to make freedom secure. Attracting users to free software takes them just part of the way to becoming defenders of their own freedom.

Sooner or later these users will be invited to switch back to proprietary software for some practical advantage. Countless companies seek to offer such temptation, some even offering copies gratis. Why would users decline? Only if they have learned to value the freedom free software gives them, to value freedom in and of itself rather than the technical and practical convenience of specific free software. To spread this idea, we have to talk about freedom. A certain amount of the "keep quiet" approach to business can be useful for the community, but it is dangerous if it becomes so common that the love of freedom comes to seem like an eccentricity.

That dangerous situation is exactly what we have. Most people involved with free software, especially its distributors, say little about freedom—usually because they seek to be "more acceptable to business." Nearly all GNU/Linux operating system distributions add proprietary packages to the basic free system, and they invite users to consider this an advantage rather than a flaw.

Proprietary add-on software and partially nonfree GNU/Linux distributions find fertile ground because most of our community does not insist on freedom with its software. This is no coincidence. Most GNU/Linux users were introduced to the system through "open source" discussion, which doesn't say that freedom is a goal. The practices that don't uphold freedom and the words that don't talk about freedom go hand in hand, each promoting the other. To overcome this tendency, we need more, not less, talk about freedom.

"FLOSS" and "FOSS"

The terms "FLOSS" and "FOSS"[12] are used to be neutral between free software and open source. If neutrality is your goal, "FLOSS" is the better of the two, since it really is neutral. But if you want to stand up for freedom, using a neutral term isn't the way. Standing up for freedom entails showing people your support for freedom.

Rivals for Mindshare

"Free" and "open" are rivals for mindshare. "Free software" and "open source" are different ideas but, in most people's way of looking at software, they compete for the same conceptual slot. When people become habituated to saying and thinking "open source," that is an obstacle to their grasping the free software movement's philosophy and thinking about it. If they have already come to associate us and our software with the word "open," we may need to shock them intellectually before they recognize that we stand for something *else.* Any activity that promotes the word "open" tends to extend the curtain that hides the ideas of the free software movement.

Thus, free software activists are well advised to decline to work on an activity that calls itself "open." Even if the activity is good in and of itself, each contribution you make does a little harm on the side. There are plenty of other good activities which call themselves "free" or "libre." Each contribution to those projects does a little extra good on the side. With so many useful projects to choose from, why not choose one which does extra good?

---

[12] See both p. 95 and the article "FLOSS and FOSS," at `http://www.gnu.org/philosophy/floss-and-foss.html`, for more on this issue.

Conclusion

As the advocates of open source draw new users into our community, we free software activists must shoulder the task of bringing the issue of freedom to their attention. We have to say, "It's free software and it gives you freedom!"—more and louder than ever. Every time you say "free software" rather than "open source," you help our cause.

Note

Karim R. Lakhani and Robert G. Wolf's paper on the motivation of free software developers ("Why Hackers Do What They Do: Understanding Motivation and Effort in Free/Open Source Software Projects," in *Perspectives on Free and Open Source Software*, edited by J. Feller and others (Cambridge: MIT Press, 2005), `http://ocw.mit.edu/courses/sloan-school-of-management/15-352-managing-innovation-emerging-trends-spring-2005/readings/lakhaniwolf.pdf`) says that a considerable fraction are motivated by the view that software should be free. This is despite the fact that they surveyed the developers on SourceForge, a site that does not support the view that this is an ethical issue.

15 Did You Say "Intellectual Property"? It's a Seductive Mirage

It has become fashionable to toss copyright, patents, and trademarks—three separate and different entities involving three separate and different sets of laws—plus a dozen other laws into one pot and call it "intellectual property." The distorting and confusing term did not become common by accident. Companies that gain from the confusion promoted it. The clearest way out of the confusion is to reject the term entirely.

According to Professor Mark Lemley, now of the Stanford Law School, the widespread use of the term "intellectual property" is a fashion that followed the 1967 founding of the World "Intellectual Property" Organization (WIPO), and only became really common in recent years. (WIPO is formally a UN organization, but in fact represents the interests of the holders of copyrights, patents, and trademarks.) Wide use dates from around 1990.

The term carries a bias that is not hard to see: it suggests thinking about copyright, patents and trademarks by analogy with property rights for physical objects. (This analogy is at odds with the legal philosophies of copyright law, of patent law, and of trademark law, but only specialists know that.) These laws are in fact not much like physical property law, but use of this term leads legislators to change them to be more so. Since that is the change desired by the companies that exercise copyright, patent and trademark powers, the bias introduced by the term "intellectual property" suits them.

The bias is reason enough to reject the term, and people have often asked me to propose some other name for the overall category—or have proposed their own alternatives (often humorous). Suggestions include IMPs, for Imposed Monopoly Privileges, and GOLEMs, for Government-Originated Legally Enforced Monopolies. Some speak of "exclusive rights regimes," but referring to restrictions as "rights" is doublethink too.

Some of these alternative names would be an improvement, but it is a mistake to replace "intellectual property" with any other term. A different name will not address the term's deeper problem: overgeneralization. There is no such unified thing as "intellectual property"—it is a mirage. The only reason people think it makes sense as a coherent category is that widespread use of the term has misled them about the laws in question.

The term "intellectual property" is at best a catch-all to lump together disparate laws. Nonlawyers who hear one term applied to these various laws tend to assume they are based on a common principle and function similarly.

This article was written in 2004 and published in *Policy Futures in Education*, vol. 4, n. 4, pp. 334–336, 2006. This version is part of *Free Software, Free Society: Selected Essays of Richard M. Stallman*, 3rd ed. (Boston: GNU Press, 2015).

Nothing could be further from the case. These laws originated separately, evolved differently, cover different activities, have different rules, and raise different public policy issues.

For instance, copyright law was designed to promote authorship and art, and covers the details of expression of a work. Patent law was intended to promote the publication of useful ideas, at the price of giving the one who publishes an idea a temporary monopoly over it—a price that may be worth paying in some fields and not in others.

Trademark law, by contrast, was not intended to promote any particular way of acting, but simply to enable buyers to know what they are buying. Legislators under the influence of the term "intellectual property," however, have turned it into a scheme that provides incentives for advertising. And these are just three out of many laws that the term refers to.

Since these laws developed independently, they are different in every detail, as well as in their basic purposes and methods. Thus, if you learn some fact about copyright law, you'd be wise to assume that patent law is different. You'll rarely go wrong!

In practice, nearly all general statements you encounter that are formulated using "intellectual property" will be false. For instance, you'll see claims that "its" purpose is to "promote innovation," but that only fits patent law and perhaps plant variety monopolies. Copyright law is not concerned with innovation; a pop song or novel is copyrighted even if there is nothing innovative about it. Trademark law is not concerned with innovation; if I start a tea store and call it "rms tea," that would be a solid trademark even if I sell the same teas in the same way as everyone else. Trade secret law is not concerned with innovation, except tangentially; my list of tea customers would be a trade secret with nothing to do with innovation.

You will also see assertions that "intellectual property" is concerned with "creativity," but really that only fits copyright law. More than creativity is needed to make a patentable invention. Trademark law and trade secret law have nothing to do with creativity; the name "rms tea" isn't creative at all, and neither is my secret list of tea customers.

People often say "intellectual property" when they really mean some larger or smaller set of laws. For instance, rich countries often impose unjust laws on poor countries to squeeze money out of them. Some of these laws are among those called "intellectual property" laws, and others are not; nonetheless, critics of the practice often grab for that label because it has become familiar to them. By using it, they misrepresent the nature of the issue. It would be better to use an accurate term, such as "legislative colonization," that gets to the heart of the matter.

Laymen are not alone in being confused by this term. Even law professors who teach these laws are lured and distracted by the seductiveness of the term "intellectual property," and make general statements that conflict with facts they know. For example, one professor wrote in 2006:

> Unlike their descendants who now work the floor at WIPO, the framers of the US constitution had a principled, procompetitive attitude to intellectual property. They knew rights might be necessary, but. . . they tied Congress's hands, restricting its power in multiple ways.

That statement refers to Article I, Section 8, Clause 8, of the US Constitution, which authorizes copyright law and patent law. That clause, though, has nothing to do with trademark law, trade secret law, or various others. The term "intellectual property" led that professor to make a false generalization.

The term "intellectual property" also leads to simplistic thinking. It leads people to focus on the meager commonality in form that these disparate laws have—that they create artificial privileges for certain parties—and to disregard the details which form their substance: the specific restrictions each law places on the public, and the consequences that result. This simplistic focus on the form encourages an "economistic" approach to all these issues.

Economics operates here, as it often does, as a vehicle for unexamined assumptions. These include assumptions about values, such as that amount of production matters while freedom and way of life do not, and factual assumptions which are mostly false, such as that copyrights on music supports musicians, or that patents on drugs support life-saving research.

Another problem is that, at the broad scale implicit in the term "intellectual property," the specific issues raised by the various laws become nearly invisible. These issues arise from the specifics of each law—precisely what the term "intellectual property" encourages people to ignore. For instance, one issue relating to copyright law is whether music sharing should be allowed; patent law has nothing to do with this. Patent law raises issues such as whether poor countries should be allowed to produce life-saving drugs and sell them cheaply to save lives; copyright law has nothing to do with such matters.

Neither of these issues is solely economic in nature, and their noneconomic aspects are very different; using the shallow economic overgeneralization as the basis for considering them means ignoring the differences. Putting the two laws in the "intellectual property" pot obstructs clear thinking about each one.

Thus, any opinions about "the issue of intellectual property" and any generalizations about this supposed category are almost surely foolish. If you think all those laws are one issue, you will tend to choose your opinions from a selection of sweeping overgeneralizations, none of which is any good.

If you want to think clearly about the issues raised by patents, or copyrights, or trademarks, or various other different laws, the first step is to forget the idea of lumping them together, and treat them as separate topics. The second step is to reject the narrow perspectives and simplistic picture the term "intellectual property" suggests. Consider each of these issues separately, in its fullness, and you have a chance of considering them well.

Notes

- See also "The Curious History of Komongistan (Busting the Term 'Intellectual Property')," at http://gnu.org/philosophy/komongistan.html.
- Countries in Africa are a lot more similar than these laws, and "Africa" is a coherent geographical concept; nonetheless, talking about "Africa" instead of a specific country causes lots of confusion.[1]
- Rickard Falkvinge supports rejection of this term.[2]

[1] Nicolas Kayser-Bril, "Africa Is Not a Country," 24 January 2014, http://theguardian.com/world/2014/jan/24/africa-clinton.

[2] "Language Matters: Framing the Copyright Monopoly So We Can Keep Our Liberties," 14 July 2013, http://torrentfreak.com/language-matters-framing-the-copyright-monopoly-so-we-can-keep-our-liberties-130714.

16 Why Call It the Swindle?

I go out of my way to call nasty things by names that criticize them. I call Apple's user-subjugating computers the "iThings," and Amazon's abusive e-reader the "Swindle." Sometimes I refer to Microsoft's operating system as "Losedows"; I referred to Microsoft's first operating system as "MS-Dog."[1] Of course, I do this to vent my feelings and have fun. But this fun is more than personal; it serves an important purpose. Mocking our enemies recruits the power of humor into our cause.

Twisting a name is disrespectful. If we respected the makers of these products, we would use the names that they chose. . . and that's exactly the point. These noxious products deserve our contempt, not our respect. Every proprietary program subjects its users to some entity's power, but nowadays most widely used ones go beyond that to spy on users, restrict them and even push them around: the trend is for products to get nastier. These products deserve to be wiped out. Those with DRM ought to be illegal.

When we mention them, we should show that we condemn them, and what easier way than by twisting their names? If we don't do that, it is all too easy to mention them and fail to present the condemnation. When the product comes up in the middle of some other topic, for instance, explaining at greater length that the product is bad might seem like a long digression.

To mention these products by name and fail to condemn them has the effect of legitimizing them, which is the opposite of what they call for.

Companies choose names for products as part of a marketing plan. They choose names they think people will be likely to repeat, then invest millions of dollars in marketing campaigns to make people repeat and think about those names. Usually these marketing campaigns are intended to convince people to admire the products based on their superficial attractions and overlook the harm they do.

Every time we call these products by the names the companies use, we contribute to their marketing campaigns. Repeating those names is active support for the products; twisting them denies the products our support.

Other terminology besides product names can raise a similar issue. For instance, DRM refers to building technology products to restrict their users for the benefit of someone else. This inexcusable practice deserves our burning hatred until we wipe it out. Naturally, those responsible gave it a name that

---

[1] Take action against iThings, at `u.fsf.org/ithings`, against the Swindle, at `u.fsf.org/swindle` and `u.fsf.org/ebookslist`, and against Windows, at `upgradefromwindows.org`.

---

frames the issue from their point of view: "Digital Rights Management." This name is the basis of a public relations campaign that aims to win support from entities ranging from governments to the W3C.[2]

To use their term is to take their side. If that's not the side you're on, why give it your implicit support?

We take the users' side, and from the users' point of view, what these malfeatures manage are not rights but restrictions. So we call them "Digital Restrictions Management."

Neither of those terms is neutral: choose a term, and you choose a side. Please choose the users' side and please let it show.

Once, a man in the audience at my speech claimed that the name "Digital Rights Management" was the official name of "DRM," the only possible correct name, because it was the first name. He argued that as a consequence it was wrong for us to say "Digital Restrictions Management."

Those who make a product or carry out a business practice typically choose a name for it before we even know it exists. If their temporal precedence obligated us to use their name, they would have an additional automatic advantage, on top of their money, their media influence and their technological position. We would have to fight them with our mouths tied behind our backs.

Some people feel a distaste for twisting names and say it sounds "juvenile" or "unprofessional." What they mean is, it doesn't sound humorless and stodgy—and that's a good thing, because we would not have laughter on our side if we tried to sound "professional." Fighting oppression is far more serious than professional work, so we've got to add comic relief. It calls for real maturity, which includes some childishness, not "acting like an adult."

If you don't like our choice of name parodies, you can invent your own. The more, the merrier. Of course, there are other ways to express condemnation. If you want to sound "professional," you can show it in other ways. They can get the point across, but they require more time and effort, especially if you don't make use of mockery. Take care this does not this lead you to skimp; don't let the pressure against such "digression" push you into insufficiently criticizing the nasty things you mention, because that would have the effect of legitimizing them. 1

---

[2] See `https://u.fsf.org/drm` for more on DRM.

17 Words to Avoid (or Use with Care) Because They Are Loaded or Confusing

There are a number of words and phrases that we recommend avoiding, or avoiding in certain contexts and usages. Some are ambiguous or misleading; others presuppose a viewpoint that we disagree with, and we hope you disagree with it too. (See also "Categories of Free and Nonfree Software" (p. 68) and "Why Call It the Swindle?" (p. 87).)

"Access"

It is a common misunderstanding to think free software means that the public has "access" to a program. That is not what free software means.

The criterion for free software[1] is not about who has "access" to the program; the four essential freedoms concern what a user that has a copy of the program can do with it. For instance, freedom 2 says that that user is free to make another copy and give or sell it to you. But no user is *obligated* to do that for you; you do not have a *right* to demand a copy of that program from any user.

In particular, if you write a program yourself and never offer a copy to anyone else, that program is free software (in a trivial way) because you (the sole user that has it) have the four essential freedoms.

In practice, when many users have copies of a program, someone is sure to post it on the internet, giving everyone access to it. We think people ought to do that, if the program is useful. But this isn't a requirement of free software.

There is one specific point in which a question of having access is directly pertinent to free software: the GNU GPL permits giving a particular user access to download a program's source code as a substitute for physically giving that user a copy of the source. This applies to the special case in which the user already has a copy of the program in non-source form.

"Alternative"

We don't describe free software as an "alternative" to proprietary, because that word presumes all the "alternatives" are legitimate and each additional one makes users better off. In effect, it assumes that free software ought to coexist with software that does not respect users' freedom.

We believe that distribution as free software is the only ethical way to make software available for others to use. The other methods, nonfree software and

[1] See p. 3 for the full definition of free software.

Service as a Software Substitute subjugate their users.[1] We do not think it is good to offer users those "alternatives" to free software.

"BSD-Style"

The expression "BSD-style license" leads to confusion because it lumps together licenses that have important differences.[2] For instance, the original BSD license with the advertising clause is incompatible with the GNU General Public License, but the revised BSD license is compatible with the GPL.

To avoid confusion, it is best to name the specific license in question[3] and avoid the vague term "BSD-style."

"Closed"

Describing nonfree software as "closed" clearly refers to the term "open source." In the free software movement, we do not want to be confused with the open source camp, so we are careful to avoid saying things that would encourage people to lump us in with them.[4] For instance, we avoid describing nonfree software as "closed." We call it "nonfree" or "proprietary."[5]

"Cloud Computing"

The term "cloud computing" (or just "cloud," in the context of computing) is a marketing buzzword with no coherent meaning. It is used for a range of different activities whose only common characteristic is that they use the internet for something beyond transmitting files. Thus, the term spreads confusion. If you base your thinking on it, your thinking will be confused.

When thinking about or responding to a statement someone else has made using this term, the first step is to clarify the topic. What scenario is the statement about? What is a good, clear term for that scenario? Once the topic is clearly formulated, coherent discussion is possible.

One of the many meanings of "cloud computing" is storing your data in online services. In most scenarios, that is foolish because it exposes you to surveillance.[6]

Another meaning (which overlaps that but is not the same thing) is Service as a Software Substitute, which denies you control over your computing. You should never use SaaSS.[7]

---

[1] See "Free Software Is Even More Important Now" (p. 28) and "Who Does That Server Really Serve?" (p. 243) for more on this.

[2] See "The BSD License Problem," at `http://gnu.org/philosophy/bsd.html`.

[3] See "Various Licenses and Comments about Them," at `http://gnu.org/licenses/license-list.html`.

[4] See "Why Open Source Misses the Point of Free Software" (p. 75).

[5] See p. 73 for more on proprietary software.

[6] John Harris, "Why Hackers and Spooks Want Our Heads in the Cloud," 25 April 2011, `http://guardian.co.uk/commentisfree/2011/apr/25/hackers-spooks-cloud-antiauthoritarian-dream`.

[7] See "Who Does That Server Really Serve?" (p. 243) for more on this issue.

Another meaning is renting a remote physical server, or virtual server. These practices are OK under certain circumstances.

Another meaning is accessing your own server from your own mobile device. That raises no particular ethical issues.

The NIST definition of "cloud computing"[8] mentions three scenarios that raise different ethical issues: Software as a Service, Platform as a Service, and Infrastructure as a Service. However, that definition does not match the common use of "cloud computing," since it does not include storing data in online services. Software as a Service as defined by NIST overlaps considerably with Service as a Software Substitute, which mistreats the user, but the two concepts are not equivalent.

These different computing practices don't even belong in the same discussion. The best way to avoid the confusion the term "cloud computing" spreads is not to use the term "cloud" in connection with computing. Talk about the scenario you mean, and call it by a specific term.

Curiously, Larry Ellison, a proprietary software developer, also noted the vacuity of the term "cloud computing."[9] He decided to use the term anyway because, as a proprietary software developer, he isn't motivated by the same ideals as we are.

"Commercial"

Please don't use "commercial" as a synonym for "nonfree." That confuses two entirely different issues.

A program is commercial if it is developed as a business activity. A commercial program can be free or nonfree, depending on its manner of distribution. Likewise, a program developed by a school or an individual can be free or nonfree, depending on its manner of distribution. The two questions—what sort of entity developed the program and what freedom its users have—are independent.

In the first decade of the free software movement, free software packages were almost always noncommercial; the components of the GNU/Linux operating system were developed by individuals or by nonprofit organizations such as the FSF and universities. Later, in the 1990s, free commercial software started to appear.

Free commercial software is a contribution to our community, so we should encourage it. But people who think that "commercial" means "nonfree" will tend to think that the "free commercial" combination is self-contradictory, and dismiss the possibility. Let's be careful not to use the word "commercial" in that way.

---

8 Peter Mell and Anthony Grance, "The NIST Definition of Cloud Computing: Recommendations of the National Institute of Standards and Technology," *NIST Special Publication* 800-145 (September 2011), `http://csrc.nist.gov/publications/nistpubs/800-145/SP800-145.pdf`.

9 Dan Farber, "Oracle's Ellison Nails Cloud Computing," 26 September 2008, `http://news.cnet.com/8301-13953_3-10052188-80.html`.

"Compensation"

To speak of "compensation for authors" in connection with copyright carries the assumptions that (1) copyright exists for the sake of authors and (2) whenever we read something, we take on a debt to the author which we must then repay. The first assumption is simply false,[10] and the second is outrageous.

"Compensating the rights-holders" adds a further swindle: you're supposed to imagine that means paying the authors, and occasionally it does, but most of the time it means a subsidy for the same publishing companies that are pushing unjust laws on us.

"Consume"

"Consume" refers to what we do with food: we ingest it, after which the food as such no longer exists. By analogy, we employ the same word for other products whose use *uses them up*. Applying it to durable goods, such as clothing or appliances, is a stretch. Applying it to published works (programs, recordings on a disk or in a file, books on paper or in a file), whose nature is to last indefinitely and which can be run, played or read any number of times, is simply an error. Playing a recording, or running a program, does not consume it.

The term "consume" is associated with the economics of uncopyable material products, and leads people to transfer its conclusions unconsciously to copyable digital works—an error that proprietary software developers (and other publishers) dearly wish to encourage. Their twisted viewpoint comes through clearly in a *Business Insider* article,[11] which also refers to publications as "content."

The narrow thinking associated with the idea that we "consume content" paves the way for laws such as the DMCA that forbid users to break the Digital Restrictions Management (DRM) facilities in digital devices. If users think what they do with these devices is "consume," they may see such restrictions as natural.

It also encourages the acceptation of "streaming" services, which use DRM to limit use of digital recordings to a form that fits the word "consume."

Why is this perverse usage spreading? Some may feel that the term sounds sophisticated; if that attracts you, rejecting it with cogent reasons can appear even more sophisticated. Others may be acting from business interests (their own, or their employers'). Their use of the term in prestigious forums gives the impression that it's the "correct" term.

To speak of "consuming" music, fiction, or any other artistic works is to treat them as products rather than as art. If you don't want to spread that attitude, you would do well to reject using the term "consume" for them. We recommend saying that someone "experiences" an artistic work or a work stating a point of view, and that someone "uses" a practical work.

---

[10] See "Misinterpreting Copyright" (p. 113) for more on this.

[11] Lara O'Reilly, "A Former Googler Has Declared War on Ad Blockers with a New Startup That Tackles Them in an Unorthodox Way," 18 June 2015, `http://uk.businessinsider.com/former-google-exec-launches-sourcepoint-with-10-million-series-a-funding-2015-6?r=US&IR=T`.

"Consumer"

The term "consumer," when used to refer to the users of computing, is loaded with assumptions we should reject. Some come from the idea that using the program "consumes" the program (see the previous entry), which leads people to impose on copyable digital works the economic conclusions that were drawn about uncopyable material products.

In addition, describing the users of software as "consumers" refers to a framing in which people are limited to selecting between whatever "products" are available in the "market." There is no room in this framing for the idea that users can directly exercise control over what a program does.[12]

To describe people who are not limited to passive use of works, we suggest terms such as "individuals" and "citizens," rather than "consumers."

This problem with the word "consumer" has been noted before.[13]

"Content"

If you want to describe a feeling of comfort and satisfaction, by all means say you are "content," but using the word as a noun to describe publications and works of authorship adopts an attitude you might rather avoid: it treats them as a commodity whose purpose is to fill a box and make money. In effect, it disparages the works themselves. If you don't agree with that attitude, you can call them "works" or "publications."

Those who use the term "content" are often the publishers that push for increased copyright power in the name of the authors ("creators," as they say) of the works. The term "content" reveals their real attitude towards these works and their authors. (See Courtney Love's open letter to Steve Case[14] and search for "content provider" in that page. Alas, Ms. Love is unaware that the term "intellectual property" is also biased and confusing.[15])

However, as long as other people use the term "content provider," political dissidents can well call themselves "malcontent providers."

The term "content management" takes the prize for vacuity. "Content" means "some sort of information," and "management" in this context means "doing something with it." So a "content management system" is a system for doing something to some sort of information. Nearly all programs fit that description.

In most cases, that term really refers to a system for updating pages on a web site. For that, we recommend the term "web site revision system" (WRS).

---

12 See "Free Software Is Even More Important Now" (p. 28) for more on this.

13 Owen Hatherley, "Be a User, Not a Consumer: How Capitalism Has Changed Our Language," 11 August 2013, `http://theguardian.com/commentisfree/2013/aug/11/capitalism-language-raymond-williams`.

14 An unedited transcript of American rock musician Courtney Love's 16 May 2000 speech to the Digital Hollywood online-entertainment conference is available at `http://www.salon.com/2000/06/14/love_7/`.

15 See p. 97 for the reason why.

"Creative Commons Licensed"

The most important licensing characteristic of a work is whether it is free. Creative Commons publishes seven licenses; three are free (CC BY, CC BY-SA and CC0) and the rest are nonfree. Thus, to describe a work as "Creative Commons licensed" fails to say whether it is free, and suggests that the question is not important. The statement may be accurate, but the omission is harmful.

To encourage people to pay attention to the most important distinction, always specify *which* Creative Commons license is used, as in "licensed under CC BY-SA." If you don't know which license a certain work uses, find out and then make your statement.

"Creator"

The term "creator" as applied to authors implicitly compares them to a deity ("the creator"). The term is used by publishers to elevate authors' moral standing above that of ordinary people in order to justify giving them increased copyright power, which the publishers can then exercise in their name. We recommend saying "author" instead. However, in many cases "copyright holder" is what you really mean. These two terms are not equivalent: often the copyright holder is not the author.

"Digital Goods"

The term "digital goods," as applied to copies of works of authorship, identifies them with physical goods—which cannot be copied, and which therefore have to be manufactured in quantity and sold. This metaphor encourages people to judge issues about software or other digital works based on their views and intuitions about physical goods. It also frames issues in terms of economics, whose shallow and limited values don't include freedom and community.

"Digital Locks"

"Digital locks" is used to refer to Digital Restrictions Management by some who criticize it. The problem with this term is that it fails to do justice to the badness of DRM. The people who adopted that term did not think it through.

Locks are not necessarily oppressive or bad. You probably own several locks, and their keys or codes as well; you may find them useful or troublesome, but they don't oppress you, because you can open and close them. Likewise, we find encryption[16] invaluable for protecting our digital files. That too is a kind of digital lock that you have control over.

DRM is like a lock placed on you by someone else, who refuses to give you the key—in other words, like *handcuffs.* Therefore, the proper metaphor for DRM is "digital handcuffs," not "digital locks."

---

[16] Cory Doctorow, "Encryption Won't Work If It Has a Back Door Only the 'Good Guys' Have Keys To," 1 May 2015, `http://theguardian.com/technology/2015/may/01/encryption-wont-work-if-it-has-a-back-door-only-the-good-guys-have-keys-to-`.

A number of opposition campaigns have chosen the unwise term "digital locks"; to get things back on the right track, we must firmly insist on correcting this mistake. The FSF can support a campaign that opposes "digital locks" if we agree on the substance; however, when we state our support, we conspicuously replace the term with "digital handcuffs" and say why.

"Digital Rights Management"

"Digital Rights Management" (abbreviated "DRM") refers to technical mechanisms designed to impose restrictions on computer users. The use of the word "rights" in this term is propaganda, designed to lead you unawares into seeing the issue from the viewpoint of the few that impose the restrictions, and ignoring that of the general public on whom these restrictions are imposed.

Good alternatives include "Digital Restrictions Management," and "digital handcuffs."

Please sign up to support our campaign to abolish DRM, at `DefectiveByDesign.org`.

"Ecosystem"

It is inadvisable to describe the free software community, or any human community, as an "ecosystem," because that word implies the absence of ethical judgment.

The term "ecosystem" implicitly suggests an attitude of nonjudgmental observation: don't ask how what *should* happen, just study and understand what *does* happen. In an ecosystem, some organisms consume other organisms. In ecology, we do not ask whether it is right for an owl to eat a mouse or for a mouse to eat a seed, we only observe that they do so. Species' populations grow or shrink according to the conditions; this is neither right nor wrong, merely an ecological phenomenon, even if it goes so far as the extinction of a species.

By contrast, beings that adopt an ethical stance towards their surroundings can decide to preserve things that, without their intervention, might vanish—such as civil society, democracy, human rights, peace, public health, a stable climate, clean air and water, endangered species, traditional arts. . . and computer users' freedom.

"FLOSS"

The term "FLOSS," meaning "Free/Libre and Open Source Software," was coined as a way to be neutral between free software and open source.[17] If neutrality is your goal, "FLOSS" is the best way to be neutral. But if you want to show you stand for freedom, don't use a neutral term.

---

[17] See `http://www.gnu.org/philosophy/floss-and-foss.html` for more on this.

“For Free”

If you want to say that a program is free software, please don’t say that it is available “for free.” That term specifically means “for zero price.” Free software is a matter of freedom, not price.

Free software copies are often available for free—for example, by downloading via FTP. But free software copies are also available for a price on CD-ROMs; meanwhile, proprietary software copies are occasionally available for free in promotions, and some proprietary packages are normally available at no charge to certain users.

To avoid confusion, you can say that the program is available “as free software.”

“FOSS”

The term “FOSS,” meaning “Free and Open Source Software,” was coined as a way to be neutral between free software and open source, but it doesn’t really do that.[18] If neutrality is your goal, “FLOSS” is better. But if you want to show you stand for freedom, don’t use a neutral term.

“Freely Available”

Don’t use “freely available software” as a synonym for “free software.” The terms are not equivalent. Software is “freely available” if anyone can easily get a copy. “Free software” is defined in terms of the freedom of users that have a copy of it. These are answers to different questions.

“Freeware”

Please don’t use the term “freeware” as a synonym for “free software.” The term “freeware” was used often in the 1980s for programs released only as executables, with source code not available. Today it has no particular agreed-on definition.

When using languages other than English, please avoid borrowing English terms such as “free software” or “freeware.” It is better to translate the term “free software” into your language. (Please see p. 274 for a list of recommended unambiguous translations for the term “free software” into various languages.)

By using a word in your own language, you show that you are really referring to freedom and not just parroting some mysterious foreign marketing concept. The reference to freedom may at first seem strange or disturbing to your compatriots, but once they see that it means exactly what it says, they will really understand what the issue is.

“Give Away Software”

It’s misleading to use the term “give away” to mean “distribute a program as free software.” This locution has the same problem as “for free”: it implies the issue is price, not freedom. One way to avoid the confusion is to say “release as free software.”

---

[18] See previous footnote.

"Google"

Please avoid using the term "google" as a verb, meaning to search for something on the internet. "Google" is just the name of one particular search engine among others. We suggest to use the term "web search" instead. Try to use a search engine that respects your privacy; DuckDuckGo claims not to track its users,[19] although we cannot confirm.

"Hacker"

A hacker is someone who enjoys playful cleverness[20]—not necessarily with computers. The programmers in the old MIT free software community of the 60s and 70s referred to themselves as hackers. Around 1980, journalists who discovered the hacker community mistakenly took the term to mean "security breaker."

Please don't spread this mistake. People who break security are "crackers."

"Intellectual Property"

Publishers and lawyers like to describe copyright as "intellectual property"—a term also applied to patents, trademarks, and other more obscure areas of law. These laws have so little in common, and differ so much, that it is ill-advised to generalize about them. It is best to talk specifically about "copyright," or about "patents," or about "trademarks."

The term "intellectual property" carries a hidden assumption—that the way to think about all these disparate issues is based on an analogy with physical objects, and our conception of them as physical property.

When it comes to copying, this analogy disregards the crucial difference between material objects and information: information can be copied and shared almost effortlessly, while material objects can't be.

To avoid spreading unnecessary bias and confusion, it is best to adopt a firm policy not to speak or even think in terms of "intellectual property."

The hypocrisy of calling these powers "rights" is starting to make the World "Intellectual Property" Organization embarrassed.[21]

"LAMP System"

"LAMP" stands for "Linux, Apache, MySQL and PHP"—a common combination of software to use on a web server, except that "Linux" in this context really refers to the GNU/Linux system. So instead of "LAMP" it should be "GLAMP": "GNU, Linux, Apache, MySQL and PHP."

---

[19] "DuckDuckGo Privacy Policy," last modified on 11 April 2012, `https://duckduckgo.com/privacy`.

[20] See my article "On Hacking," at `http://stallman.org/articles/on-hacking.html`.

[21] Richard Stallman, "Public Awareness of Copyright, WIPO, June 2002," last updated in 2014, `http://gnu.org/philosophy/wipo-PublicAwarenessOfCopyright-2002.html`.

"Linux System"

Linux is the name of the kernel that Linus Torvalds developed starting in 1991. The operating system in which Linux is used is basically GNU with Linux added. To call the whole system "Linux" is both unfair and confusing. Please call the complete system GNU/Linux, both to give the GNU Project credit and to distinguish the whole system from the kernel alone.[22]

"Market"

It is misleading to describe the users of free software, or the software users in general, as a "market."

This is not to say there is no room for markets in the free software community. If you have a free software support business, then you have clients, and you trade with them in a market. As long as you respect their freedom, we wish you success in your market.

But the free software movement is a social movement, not a business, and the success it aims for is not a market success. We are trying to serve the public by giving it freedom—not competing to draw business away from a rival. To equate this campaign for freedom to a business's efforts for mere success is to deny the importance of freedom and legitimize proprietary software.

"Monetize"

The proper definition of "monetize" is "to use something as currency." For instance, human societies have monetized gold, silver, copper, printed paper, special kinds of seashells, and large rocks. However, we now see a tendency to use the word in another way, meaning "to use something as a basis for profit."

That usage casts the profit as primary, and the thing used to get the profit as secondary. That attitude applied to a software project is objectionable because it would lead the developers to make the program proprietary, if they conclude that making it free/libre isn't sufficiently profitable.

A productive and ethical business can make money, but if it subordinates all else to profit, it is not likely to remain ethical.

"MP3Player"

In the late 1990s it became feasible to make portable, solid-state digital audio players. Most support the patented MP3 codec, but not all. Some support the patent-free audio codecs Ogg Vorbis and FLAC, and may not even support MP3-encoded files at all, precisely to avoid these patents. To call such players "MP3 players" is not only confusing, it also privileges the MP3 that we ought to reject. We suggest the terms "digital audio player," or simply "audio player" if context permits.

---

[22] See also "Linux and the GNU System" (p. 64) for more on the history of the GNU/Linux system as it relates to this issue of naming.

"Open"

Please avoid using the term "open" or "open source" as a substitute for "free software." Those terms refer to a different position[23] based on different values. Free software is a political movement; open source is a development model.

When referring to the open source position, using its name is appropriate; but please do not use it to label us or our work—that leads people to think we share those views.

"PC"

It's OK to use the abbreviation "PC" to refer to a certain kind of computer hardware, but please don't use it with the implication that the computer is running Microsoft Windows. If you install GNU/Linux on the same computer, it is still a PC.

The term "WC" has been suggested for a computer running Windows.

"Photoshop"

Please avoid using the term "photoshop" as a verb, meaning any kind of photo manipulation or image editing in general. Photoshop is just the name of one particular image editing program, which should be avoided since it is proprietary. There are plenty of free programs for editing images, such as the GIMP.[24]

"Piracy"

Publishers often refer to copying they don't approve of as "piracy." In this way, they imply that it is ethically equivalent to attacking ships on the high seas, kidnapping and murdering the people on them. Based on such propaganda, they have procured laws in most of the world to forbid copying in most (or sometimes all) circumstances. (They are still pressuring to make these prohibitions more complete.)

If you don't believe that copying not approved by the publisher is just like kidnapping and murder, you might prefer not to use the word "piracy" to describe it. Neutral terms such as "unauthorized copying" (or "prohibited copying" for the situation where it is illegal) are available for use instead. Some of us might even prefer to use a positive term such as "sharing information with your neighbor."

A US judge, presiding over a trial for copyright infringement, recognized that "piracy" and "theft" are smear words.[25]

---

[23] See "Why Open Source Misses the Point of Free Software" (p. 75) for a complete explanation.

[24] See `http://directory.fsf.org/wiki/GIMP`.

[25] Ernesto Van der Sar, "MPAA Banned from Using Piracy and Theft Terms in Hotfile Trial," 29 November 2013, `http://torrentfreak.com/mpaa-banned-from-using-piracy-and-theft-terms-in-hotfile-trial-131129`.

"PowerPoint"

Please avoid using the term "PowerPoint" to mean any kind of slide presentation. "PowerPoint" is just the name of one particular proprietary program to make presentations. For your freedom's sake, you should use only free software to make your presentations. Recommended options include TEX's `beamer` class and OpenOffice.org's Impress.

"Protection"

Publishers' lawyers love to use the term "protection" to describe copyright. This word carries the implication of preventing destruction or suffering; therefore, it encourages people to identify with the owner and publisher who benefit from copyright, rather than with the users who are restricted by it.

It is easy to avoid "protection" and use neutral terms instead. For example, instead of saying, "Copyright protection lasts a very long time," you can say, "Copyright lasts a very long time."

Likewise, instead of saying, "protected by copyright," you can say, "covered by copyright" or just "copyrighted."

If you want to criticize copyright rather than be neutral, you can use the term "copyright restrictions." Thus, you can say, "Copyright restrictions last a very long time."

The term "protection" is also used to describe malicious features. For instance, "copy protection" is a feature that interferes with copying. From the user's point of view, this is obstruction. So we could call that malicious feature "copy obstruction." More often it is called Digital Restrictions Management (DRM)—see the Defective by Design campaign, at `DefectiveByDesign.org`.

"RAND (Reasonable and Non-Discriminatory)"

Standards bodies that promulgate patent-restricted standards that prohibit free software typically have a policy of obtaining patent licenses that require a fixed fee per copy of a conforming program. They often refer to such licenses by the term "RAND," which stands for "reasonable and non-discriminatory."

That term whitewashes a class of patent licenses that are normally neither reasonable nor nondiscriminatory. It is true that these licenses do not discriminate against any specific person, but they do discriminate against the free software community, and that makes them unreasonable. Thus, half of the term "RAND" is deceptive and the other half is prejudiced.

Standards bodies should recognize that these licenses are discriminatory, and drop the use of the term "reasonable and non-discriminatory" or "RAND" to describe them. Until they do so, writers who do not wish to join in the whitewashing would do well to reject that term. To accept and use it merely because patent-wielding companies have made it widespread is to let those companies dictate the views you express.

We suggest the term "uniform fee only," or "UFO" for short, as a replacement. It is accurate because the only condition in these licenses is a uniform royalty fee.

"SaaS" or "Software as a Service"

We used to say that SaaS (short for "Software as a Service") is an injustice, but then we found that there was a lot of variation in people's understanding of which activities count as SaaS. So we switched to a new term, "Service as a Software Substitute" or "SaaSS." This term has two advantages: it wasn't used before, so our definition is the only one, and it explains what the injustice consists of.

See "Who Does That Server Really Serve?" (p. 243) for discussion of this issue.

In Spanish we continue to use the term "software como servicio" because the joke of "software como ser vicio"[26] is too good to give up.

"Sell Software"

The term "sell software" is ambiguous. Strictly speaking, exchanging a copy of a free program for a sum of money is selling the program, and there is nothing wrong with doing that. However, people usually associate the term "selling software" with proprietary restrictions on the subsequent use of the software. You can be clear, and prevent confusion, by saying either "distributing copies of a program for a fee" or "imposing proprietary restrictions on the use of a program."

See "Selling Free Software" (p. 43) for further discussion of this issue.

"Sharing Economy"

The term "sharing economy" is not a good way to refer to services such as Uber and Airbnb that arrange business transactions between people. We use the term "sharing" to refer to noncommercial cooperation, including noncommercial redistribution of exact copies of published works. Stretching the word "sharing" to include these transactions undermines its meaning, so we don't use it in this context.

A more suitable term for businesses like Uber is the "piecework service economy."

"Skype"

Please avoid using the term "skype" as a verb, meaning any kind of video communication or telephony over the internet in general. "Skype" is just the name of one particular proprietary program, one that spies on its users.[27] If you want to make video and voice calls over the internet in a way that respects both your freedom and your privacy, try one of the numerous free Skype replacements, at `https://libreplanet.org/wiki/Group:Skype_Replacement`.

---

[26] "software, as being pernicious" (*sp.*)

[27] See `http://gnu.org/proprietary/proprietary-surveillance.html#SpywareInSkype` for more on this.

"Software Industry"

The term "software industry" encourages people to imagine that software is always developed by a sort of factory and then delivered to "consumers." The free software community shows this is not the case. Software businesses exist, and various businesses develop free and/or nonfree software, but those that develop free software are not run like factories.

The term "industry" is being used as propaganda by advocates of software patents. They call software development "industry" and then try to argue that this means it should be subject to patent monopolies. The European Parliament, rejecting software patents in 2003, voted to define "industry" as "automated production of material goods."[28]

"Source Model"

Wikipedia uses the term "source model" in a confused and ambiguous way. Ostensibly it refers to how a program's source is distributed, but the text confuses this with the development methodology. It distinguishes "open source" and "shared source" as answers, but they overlap— Microsoft uses the latter as a marketing term to cover a range of practices, some of which are "open source." Thus, this term really conveys no coherent information, but it provides an opportunity to say "open source" in pages describing free software programs.

"Terminal"

Mobile phones and tablets are computers, and people should be able to do their computing on them using free software. To call them "terminals" supposes that all they are good for is to connect to servers, which is a bad way to do your own computing.

"Theft"

The supporters of a too-strict, repressive form of copyright often use words like "stolen" and "theft" to refer to copyright infringement. This is spin, but they would like you to take it for objective truth.

Under the US legal system, copyright infringement is not theft. Laws about theft are not applicable to copyright infringement. The supporters of repressive copyright are making an appeal to authority—and misrepresenting what authority says.[29] which shows what can properly be described as "copyright theft."

Unauthorized copying is forbidden by copyright law in many circumstances (not all!), but being forbidden doesn't make it wrong. In general, laws don't define right and wrong. Laws, at their best, attempt to implement justice. If

---

[28] European Parliament, "Directive on the Patentability of Computer-Implemented Inventions," 24 September 2003, `http://web.archive.org/web/20071222001014/http://www.swpat.ffii.org/papers/europarl0309`.

[29] To refute them, you can point to the real case of Harper Lee suing her agent for allegedly duping her into assigning him the copyright on *To Kill a Mockingbird*.

the laws (the implementation) don't fit our ideas of right and wrong (the spec), the laws are what should change.

A US judge, presiding over a trial for copyright infringement, recognized that "piracy" and "theft" are smear words.[30]

"Trusted Computing"

"Trusted computing" is the proponents' name for a scheme to redesign computers so that application developers can trust your computer to obey them instead of you.[31] From their point of view, it is "trusted"; from your point of view, it is "treacherous."

"Vendor"

Please don't use the term "vendor" to refer generally to anyone that develops or packages software. Many programs are developed in order to sell copies, and their developers are therefore their vendors; this even includes some free software packages. However, many programs are developed by volunteers or organizations which do not intend to sell copies. These developers are not vendors. Likewise, only some of the packagers of GNU/Linux distributions are vendors. We recommend the general term "supplier" instead.

[30] See footnote 25, on p. 99.

[31] See "Can You Trust Your Computer?" (p. 225) for more on this issue.

Part III:
Copyright and Injustice

18 The Right to Read

From The Road to Tycho, *a collection of articles about the antecedents of the Lunarian Revolution, published in Luna City in 2096.*

For Dan Halbert, the road to Tycho began in college—when Lissa Lenz asked to borrow his computer. Hers had broken down, and unless she could borrow another, she would fail her midterm project. There was no one she dared ask, except Dan.

This put Dan in a dilemma. He had to help her—but if he lent her his computer, she might read his books. Aside from the fact that you could go to prison for many years for letting someone else read your books, the very idea shocked him at first. Like everyone, he had been taught since elementary school that sharing books was nasty and wrong—something that only pirates would do.

And there wasn't much chance that the SPA—the Software Protection Authority—would fail to catch him. In his software class, Dan had learned that each book had a copyright monitor that reported when and where it was read, and by whom, to Central Licensing. (They used this information to catch reading pirates, but also to sell personal interest profiles to retailers.) The next time his computer was networked, Central Licensing would find out. He, as computer owner, would receive the harshest punishment—for not taking pains to prevent the crime.

Of course, Lissa did not necessarily intend to read his books. She might want the computer only to write her midterm. But Dan knew she came from a middle-class family and could hardly afford the tuition, let alone her reading fees. Reading his books might be the only way she could graduate. He understood this situation; he himself had had to borrow to pay for all the research papers he read. (Ten percent of those fees went to the researchers who wrote the papers; since Dan aimed for an academic career, he could hope that his own research papers, if frequently referenced, would bring in enough to repay this loan.)

Later on, Dan would learn there was a time when anyone could go to the library and read journal articles, and even books, without having to pay. There were independent scholars who read thousands of pages without government library grants. But in the 1990s, both commercial and nonprofit journal publishers had begun charging fees for access. By 2047, libraries offering free public access to scholarly literature were a dim memory.

This essay was written in 1996 and was published as "The Right to Read: A Dystopian Short Story" in *Communications of the ACM,* vol. 40, n. 2, February 1997. This version is part of *Free Software, Free Society: Selected Essays of Richard M. Stallman,* 3rd ed. (Boston: GNU Press, 2015).

Later, Dan would learn that this kind of university policy started only in the 1980s, when university students in large numbers began using computers. Previously, universities maintained a different approach to student discipline; they punished activities that were harmful, not those that merely raised suspicion.

Lissa did not report Dan to the SPA. His decision to help her led to their marriage, and also led them to question what they had been taught about piracy as children. The couple began reading about the history of copyright, about the Soviet Union and its restrictions on copying, and even the original United States Constitution. They moved to Luna, where they found others who had likewise gravitated away from the long arm of the SPA. When the Tycho Uprising began in 2062, the universal right to read soon became one of its central aims.

Author's Notes

- This story is supposedly a historical article that will be written in the future by someone else, describing Dan Halbert's youth under a repressive society shaped by the enemies that use "pirate" as propaganda. So it uses the terminology of that society. I have tried to project it from today so as to sound even more oppressive. See "Piracy," on p. 99.
- The following note has been updated several times since the first publication of the story.

  The right to read is a battle being fought today. Although it may take 50 years for our present way of life to fade into obscurity, most of the specific laws and practices described above have already been proposed; many have been enacted into law in the US and elsewhere. In the US, the 1998 Digital Millennium Copyright Act (DMCA) established the legal basis to restrict the reading and lending of computerized books (and other works as well). The European Union imposed similar restrictions in a 2001 copyright directive. In France, under the DADVSI law adopted in 2006, mere possession of a copy of DeCSS, the free program to decrypt video on a DVD, is a crime.

  In 2001, Disney-funded Senator Hollings proposed a bill called the SSSCA that would require every new computer to have mandatory copy-restriction facilities that the user cannot bypass. Following the Clipper chip and similar US government key-escrow proposals, this shows a long-term trend: computer systems are increasingly set up to give absentees with clout control over the people actually using the computer system. The SSSCA was later renamed to the unpronounceable CBDTPA, which was glossed as the "Consume But Don't Try Programming Act."

  The Republicans took control of the US Senate shortly thereafter. They are less tied to Hollywood than the Democrats, so they did not press these proposals. Now that the Democrats are back in control, the danger is once again higher.

  In 2001 the US began attempting to use the proposed "Free Trade" Area of the Americas (FTAA) treaty to impose the same rules on all the countries in the Western Hemisphere. The FTAA is one of the so-called "free trade" treaties, which are actually designed to give business increased power over democratic governments; imposing laws like the DMCA is typical of this spirit. The FTAA was effectively killed by Lula, President of Brazil, who rejected the DMCA requirement and others.

Since then, the US has imposed similar requirements on countries such as Australia and Mexico through bilateral "free trade" agreements, and on countries such as Costa Rica through another treaty, CAFTA. Ecuador's President Correa refused to sign a "free trade" agreement with the US, but I've heard Ecuador had adopted something like the DMCA in 2003.

One of the ideas in the story was not proposed in reality until 2002. This is the idea that the FBI and Microsoft will keep the root passwords for your personal computers, and not let you have them.

The proponents of this scheme have given it names such as "trusted computing" and "Palladium." We call it "treacherous computing"[1] because the effect is to make your computer obey companies even to the extent of disobeying and defying you. This was implemented in 2007 as part of Windows Vista;[2] we expect Apple to do something similar. In this scheme, it is the manufacturer that keeps the secret code, but the FBI would have little trouble getting it.

What Microsoft keeps is not exactly a password in the traditional sense; no person ever types it on a terminal. Rather, it is a signature and encryption key that corresponds to a second key stored in your computer. This enables Microsoft, and potentially any web sites that cooperate with Microsoft, the ultimate control over what the user can do on his own computer.

Vista also gives Microsoft additional powers; for instance, Microsoft can forcibly install upgrades, and it can order all machines running Vista to refuse to run a certain device driver. The main purpose of Vista's many restrictions is to impose DRM (Digital Restrictions Management) that users can't overcome. The threat of DRM is why we have established the Defective by Design campaign, at `DefectiveByDesign.org`.

When this story was first written, the SPA was threatening small Internet service providers, demanding they permit the SPA to monitor all users. Most ISPs surrendered when threatened, because they cannot afford to fight back in court. One ISP, Community ConneXion in Oakland, California, refused the demand and was actually sued. The SPA later dropped the suit, but obtained the DMCA, which gave them the power they sought. The SPA, which actually stands for Software Publishers Association, has been replaced in its police-like role by the Business Software Alliance. The BSA is not, today, an official police force; unofficially, it acts like one.

[1] See "Can You Trust Your Computer?" (p. 225) for more on "trusted computing."

[2] See `http://badvista.fsf.org/` for our campaigns against Windows Vista.

Using methods reminiscent of the erstwhile Soviet Union, it invites people to inform on their coworkers and friends. A BSA terror campaign in Argentina in 2001 made slightly veiled threats that people sharing software would be raped.

The university security policies described above are not imaginary. For example, a computer at one Chicago-area university displayed this message upon login:

> This system is for the use of authorized users only. Individuals using this computer system without authority or in the excess of their authority are subject to having all their activities on this system monitored and recorded by system personnel. In the course of monitoring individuals improperly using this system or in the course of system maintenance, the activities of authorized user may also be monitored. Anyone using this system expressly consents to such monitoring and is advised that if such monitoring reveals possible evidence of illegal activity or violation of University regulations system personnel may provide the evidence of such monitoring to University authorities and/or law enforcement officials.

This is an interesting approach to the Fourth Amendment: pressure most everyone to agree, in advance, to waive their rights under it.

Bad News

The battle for the right to read is already in progress. The enemy is is organized, while we are not, so it is going against us. Examples of bad things that have happened since the original publication of this article include:

- Today's commercial e-books abolish readers' traditional freedoms. See "The Danger of E-Books" (p. 238) for more on this.
- The publication of a "biology textbook" web site[3] that you can access only by signing a contract not to lend it to anyone else,[4] which the publisher can revoke at will.
- Electronic publishing's curtailment of user freedom.[5]
- Books inside computers:[6] software to control who can read books and documents on a computer.

---

[3] *Nature America Inc.*, "Announcing Principles of Biology, an Interactive Textbook by Nature Education," `http://nature.com/nature_education/biology.html`.

[4] Nature America Inc., "Principles of Science Privacy Notice," accessed August 2015, `http://nature.com/principles/viewTermsOfUse`.

[5] See Don Clark's article "Seybold Opens Chapter on Digital Books" (31 August 1999, `http://www.zdnet.com/article/seybold-opens-chapter-on-digital-books/`), about distribution of books in electronic form and copyright issues affecting the right to read a copy.

[6] "Microsoft Announces New Software for Reading on Screen," 30 August 1999, `http://microsoft.com/en-us/news/press/1999/Aug99/SeyboldPR.aspx`.

If we want to stop the bad news and create some good news, we need to organize and fight. The FSF's Defective by Design campaign has made a start; subscribe to the campaign's mailing list to lend a hand. And join the FSF, at http://my.fsf.org/join, to help fund our work.

References

- United States Patent and Trademark Office, *Intellectual Property [sic] and the National Information Infrastructure: The Report of the Working Group on Intellectual Property [sic] Rights*, Washington, DC: GPO, 1995. (See "Did You Say 'Intellectual Property'? It's a Seductive Mirage" (p. 83) for why the term "Intellectual Property" is incoherent and should never be used.)
- Samuelson, Pamela, "The Copyright Grab," *Wired*, January 1996, 4.01, http://wired.com/wired/archive/4.01/white.paper_pr.html.
- Boyle, James, "Sold Out," *New York Times*, 31 March 1996, sec. 4, p. 15; also available at https://law.duke.edu/boylesite/sold_out.htm.
- Editorial, *Washington Post*, "Public Data or Private Data," 3 November 1996, sec. C, p. 6, http://web.archive.org/web/20130508120533/http://www.interesting-people.org/archives/interesting-people/199611/msg00012.html.
- Union for the Public Domain—an organization which aims to resist and reverse the overextension of copyright and patent powers.

19 Misinterpreting Copyright—A Series of Errors

Something strange and dangerous is happening in copyright law. Under the US Constitution, copyright exists to benefit users—those who read books, listen to music, watch movies, or run software—not for the sake of publishers or authors. Yet even as people tend increasingly to reject and disobey the copyright restrictions imposed on them "for their own benefit," the US government is adding more restrictions, and trying to frighten the public into obedience with harsh new penalties.

How did copyright policies come to be diametrically opposed to their stated purpose? And how can we bring them back into alignment with that purpose? To understand, we should start by looking at the root of United States copyright law: the US Constitution.

Copyright in the US Constitution

When the US Constitution was drafted, the idea that authors were entitled to a copyright monopoly was proposed—and rejected. The founders of our country adopted a different premise, that copyright is not a natural right of authors, but an artificial concession made to them for the sake of progress. The Constitution gives permission for a copyright system with this clause (Article I, Section 8, Clause 8):

> [Congress shall have the power] to promote the Progress of Science and the useful Arts, by securing for limited Times to Authors and Inventors the exclusive Right to their respective Writings and Discoveries.

The Supreme Court has repeatedly affirmed that promoting progress means benefit for the users of copyrighted works. For example, in *Fox Film v. Doyal,*[1] the court said,

> The sole interest of the United States and the primary object in conferring the [copyright] monopoly lie in the general benefits derived by the public from the labors of authors.

This fundamental decision explains why copyright is not *required* by the Constitution, only *permitted* as an option—and why it is supposed to last for "limited times." If copyright were a natural right, something that authors have because they deserve it, nothing could justify terminating this right after a certain period of time, any more than everyone's house should become public property after a certain lapse of time from its construction.

[1] *Fox Film Corp. v. Doyal,* 286 US 123, 1932.

This essay was first published on `http://gnu.org`, in 2002. This version is part of *Free Software, Free Society: Selected Essays of Richard M. Stallman,* 3rd ed. (Boston: GNU Press, 2015).

There were ways, of course, to get around the SPA and Central Licensing. They were themselves illegal. Dan had had a classmate in software, Frank Martucci, who had obtained an illicit debugging tool, and used it to skip over the copyright monitor code when reading books. But he had told too many friends about it, and one of them turned him in to the SPA for a reward (students deep in debt were easily tempted into betrayal). In 2047, Frank was in prison, not for pirate reading, but for possessing a debugger.

Dan would later learn that there was a time when anyone could have debugging tools. There were even free debugging tools available on CD or downloadable over the net. But ordinary users started using them to bypass copyright monitors, and eventually a judge ruled that this had become their principal use in actual practice. This meant they were illegal; the debuggers' developers were sent to prison.

Programmers still needed debugging tools, of course, but debugger vendors in 2047 distributed numbered copies only, and only to officially licensed and bonded programmers. The debugger Dan used in software class was kept behind a special firewall so that it could be used only for class exercises.

It was also possible to bypass the copyright monitors by installing a modified system kernel. Dan would eventually find out about the free kernels, even entire free operating systems, that had existed around the turn of the century. But not only were they illegal, like debuggers—you could not install one if you had one, without knowing your computer's root password. And neither the FBI nor Microsoft Support would tell you that.

Dan concluded that he couldn't simply lend Lissa his computer. But he couldn't refuse to help her, because he loved her. Every chance to speak with her filled him with delight. And that she chose him to ask for help, that could mean she loved him too.

Dan resolved the dilemma by doing something even more unthinkable—he lent her the computer, and told her his password. This way, if Lissa read his books, Central Licensing would think he was reading them. It was still a crime, but the SPA would not automatically find out about it. They would only find out if Lissa reported him.

Of course, if the school ever found out that he had given Lissa his own password, it would be curtains for both of them as students, regardless of what she had used it for. School policy was that any interference with their means of monitoring students' computer use was grounds for disciplinary action. It didn't matter whether you did anything harmful—the offense was making it hard for the administrators to check on you. They assumed this meant you were doing something else forbidden, and they did not need to know what it was.

Students were not usually expelled for this—not directly. Instead they were banned from the school computer systems, and would inevitably fail all their classes.

The "Copyright Bargain"

The copyright system works by providing privileges and thus benefits to publishers and authors; but it does not do this for their sake. Rather, it does this to modify their behavior: to provide an incentive for authors to write more and publish more. In effect, the government spends the public's natural rights, on the public's behalf, as part of a deal to bring the public more published works. Legal scholars call this concept the "copyright bargain." It is like a government purchase of a highway or an airplane using taxpayers' money, except that the government spends our freedom instead of our money.

But is the bargain as it exists actually a good deal for the public? Many alternative bargains are possible; which one is best? Every issue of copyright policy is part of this question. If we misunderstand the nature of the question, we will tend to decide the issues badly.

The Constitution authorizes granting copyright powers to authors. In practice, authors typically cede them to publishers; it is usually the publishers, not the authors, who exercise these powers and get most of the benefits, though authors may get a small portion. Thus it is usually the publishers that lobby to increase copyright powers. To better reflect the reality of copyright rather than the myth, this article refers to publishers rather than authors as the holders of copyright powers. It also refers to the users of copyrighted works as "readers," even though using them does not always mean reading, because "the users" is remote and abstract.

The First Error: "Striking a Balance"

The copyright bargain places the public first: benefit for the reading public is an end in itself; benefits (if any) for publishers are just a means toward that end. Readers' interests and publishers' interests are thus qualitatively unequal in priority. The first step in misinterpreting the purpose of copyright is the elevation of the publishers to the same level of importance as the readers.

It is often said that US copyright law is meant to "strike a balance" between the interests of publishers and readers. Those who cite this interpretation present it as a restatement of the basic position stated in the Constitution; in other words, it is supposed to be equivalent to the copyright bargain.

But the two interpretations are far from equivalent; they are different conceptually, and different in their implications. The balance concept assumes that the readers' and publishers' interests differ in importance only quantitatively, in *how much weight* we should give them, and in what actions they apply to. The term "stakeholders" is often used to frame the issue in this way; it assumes that all kinds of interest in a policy decision are equally important. This view rejects the qualitative distinction between the readers' and publishers' interests which is at the root of the government's participation in the copyright bargain.

The consequences of this alteration are far-reaching, because the great protection for the public in the copyright bargain—the idea that copyright privileges can be justified only in the name of the readers, never in the name of the publishers—is discarded by the "balance" interpretation. Since the interest of the publishers is regarded as an end in itself, it can justify copyright privileges; in other words, the "balance" concept says that privileges can be justified in the name of someone other than the public.

As a practical matter, the consequence of the "balance" concept is to reverse the burden of justification for changes in copyright law. The copyright bargain places the burden on the publishers to convince the readers to cede certain freedoms. The concept of balance reverses this burden, practically speaking, because there is generally no doubt that publishers will benefit from additional privilege. Unless harm to the readers can be proved, sufficient to "outweigh" this benefit, we are led to conclude that the publishers are entitled to almost any privilege they request.

Since the idea of "striking a balance" between publishers and readers denies the readers the primacy they are entitled to, we must reject it.

Balancing against What?

When the government buys something for the public, it acts on behalf of the public; its responsibility is to obtain the best possible deal—best for the public, not for the other party in the agreement.

For example, when signing contracts with construction companies to build highways, the government aims to spend as little as possible of the public's money. Government agencies use competitive bidding to push the price down.

As a practical matter, the price cannot be zero, because contractors will not bid that low. Although not entitled to special consideration, they have the usual rights of citizens in a free society, including the right to refuse disadvantageous contracts; even the lowest bid will be high enough for some contractor to make money. So there is indeed a balance, of a kind. But it is not a deliberate balancing of two interests each with claim to special consideration. It is a balance between a public goal and market forces. The government tries to obtain for the taxpaying motorists the best deal they can get in the context of a free society and a free market.

In the copyright bargain, the government spends our freedom instead of our money. Freedom is more precious than money, so government's responsibility to spend our freedom wisely and frugally is even greater than its responsibility to spend our money thus. Governments must never put the publishers' interests on a par with the public's freedom.

Not "Balance" but "Trade-Off"

The idea of balancing the readers' interests against the publishers' is the wrong way to judge copyright policy, but there are indeed two interests to be weighed: two interests *of the readers.* Readers have an interest in their own freedom in using published works; depending on circumstances, they may also have an interest in encouraging publication through some kind of incentive system.

The word "balance," in discussions of copyright, has come to stand as shorthand for the idea of "striking a balance" between the readers and the publishers.

Therefore, to use the word "balance" in regard to the readers' two interests would be confusing.[2] We need another term.

In general, when one party has two goals that partly conflict, and cannot completely achieve both of them, we call this a "trade-off." Therefore, rather than speaking of "striking the right balance" between parties, we should speak of "finding the right trade-off between spending our freedom and keeping it."

The Second Error: Maximizing One Output

The second mistake in copyright policy consists of adopting the goal of maximizing—not just increasing—the number of published works. The erroneous concept of "striking a balance" elevated the publishers to parity with the readers; this second error places them far above the readers.

When we purchase something, we do not generally buy the whole quantity in stock or the most expensive model. Instead we conserve funds for other purchases, by buying only what we need of any particular good, and choosing a model of sufficient rather than highest quality. The principle of diminishing returns suggests that spending all our money on one particular good is likely to be an inefficient allocation of resources; we generally choose to keep some money for another use.

Diminishing returns applies to copyright just as to any other purchase. The first freedoms we should trade away are those we miss the least, and whose sacrifice gives the largest encouragement to publication. As we trade additional freedoms that cut closer to home, we find that each trade is a bigger sacrifice than the last, while bringing a smaller increment in literary activity. Well before the increment becomes zero, we may well say it is not worth its incremental price; we would then settle on a bargain whose overall result is to increase the amount of publication, but not to the utmost possible extent.

Accepting the goal of maximizing publication rejects all these wiser, more advantageous bargains in advance—it dictates that the public must cede nearly all of its freedom to use published works, for just a little more publication.

The Rhetoric of Maximization

In practice, the goal of maximizing publication regardless of the cost to freedom is supported by widespread rhetoric which asserts that public copying is illegitimate, unfair, and intrinsically wrong. For instance, the publishers call people who copy "pirates," a smear term designed to equate sharing information with your neighbor with attacking a ship. (This smear term was formerly used by authors to describe publishers who found lawful ways to publish unauthorized editions; its modern use by the publishers is almost the reverse.) This rhetoric directly rejects the constitutional basis for copyright, but presents itself as representing the unquestioned tradition of the American legal system.

[2] See Julian Sanchez's article "The Trouble with 'Balance' Metaphors" (4 February 2011, `http://juliansanchez.com/2011/02/04/the-trouble-with-balance-metaphors/`) for an examination of "how the analogy between sound judgment and balancing weights may constrain our thinking in unhealthy ways."

The "pirate" rhetoric is typically accepted because it so pervades the media that few people realize how radical it is. It is effective because if copying by the public is fundamentally illegitimate, we can never object to the publishers' demand that we surrender our freedom to do so. In other words, when the public is challenged to show why publishers should not receive some additional power, the most important reason of all—"We want to copy"—is disqualified in advance.

This leaves no way to argue against increasing copyright power except using side issues. Hence, opposition to stronger copyright powers today almost exclusively cites side issues, and never dares cite the freedom to distribute copies as a legitimate public value.

As a practical matter, the goal of maximization enables publishers to argue that "A certain practice is reducing our sales—or we think it might—so we presume it diminishes publication by some unknown amount, and therefore it should be prohibited." We are led to the outrageous conclusion that the public good is measured by publishers' sales: What's good for General Media is good for the USA.

The Third Error: Maximizing Publishers' Power

Once the publishers have obtained assent to the policy goal of maximizing publication output at any cost, their next step is to infer that this requires giving them the maximum possible powers—making copyright cover every imaginable use of a work, or applying some other legal tool such as "shrink wrap" licenses to equivalent effect. This goal, which entails the abolition of "fair use" and the "right of first sale," is being pressed at every available level of government, from states of the US to international bodies.

This step is erroneous because strict copyright rules obstruct the creation of useful new works. For instance, Shakespeare borrowed the plots of some of his plays from works others had published a few decades before, so if today's copyright law had been in effect, his plays would have been illegal.

Even if we wanted the highest possible rate of publication, regardless of cost to the public, maximizing publishers' power is the wrong way to get it. As a means of promoting progress, it is self-defeating.

The Results of the Three Errors

The current trend in copyright legislation is to hand publishers broader powers for longer periods of time. The conceptual basis of copyright, as it emerges distorted from the series of errors, rarely offers a basis for saying no. Legislators give lip service to the idea that copyright serves the public, while in fact giving publishers whatever they ask for.

For example, here is what Senator Hatch said when introducing S. 483,[3] a 1995 bill to increase the term of copyright by 20 years:

---

[3] *Congressional Record*, S. 483, "The Copyright Term Extension Act of 1995," 2 March 1995, pp. S3390–4.

> I believe we are now at such a point with respect to the question of whether the current term of copyright adequately protects the interests of authors and the related question of whether the term of protection continues to provide a sufficient incentive for the creation of new works of authorship.[4]

This bill extended the copyright on already published works written since the 1920s. This change was a giveaway to publishers with no possible benefit to the public, since there is no way to retroactively increase now the number of books published back then. Yet it cost the public a freedom that is meaningful today—the freedom to redistribute books from that era. Note the use of the propaganda term, "protect,"[5] which embodies the second of the three errors.

The bill also extended the copyrights of works yet to be written. For works made for hire, copyright would last 95 years instead of the present 75 years. Theoretically this would increase the incentive to write new works; but any publisher that claims to need this extra incentive should be required to substantiate the claim with projected balance sheets for 75 years in the future.

Needless to say, Congress did not question the publishers' arguments: a law extending copyright was enacted in 1998. It was officially called the Sonny Bono Copyright Term Extension Act, named after one of its sponsors who died earlier that year. We usually call it the Mickey Mouse Copyright Act, since we presume its real motive was to prevent the copyright on the appearance of Mickey Mouse from expiring. Bono's widow, who served the rest of his term, made this statement:

> Actually, Sonny wanted the term of copyright protection to last forever. I am informed by staff that such a change would violate the Constitution. I invite all of you to work with me to strengthen our copyright laws in all of the ways available to us. As you know, there is also Jack Valenti's[6] proposal for term to last forever less one day. Perhaps the Committee may look at that next Congress.[7]

The Supreme Court later heard a case that sought to overturn the law on the grounds that the retroactive extension fails to serve the Constitution's goal of promoting progress. The court responded by abdicating its responsibility to judge the question; on copyright, the Constitution requires only lip service.

Another law, passed in 1997, made it a felony to make sufficiently many copies of any published work, even if you give them away to friends just to be nice. Previously this was not a crime in the US at all.

An even worse law, the Digital Millennium Copyright Act (DMCA), was designed to bring back what was then called "copy protection"—now known

---

[4] *Congressional Record,* "Statement on Introduced Bills and Joint Resolutions," 2 March 1995, p. S3390, `http://gpo.gov/fdsys/pkg/CREC-1995-03-02/pdf/CREC-1995-03-02-pt1-PgS3390-2.pdf`.

[5] See p. 100 for why use the term "protect" should be avoided in connection with copyright.

[6] Jack Valenti was a longtime president of the Motion Picture Association of America.

[7] *Congressional Record,* remarks of Rep. Bono, 7 October 1998, p. H9952, `http://gpo.gov/fdsys/pkg/CREC-1998-10-07/pdf/CREC-1998-10-07-pt1-PgH9946.pdf`.

as DRM (Digital Restrictions Management)[8]—which users already detested, by making it a crime to defeat the restrictions, or even publish information about how to defeat them. This law ought to be called the "Domination by Media Corporations Act" because it effectively offers publishers the chance to write their own copyright law. It says they can impose any restrictions whatsoever on the use of a work, and these restrictions take the force of law provided the work contains some sort of encryption or license manager to enforce them.

One of the arguments offered for this bill was that it would implement a recent treaty to increase copyright powers. The treaty was promulgated by the World "Intellectual Property"[9] Organization, an organization dominated by copyright- and patent-holding interests, with the aid of pressure from the Clinton administration; since the treaty only increases copyright power, whether it serves the public interest in any country is doubtful. In any case, the bill went far beyond what the treaty required.

Libraries were a key source of opposition to this bill, especially to the aspects that block the forms of copying that are considered fair use. How did the publishers respond? Former representative Pat Schroeder, now a lobbyist for the Association of American Publishers, said that the publishers "could not live with what [the libraries were] asking for." Since the libraries were asking only to preserve part of the status quo, one might respond by wondering how the publishers had survived until the present day.

Congressman Barney Frank, in a meeting with me and others who opposed this bill, showed how far the US Constitution's view of copyright has been disregarded. He said that new powers, backed by criminal penalties, were needed urgently because the "movie industry is worried," as well as the "music industry" and other "industries." I asked him, "But is this in the public interest?" His response was telling: "Why are you talking about the public interest? These creative people don't have to give up their rights for the public interest!" The "industry" has been identified with the "creative people" it hires, copyright has been treated as its entitlement, and the Constitution has been turned upside down.

The DMCA was enacted in 1998. As enacted, it says that fair use remains nominally legitimate, but allows publishers to prohibit all software or hardware that you could practice it with. Effectively, fair use is prohibited.

Based on this law, the movie industry has imposed censorship on free software for reading and playing DVDs, and even on the information about how to read them. In April 2001, Professor Edward Felten of Princeton University was intimidated by lawsuit threats from the Recording Industry Association of America (RIAA) into withdrawing a scientific paper stating what he had learned about a proposed encryption system for restricting access to recorded music.

We are also beginning to see e-books that take away many of readers' traditional freedoms—for instance, the freedom to lend a book to your friend, to

---

8 See `http://gnu.org/proprietary/proprietary-drm.html` for more on this issue.

9 See "Did You Say "Intellectual Property"? It's a Seductive Mirage" (p. 83) for an explanation of why this term is problematic.

sell it to a used book store, to borrow it from a library, to buy it without giving your name to a corporate data bank, even the freedom to read it twice. Encrypted e-books generally restrict all these activities—you can read them only with special secret software designed to restrict you.

I will never buy one of these encrypted, restricted e-books, and I hope you will reject them too. If an e-book doesn't give you the same freedoms as a traditional paper book, don't accept it!

Anyone independently releasing software that can read restricted e-books risks prosecution. A Russian programmer, Dmitry Sklyarov, was arrested in 2001 while visiting the US to speak at a conference, because he had written such a program in Russia, where it was lawful to do so. Now Russia is preparing a law to prohibit it too, and the European Union recently adopted one.

Mass-market e-books have been a commercial failure so far, but not because readers chose to defend their freedom; they were unattractive for other reasons, such as that computer display screens are not easy surfaces to read from. We can't rely on this happy accident to protect us in the long term; the next attempt to promote e-books will use "electronic paper"—book-like objects into which an encrypted, restricted e-book can be downloaded. If this paper-like surface proves more appealing than today's display screens, we will have to defend our freedom in order to keep it. Meanwhile, e-books are making inroads in niches: NYU and other dental schools require students to buy their textbooks in the form of restricted e-books.

The media companies are not satisfied yet. In 2001, Disney-funded Senator Hollings proposed a bill called the "Security Systems Standards and Certification Act" (SSSCA),[10] which would require all computers (and other digital recording and playback devices) to have government-mandated copy-restriction systems. That is their ultimate goal, but the first item on their agenda is to prohibit any equipment that can tune digital HDTV unless it is designed to be impossible for the public to "tamper with" (i.e., modify for their own purposes). Since free software is software that users can modify, we face here for the first time a proposed law that explicitly prohibits free software for a certain job. Prohibition of other jobs will surely follow. If the FCC adopts this rule, existing free software such as GNU Radio would be censored.

To block these bills and rules requires political action.[11]

---

[10] Since renamed to the unpronounceable CBDTPA, for which a good mnemonic is "Consume, But Don't Try Programming Anything," but it really stands for the "Consumer Broadband and Digital Television Promotion Act."

[11] If you would like to help, I recommend the web sites `http://defectivebydesign.org`, `http://publicknowledge.org`, and `http://eff.org`.

Finding the Right Bargain

What is the proper way to decide copyright policy? If copyright is a bargain made on behalf of the public, it should serve the public interest above all. The government's duty when selling the public's freedom is to sell only what it must, and sell it as dearly as possible. At the very least, we should pare back the extent of copyright as much as possible while maintaining a comparable level of publication.

Since we cannot find this minimum price in freedom through competitive bidding, as we do for construction projects, how can we find it?

One possible method is to reduce copyright privileges in stages, and observe the results. By seeing if and when measurable diminutions in publication occur, we will learn how much copyright power is really necessary to achieve the public's purposes. We must judge this by actual observation, not by what publishers say will happen, because they have every incentive to make exaggerated predictions of doom if their powers are reduced in any way.

Copyright policy includes several independent dimensions, which can be adjusted separately. After we find the necessary minimum for one policy dimension, it may still be possible to reduce other dimensions of copyright while maintaining the desired publication level.

One important dimension of copyright is its duration, which is now typically on the order of a century. Reducing the monopoly on copying to ten years, starting from the date when a work is published, would be a good first step. Another aspect of copyright, which covers the making of derivative works, could continue for a longer period.

Why count from the date of publication? Because copyright on unpublished works does not directly limit readers' freedom; whether we are free to copy a work is moot when we do not have copies. So giving authors a longer time to get a work published does no harm. Authors (who generally do own the copyright prior to publication) will rarely choose to delay publication just to push back the end of the copyright term.

Why ten years? Because that is a safe proposal; we can be confident on practical grounds that this reduction would have little impact on the overall viability of publishing today. In most media and genres, successful works are very profitable in just a few years, and even successful works are usually out of print well before ten. Even for reference works, whose useful life may be many decades, ten-year copyright should suffice: updated editions are issued regularly, and many readers will buy the copyrighted current edition rather than copy a ten-year-old public domain version.

Ten years may still be longer than necessary; once things settle down, we could try a further reduction to tune the system. At a panel on copyright at a literary convention, where I proposed the ten-year term, a noted fantasy author sitting beside me objected vehemently, saying that anything beyond five years was intolerable.

But we don't have to apply the same time span to all kinds of works. Maintaining the utmost uniformity of copyright policy is not crucial to the public interest, and copyright law already has many exceptions for specific uses and media. It would be foolish to pay for every highway project at the rates necessary for the most difficult projects in the most expensive regions of the country; it is equally foolish to "pay" for all kinds of art with the greatest price in freedom that we find necessary for any one kind.

So perhaps novels, dictionaries, computer programs, songs, symphonies, and movies should have different durations of copyright, so that we can reduce the duration for each kind of work to what is necessary for many such works to be published. Perhaps movies over one hour long could have a 20-year copyright, because of the expense of producing them. In my own field, computer programming, three years should suffice, because product cycles are even shorter than that.

Another dimension of copyright policy is the extent of fair use: some ways of reproducing all or part of a published work that are legally permitted even though it is copyrighted. The natural first step in reducing this dimension of copyright power is to permit occasional private small-quantity noncommercial copying and distribution among individuals. This would eliminate the intrusion of the copyright police into people's private lives, but would probably have little effect on the sales of published works. (It may be necessary to take other legal steps to ensure that shrink-wrap licenses cannot be used to substitute for copyright in restricting such copying.) The experience of Napster shows that we should also permit noncommercial verbatim redistribution to the general public—when so many of the public want to copy and share, and find it so useful, only draconian measures will stop them, and the public deserves to get what it wants.

For novels, and in general for works that are used for entertainment, noncommercial verbatim redistribution may be sufficient freedom for the readers. Computer programs, being used for functional purposes (to get jobs done), call for additional freedoms beyond that, including the freedom to publish an improved version. See "The Free Software Definition," in this book, for an explanation of the freedoms that software users should have. But it may be an acceptable compromise for these freedoms to be universally available only after a delay of two or three years from the program's publication.

Changes like these could bring copyright into line with the public's wish to use digital technology to copy. Publishers will no doubt find these proposals "unbalanced"; they may threaten to take their marbles and go home, but they won't really do it, because the game will remain profitable and it will be the only game in town.

As we consider reductions in copyright power, we must make sure media companies do not simply replace it with end-user license agreements. It would be necessary to prohibit the use of contracts to apply restrictions on copying that go beyond those of copyright. Such limitations on what mass-market nonnegotiated contracts can require are a standard part of the US legal system.

A Personal Note

I am a software designer, not a legal scholar. I've become concerned with copyright issues because there's no avoiding them in the world of computer networks, such as the Internet. As a user of computers and networks for 30 years, I value the freedoms that we have lost, and the ones we may lose next. As an author, I can reject the romantic mystique of the author as semidivine creator, often cited by publishers to justify increased copyright powers for authors—powers which these authors will then sign away to publishers.

Most of this article consists of facts and reasoning that you can check, and proposals on which you can form your own opinions. But I ask you to accept one thing on my word alone: that authors like me don't deserve special power over you. If you wish to reward me further for the software or books I have written, I would gratefully accept a check—but please don't surrender your freedom in my name.

20 Science Must Push Copyright Aside

Many points that lead to a conclusion that software freedom must be universal often apply to other forms of expressive works, albeit in different ways. This essay concerns the application of principles related to software freedom to the area of literature. Generally, such issues are orthogonal to software freedom, but we include essays like this here since many people interested in Free Software want to know more about how the principles can be applied to areas other than software.

It should be a truism that the scientific literature exists to disseminate scientific knowledge, and that scientific journals exist to facilitate the process. It therefore follows that rules for use of the scientific literature should be designed to help achieve that goal.

The rules we have now, known as copyright, were established in the age of the printing press, an inherently centralized method of mass-production copying. In a print environment, copyright on journal articles restricted only journal publishers—requiring them to obtain permission to publish an article—and would-be plagiarists. It helped journals to operate and disseminate knowledge, without interfering with the useful work of scientists or students, either as writers or readers of articles. These rules fit that system well.

The modern technology for scientific publishing, however, is the World Wide Web. What rules would best ensure the maximum dissemination of scientific articles, and knowledge, on the web? Articles should be distributed in nonproprietary formats, with open access for all. And everyone should have the right to "mirror" articles—that is, to republish them verbatim with proper attribution.

These rules should apply to past as well as future articles, when they are distributed in electronic form. But there is no crucial need to change the present copyright system as it applies to paper publication of journals because the problem is not in that domain.

Unfortunately, it seems that not everyone agrees with the truisms that began this article. Many journal publishers appear to believe that the purpose of scientific literature is to enable them to publish journals so as to collect subscriptions from scientists and students. Such thinking is known as "confusion of the means with the ends."

Their approach has been to restrict access even to read the scientific literature to those who can and will pay for it. They use copyright law, which is still in force despite its inappropriateness for computer networks, as an excuse to stop scientists from choosing new rules.

This essay was first published in *Nature* magazine's *Web Debates* forum, on 8 June 2001. This version is part of *Free Software, Free Society: Selected Essays of Richard M. Stallman*, 3rd ed. (Boston: GNU Press, 2015).

For the sake of scientific cooperation and humanity's future, we must reject that approach at its root—not merely the obstructive systems that have been instituted, but the mistaken priorities that inspired them.

Journal publishers sometimes claim that online access requires expensive high-powered server machines, and that they must charge access fees to pay for these servers. This "problem" is a consequence of its own "solution." Give everyone the freedom to mirror, and libraries around the world will set up mirror sites to meet the demand. This decentralized solution will reduce network bandwidth needs and provide faster access, all the while protecting the scholarly record against accidental loss.

Publishers also argue that paying the editors requires charging for access. Let us accept the assumption that editors must be paid; this tail need not wag the dog. The cost of editing for a typical paper is between 1 percent and 3 percent of the cost of funding the research to produce it. Such a small percentage of the cost can hardly justify obstructing the use of the results.

Instead, the cost of editing could be recovered, for example, through page charges to the authors, who can pass these on to the research sponsors. The sponsors should not mind, given that they currently pay for publication in a more cumbersome way, through overhead fees for the university library's subscription to the journal. By changing the economic model to charge editing costs to the research sponsors, we can eliminate the apparent need to restrict access. The occasional author who is not affiliated with an institution or company, and who has no research sponsor, could be exempted from page charges, with costs levied on institution-based authors.

Another justification for access fees to online publications is to fund conversion of the print archives of a journal into online form. That work needs to be done, but we should seek alternative ways of funding it that do not involve obstructing access to the result. The work itself will not be any more difficult, or cost any more. It is self-defeating to digitize the archives and waste the results by restricting access.

The US Constitution says that copyright exists "to promote the Progress of Science." When copyright impedes the progress of science, science must push copyright out of the way.

Later Developments

Some universities—MIT for instance[1]—have adopted policies to thwart the journal publishers' power. Stronger policies are needed, however, as ones like MIT's permit individual authors to "opt out" (i.e., cave in).

The US government has imposed a requirement known as "public access" on some funded research. This requires publication within a certain period in a site that allows anyone to view the article. This requirement is a positive step, but inadequate because it does not include freedom to redistribute the article.

---

[1] "MIT Faculty Open Access Policy," adopted by unanimous faculty vote on 18 March 2009, `http://libraries.mit.edu/scholarly/mit-open-access/open-access-at-mit/mit-open-access-policy/`.

Curiously, the concept of “open access” in the 2002 Budapest Open Access Initiative did include freedom to redistribute. I signed that declaration, despite my distaste for the word “open,” because the substance of the position was right.

However, the word “open” had the last laugh: influential campaigners for “open access” subsequently dropped freedom to redistribute from their goals. I stand by the position of the BOAI,[2] but now that “open access” means something else, I refer to it as “redistributable publication” or “free-to-mirror publication.”

[2] See `http://www.budapestopenaccessinitiative.org/` for the BOAI guidelines.

21 Copyright vs. Community in the Age of Computer Networks

This is a transcript of the keynote speech presented by Richard Stallman, on 12 October 2009, at the LIANZA conference, at the Christchurch Convention Centre, in Christchurch, New Zealand.

Brenda Chawner: Tena koutou, tena koutou, tena koutou katoa. Today I have the privilege of introducing Richard Stallman, whose keynote speech is being sponsored by the School of Information Management at Victoria University of Wellington.

Richard has been working to promote software freedom for over 25 years. In 1983 he started the GNU Project to develop a free operating system [the GNU system], and in 1985 he set up the Free Software Foundation. Every time you read or send a message to nz-libs, you use the Mailman software which is part of the GNU Project. So whether you realize it or not, Richard's work has touched all of your lives.

I like to describe him as the most influential person most people have never heard of, although he tells me that that cannot possibly be true because it cannot be tested.

RMS: We can't tell.

BC: I said that—I still like it. His ideas about software freedom and free access to information were used by Tim Berners-Lee when he created the world's first web server, and in 1999 his musings about a free online encyclopedia inspired Jimmy Wales to set up what is now Wikipedia.

Today Richard will be talking to us about copyright vs. community in the age of computer networks, and their implications for libraries. Richard.

RMS: I've been in New Zealand for a couple of weeks, and in the North Island it was raining most of the time. Now I know why they call gumboots "Wellingtons." And then I saw somebody who was making chairs and tables out of ponga wood, and he called it fern-iture. Then we took the ferry to get here, and as soon as we got off, people started mocking and insulting us; but there were no hard feelings, they just wanted to make us really feel Picton.

The reason people usually invite me to give speeches is because of my work on free software. This is not a talk about free software; this talk answers the question whether the ideas of free software extend to other kinds of works. But in order for that to make sense, I'd better tell you briefly what free software means.

Free software is a matter of freedom, not price, so think of "free speech," not "free beer." Free software is software that respects the user's freedom, and there are four specific freedoms that the user deserves always to have:

Thank you to Bookman for the original transcript. This version of it is part of *Free Software, Free Society: Selected Essays of Richard M. Stallman*, 3rd ed. (Boston: GNU Press, 2015).

- Freedom 0 is the freedom to run the program as you wish.
- Freedom 1 is the freedom to study the source code of the program and change it to make the program do what you wish.
- Freedom 2 is the freedom to help your neighbor—that is, the freedom to redistribute copies of the program, exact copies when you wish.
- And freedom 3 is the freedom to contribute to your community. That's the freedom to publish your modified versions when you wish.

If the program gives you these four freedoms then it's free software, which means the social system of its distribution and use is an ethical system, one which respects the user's freedom and the social solidarity of the user's community. But if one of these freedoms is missing or insufficient, then it's proprietary software, nonfree software, user-subjugating software. It's unethical. It's not a contribution to society. It's a power grab. This unethical practice should not exist; the goal of the free software movement is to put an end to it. All software should be free, so that all users can be free.

Proprietary software keeps the users divided and helpless: divided, because they're forbidden to share it, and helpless, because they don't have the source code so they can't change it. They can't even study it to verify what it's really doing to them, and many proprietary programs have malicious features which spy on the user, restrict the user, even back doors to attack the user.

For instance, Microsoft Windows has a back door with which Microsoft can forcibly install software changes, without getting permission from the supposed owner of the computer. You may think it's your computer, but if you've made the mistake of having Windows running in it, then really Microsoft has owned your computer. Computers need to be defenestrated, which means either throw Windows out of the computer, or throw the computer out the window.

But any proprietary software gives the developers unjust power over the users. Some of the developers abuse this power more, and some abuse it less, but none of them ought to have it. You deserve to have control of your computing, and not be forcibly dependent on a particular company. So you deserve free software.

At the end of speeches about free software, people sometimes ask whether these same freedoms and ideas apply to other things. If you have a copy of a published work on your computer, it makes sense to ask whether you should have the same four freedoms—whether it's ethically essential that you have them or not. And that's the question that I'm going to address today.

If you have a copy of something that's not software, for the most part, the only thing that might deny you any of these freedoms is copyright law. With software that's not so. The main ways of making software nonfree are contracts and withholding the source code from the users. Copyright is a sort of secondary, back up method. For other things there's no such distinction as between source code and executable code.

For instance, if we're talking about a text, if you can see the text to read it, there's nothing in the text that you can't see. So it's not the same kind of issue exactly as software. It's for the most part only copyright that might deny you these freedoms.

So the question can be restated: "What should copyright law allow you to do with published works? What should copyright law say?"

Copyright has developed along with copying technology, so it's useful to review the history of copying technology. Copying developed in the ancient world, where you'd use a writing instrument on a writing surface. You'd read one copy and write another.

This technology was rather inefficient, but another interesting characteristic was that it had no economy of scale. To write ten copies would take ten times as long as to write one copy. It required no special equipment other than the equipment for writing, and it required no special skill other than literacy itself. The result was that copies of any particular book were made in a decentralized manner. Wherever there was a copy, if someone wanted to copy it, he could.

There was nothing like copyright in the ancient world. If you had a copy and wanted to copy it, nobody was going to tell you you weren't allowed—except if the local prince didn't like what the book said, in which case he might punish you for copying it. But that's not copyright, but rather something closely related, namely censorship. To this day, copyright is often used in attempts to censor people.

That went on for thousands of years, but then there was a big advance in copying technology, namely the printing press. The printing press made copying more efficient, but not uniformly. [This was] because mass production copying became a lot more efficient, but making one copy at a time didn't benefit from the printing press. In fact, you were better off just writing it by hand; that would be faster than trying to print one copy.

The printing press has an economy of scale: it takes a lot of work to set the type, but then you can make many copies very fast. Also, the printing press and the type were expensive equipment that most people didn't own; and the ability to use them, most literate people didn't know. Using a press was a different skill from writing. The result was a centralized manner of producing copies: the copies of any given book would be made in a few places, and then they would be transported to wherever someone wanted to buy copies.

Copyright began in the age of the printing press. Copyright in England began as a system of censorship in the 1500s. I believe it was originally meant to censor Protestants, but it was turned around and used to censor Catholics and presumably lots of others as well. According to this law, in order to publish a book you had to get permission from the Crown, and this permission was granted in the form of a perpetual monopoly to publish it. This was allowed to lapse in the 1680s, I believe [it expired in 1695 according to the Wikipedia entry]. The publishers wanted it back again, but what they got was something somewhat different. The Statute of Anne gave authors a copyright, and only for 14 years, although the author could renew it once.

This was a totally different idea—a temporary monopoly for the author, instead of a perpetual monopoly for the publisher. The idea developed that copyright was a means of promoting writing.

When the US constitution was written, some people wanted authors to be entitled to a copyright, but that was rejected. Instead, the US Constitution says that Congress can optionally adopt a copyright law, and if there is a copyright law, its purpose is to promote progress. In other words, the purpose is not benefits for copyright holders or anybody they do business with, but for the general public. Copyright has to last a limited time; publishers keep hoping for us to forget about this.

Here we have an idea of copyright which is an industrial regulation on publishers, controlled by authors, and designed to provide benefits to the public at large. It functioned this way because it didn't restrict the readers.

Now in the early centuries of printing, and still I believe in the 1790s, lots of readers wrote copies by hand because they couldn't afford printed copies. Nobody ever expected copyright law to be something other than an industrial regulation. It wasn't meant to stop people from writing copies, it was meant to regulate the publishers. Because of this it was easy to enforce, uncontroversial, and arguably beneficial for society.

It was easy to enforce, because it only had to be enforced against publishers. And it's easy to find the unauthorized publishers of a book—you go to a bookstore and say, "Where do these copies come from?" You don't have to invade everybody's home and everybody's computer to do that.

It was uncontroversial because, as the readers were not restricted, they had nothing to complain about. Theoretically they were restricted from publishing, but not being publishers and not having printing presses, they couldn't do that anyway. In what they actually could do, they were not restricted.

It was arguably beneficial because the general public, according to the concepts of copyright law, traded away a theoretical right they were not in a position to exercise. In exchange, they got the benefits of more writing.

Now if you trade away something you have no possible use for, and you get something you can use in exchange, it's a positive trade. Whether or not you could have gotten a better deal some other way, that's a different question, but at least it's positive.

So if this were still in the age of the printing press, I don't think I'd be complaining about copyright law. But the age of the printing press is gradually giving way to the age of the computer networks—another advance in copying technology that makes copying more efficient, and once again not uniformly so.

Here's what we had in the age of the printing press: mass production very efficient, one at a time copying still just as slow as the ancient world. Digital technology gets us here: they've both benefited, but one-off copying has benefited the most.

We get to a situation much more like the ancient world, where one at a time copying is not so much worse [i.e., harder] than mass production copying. It's a little bit less efficient, a little bit less good, but it's perfectly cheap enough that hundreds of millions of people do it. Consider how many people write CDs once in a while, even in poor countries. You may not have a CD-writer yourself, so you go to a store where you can do it.

This means that copyright no longer fits in with the technology as it used to. Even if the words of copyright law had not changed, they wouldn't have the same effect. Instead of an industrial regulation on publishers controlled by authors, with the benefits set up to go to the public, it is now a restriction on the general public, controlled mainly by the publishers, in the name of the authors.

In other words, it's tyranny. It's intolerable and we can't allow it to continue this way.

As a result of this change, [copyright] is no longer easy to enforce, no longer uncontroversial, and no longer beneficial.

It's no longer easy to enforce because now the publishers want to enforce it against each and every person, and to do this requires cruel measures, draconian punishments, invasions of privacy, abolition of our basic ideas of justice. There's almost no limit to how far they will propose to go to prosecute the War on Sharing.

It's no longer uncontroversial. There are political parties in several countries whose basic platform is "freedom to share."

It's no longer beneficial because the freedoms that we conceptually traded away (because we couldn't exercise them), we now can exercise. They're tremendously useful, and we want to exercise them.

What would a democratic government do in this situation?

It would reduce copyright power. It would say: "The trade we made on behalf of our citizens, trading away some of their freedom which now they need, is intolerable. We have to change this; we can't trade away the freedom that is important." We can measure the sickness of democracy by the tendency of governments to do the exact opposite around the world, extending copyright power when they should reduce it.

One example is in the dimension of time. Around the world we see pressure to make copyright last longer and longer and longer.

A wave of this started in the US in 1998. Copyright was extended by 20 years on both past and future works. I do not understand how they hope to convince the now dead or senile writers of the 20s and 30s to write more back then by extending copyright on their works now. If they have a time machine with which to inform them, they haven't used it. Our history books don't say that there was a burst of vigor in the arts in the 20s when all the artists found out that their copyrights would be extended in 1998.

It's theoretically conceivable that 20 years more copyright on future works would convince people to make more effort in producing those works. But not anyone rational, because the discounted present value of 20 more years of copyright starting 75 years in the future—if it's a work made for hire—and probably even longer if it's a work with an individual copyright holder, is so small it couldn't persuade any rational person to do anything different. Any business that wants to claim otherwise ought to present its projected balance sheets for

75 years in the future, which of course they can't do because none of them really looks that far ahead.

The real reason for this law, the desire that prompted various companies to purchase this law in the US Congress, which is how laws are decided on for the most part, was they had lucrative monopolies and they wanted those monopolies to continue.

For instance, Disney was aware that the first film in which Mickey Mouse appeared would go into the public domain in a few years, and then anybody would be free to draw that same character as part of other works. Disney didn't want that to happen. Disney borrows a lot from the public domain, but is determined never to give the slightest thing back. So Disney paid for this law, which we refer to as the Mickey Mouse Copyright Act.

The movie companies say they want perpetual copyright, but the US Constitution won't let them get that officially. So they came up with a way to get the same result unofficially: "perpetual copyright on the installment plan." Every 20 years they extend copyright for 20 more years. So that at any given time, any given work has a date when it will supposedly fall into the public domain. But that date is like tomorrow, it never comes. By the time you get there they will have postponed it, unless we stop them next time.

That's one dimension, the dimension of duration. But even more important is the dimension of breadth: which uses of the work does copyright cover?

In the age of the printing press, copyright wasn't supposed to cover all uses of a copyrighted work, because copyright regulated certain uses that were the exceptions in a broader space of unregulated uses. There were certain things you were simply allowed to do with your copy of a book.

Now the publishers have got the idea that they can turn our computers against us, and use them to seize total power over all use of published works. They want to set up a pay-per-view universe. They're doing it with DRM (Digital Restrictions Management)—the intentional features of software that's designed to restrict the user. And often the computer itself is designed to restrict the user.

The first way in which the general public saw this was in DVDs. A movie on a DVD was usually encrypted, and the format was secret. The DVD conspiracy kept this secret because they said anyone that wants to make DVD players has to join the conspiracy, promise to keep the format secret, and promise to design the DVD players to restrict the users according to the rules, which say it has to stop the user from doing this, from doing that, from doing that—a precise set of requirements, all of which are malicious towards us.

It worked for a while, but then some people figured out the secret format, and published free software capable of reading the movie on a DVD and playing it. Then the publishers said, "Since we can't actually stop them, we have to make it a crime." And they started that in the US in 1998 with the Digital Millennium Copyright Act, which imposed censorship on software capable of doing such jobs.

So that particular piece of free software was the subject of a court case. Its distribution in the US is forbidden; the US practices censorship of software.

The movie companies are well aware that they can't really make that program disappear—it's easy enough to find it. So they designed another encryption system, which they hoped would be harder to break, and it's called AACS, or the axe.

The AACS conspiracy makes precise rules about all players. For instance, in 2011 it's going to be forbidden to make analog video outputs. So all video outputs will have to be digital, and they will carry the signal encrypted into a monitor specially designed to keep secrets from the user. That is malicious hardware. They say that the purpose of this is to "close the analog hole." *[Stallman takes off his glasses.]* Here's one and here's another, that they'd like to poke out permanently.[1]

How do I know about these conspiracies? The reason is they're not secret—they have web sites. The AACS web site proudly describes the contracts that manufacturers have to sign, which is how I know about this requirement. It proudly states the names of the companies that have established this conspiracy, which include Microsoft and Apple, and Intel, and Sony, and Disney, and IBM.

A conspiracy of companies designed to restrict the public's access to technology ought to be prosecuted as a serious crime, like a conspiracy to fix prices, except it's worse, so the prison sentences for this should be longer. But these companies are quite confident that our governments are on their side against us. They have no fear against being prosecuted for these conspiracies, which is why they don't bother to hide them.

In general, DRM is set up by a conspiracy of companies. Once in a while a single company can do it, but generally it requires a conspiracy between technology companies and publishers, so [it's] almost always a conspiracy.

They thought that nobody would ever be able to break the AACS, but about three and a half years ago someone released a free program capable of decrypting that format. However, it was totally useless, because in order to run it you need to know the key.

And then, six months later, I saw a photo of two adorable puppies, with 32 hex digits above them, and I wondered, "Why put those two things together? I wonder if those numbers are some important key, and someone could have put the numbers together with the puppies, figuring people would copy the photo of the puppies because they were so cute. This would protect the key from being wiped out."

And that's what it was—that was the key to break the axe. People posted it, and editors deleted it, because laws in many countries now conscript them to censor this information. It was posted again, they deleted it; eventually they gave up, and in two weeks this number was posted in over 700,000 web sites.

---

[1] In 2010, the encryption system for digital video output was definitively cracked. (See Mark Hachman's "HDCP Master Key Confirmed; Blu-Ray Content Vulnerable" (September 16 2010), at `http://pcmag.com/article2/0,2817,2369280,00.asp`, for more information.)

That's a big outpouring of public disgust with DRM. But it didn't win the war, because the publishers changed the key. Not only that: with HD DVD, this was adequate to break the DRM, but not with Blu-ray. Blu-ray has an additional level of DRM and so far there is no free software that can break it, which means that you must regard Blu-ray disks as something incompatible with your own freedom. They are an enemy with which no accommodation is possible, at least not with our present level of knowledge.

Never accept any product designed to attack your freedom. If you don't have the free software to play a DVD, you mustn't buy or rent any DVDs, or accept them even as gifts, except for the rare non-encrypted DVDs, which there are a few of. I actually have a few [of these]—I don't have any encrypted DVDs, I won't take them.

So this is how things stand in video, but we've also seen DRM in music.

For instance, about ten years ago we started to see things that looked like compact disks, but they weren't written quite like compact disks. They didn't follow the standard. We called them "corrupt disks," and the idea of them was that they would play in an audio player, but it was impossible to read them on a computer. These different methods had various problems.

Eventually Sony came up with a clever idea. They put a program on the disk, so that if you stuck the disk into a computer, the disk would install the program. This program was designed like a virus to take control of the system. It's called a "root kit," meaning that it has things in it to break the security of the system so that it can install the software deep inside the system, and modify various parts of the system.

For instance, it modified the command you could use to examine the system to see if the software was present, so as to disguise itself. It modified the command you could use to delete some of these files, so that it wouldn't really delete them. Now all of this is a serious crime, but it's not the only one Sony committed, because the software also included free software code—code that had been released under the GNU General Public License.

Now the GNU GPL is a copyleft license, and that means it says, "Yes, you're free to put this code into other things, but when you do, the entire program that you put things into you must release as free software under the same license. And you must make the source code available to users, and to inform them of their rights you must give them a copy of this license when they get the software."

Sony didn't comply with all that. That's commercial copyright infringement, which is a felony. They're both felonies, but Sony wasn't prosecuted because the government understands that the purpose of the government and the law is to maintain the power of those companies over us, not to help defend our freedom in any way.

People got angry and they sued Sony. However, they made a mistake. They focused their condemnation not on the evil purpose of this scheme, but only on the secondary evils of the various methods that Sony used. So Sony settled the lawsuits and promised that in the future, when it attacks our freedom, it will not do those other things.

Actually, that particular corrupt disk scheme was not so bad, because if you were not using Windows it would not affect you at all. Even if you were using Windows, there's a key on the keyboard—if you remembered every time to hold it down, then the disk wouldn't install the software. But of course it's hard to remember that every time; you're going to slip up some day. This shows the kind of thing we've had to deal with.

Fortunately music DRM is receding. Even the main record companies sell downloads without DRM. But we see a renewed effort to impose DRM on books.

You see, the publishers want to take away the traditional freedoms of book readers—freedom to do things such as borrow a book from the public library, or lend it to a friend; to sell a book to a used book store, or buy it anonymously paying cash (which is the only way I buy books—we've got to resist the temptations to let Big Brother know everything that we're doing.)

Even the freedom to keep the book as long as you wish, and read it as many times as you wish, they plan to get rid of.

The way they do it is with DRM. They knew that so many people read books and would get angry if these freedoms were taken away that they didn't believe they could buy a law specifically to abolish these freedoms—there would be too much opposition. Democracy is sick, but once in a while people manage to demand something. So they came up with a two-stage plan.

First, take away these freedoms from e-books, and second, convince people to switch from paper books to e-books. They've succeeded with stage 1.

In the US they did it with the Digital Millennium Copyright Act, and in New Zealand, that was part of the Copyright Act [of 2008]; censorship on software that can break DRM was part of that law. That's an unjust provision; it's got to be repealed.

The second stage is convince people to switch from printed books to e-books; that didn't go so well.

One publisher in 2001 had the idea they would make their line of e-books really popular if they started it with my biography. So they found an author and the author asked me if I'd cooperate, and I said, "Only if this e-book is published without encryption, without DRM." The publisher wouldn't go along with that, and I just stuck to it—I said no. Eventually we found another publisher who was willing to do this—in fact willing to publish the book under a free license giving you the four freedoms—so the book was then published, and sold a lot of copies on paper.

But in any case, e-books failed at the beginning of this decade. People just didn't want to read them very much. And I said, "They will try again." We saw an amazing number of news articles about electronic ink (or is it electronic paper, I can never remember which), and it occurred to me probably the reason there's so many is the publishers want us to think about this. They want us to be eager for the next generation of e-book readers.

Now they're upon us. Things like the Sony Shreader (its official name is the Sony Reader, but if you put on 'sh' it explains what it's designed to do to your books), and the Amazon Swindle, designed to swindle you out of your traditional freedoms without your noticing. Of course, they call it the Kindle which is what it's going to do to your books.

The Kindle is an extremely malicious product, almost as malicious as Microsoft Windows. They both have spy features, they both have Digital Restrictions Management, and they both have back doors.

In the case of the Kindle, the only way you can buy a book is to buy it from Amazon, and Amazon requires you to identify yourself, so they know everything that you've bought.

Then there is Digital Restrictions Management, so you can't lend the book or sell it to a used bookstore, and the library can't lend it either.

And then there's the back door, which we found out about about three months ago, because Amazon used it. Amazon sent a command to all the Kindles to erase a particular book, namely *1984*, by George Orwell. Yes, they couldn't have picked a more ironic book to erase. So that's how we know that Amazon has a back door with which it can erase books remotely.

What else it can do, who knows? Maybe it's like Microsoft Windows. Maybe Amazon can remotely upgrade the software, which means that whatever malicious things are not in it now, they could put them in it tomorrow.

This is intolerable—any one of these restrictions is intolerable. They want to create a world where nobody lends books to anybody anymore.

Imagine that you visit a friend and there are no books on the shelf. It's not that your friend doesn't read, but his books are all inside a device, and of course he can't lend you those books. The only way he could lend you any one of those books is to lend you his whole library, which is obviously a ridiculous thing to ask anybody to do. So there goes friendship for people who love books.

Make sure that you inform people what this device implies. It means other readers will no longer be your friends, because you will be acting like a jerk toward them. Spread the word preemptively. This device is your enemy. It's the enemy of everyone who reads. The people who don't recognize that are the people who are thinking so short-term that they don't see it. It's our job to help them see beyond the momentary convenience to the implications of this device.

I have nothing against distributing books in digital form, if they are not designed to take away our freedom. Strictly speaking, it is possible to have an e-book reader:

- that is not designed to attack you,
- which runs free software and not proprietary software,
- which doesn't have DRM,
- which doesn't make people identify yourself to get a book,
- which doesn't have a back door, [and]
- which doesn't restrict what you can do with the files on your machine.

It's possible, but the big companies really pushing e-books are doing it to attack our freedom, and we mustn't stand for that. This is what governments are doing in cahoots with big business to attack our freedom, by making copyright harsher and nastier, more restrictive than ever before.

But what should they do? Governments should make copyright power less. Here are my specific proposals.

First of all, there is the dimension of time. I propose copyright should last ten years, starting from the date of publication of a work.

Why from the date of publication? Because before that, we don't have copies. It doesn't matter to us whether we would have been allowed to copy our copies that we don't have, so I figure we might as well let the authors have as much time as it takes to arrange publication, and then start the clock.

But why ten years? I don't know about in this country, but in the US, the publication cycle has got shorter and shorter. Nowadays almost all books are remaindered within two years and out-of-print within three. So ten years is more than three times the usual publication cycle—that should be plenty comfortable.

But not everybody agrees. I once proposed this in a panel discussion with fiction writers, and the award-winning fantasy writer next to me said, "Ten years? No way. Anything more than five years is intolerable." You see, he had a legal dispute with his publisher. His books seemed to be out of print, but the publisher wouldn't admit it. The publisher was using the copyright on his own book to stop him from distributing copies himself, which he wanted to do so people could read it.

This is what every artist starts out wanting—wanting to distribute her work so it will get read and appreciated. Very few make a lot of money. That tiny fraction face the danger of being morally corrupted, like JK Rowling.

JK Rowling, in Canada, got an injunction against people who had bought her book in a bookstore, ordering them not to read it. So in response I call for a boycott of *Harry Potter* books. But I don't say you shouldn't read them; I leave that to the author and the publisher. I just say you shouldn't buy them.

It's few authors that make enough money that they can be corrupted in this way. Most of them don't get anywhere near that, and continue wanting the same thing they wanted at the outset: they want their work to be appreciated.

He wanted to distribute his own book, and copyright was stopping him. He realized that more than five years of copyright was unlikely to ever do him any good.

If people would rather have copyright last five years, I won't be against it. I propose ten as a first stab at the problem. Let's reduce it to ten years and then take stock for a while, and we could adjust it after that. I don't say I think ten years is the exact right number—I don't know.

What about the dimension of breadth? Which activities should copyright cover? I distinguish three broad categories of works.

First of all, there are the functional works that you use to do a practical job in your life. This includes software, recipes, educational works, reference works, text fonts, and other things you can think of. These works should be free.

If you use the work to do a job in your life, then if you can't change the work to suit you, you don't control your life. Once you have changed the work to suit you, then you've got to be free to publish it—publish your version—because there will be others who will want the changes you've made.

This leads quickly to the conclusion that users have to have the same four freedoms [for all functional works], not just for software. And you'll notice that for recipes, practically speaking, cooks are always sharing and changing recipes just as if the recipes were free. Imagine how people would react if the government tried to stamp out so-called recipe piracy.

The term "pirate" is pure propaganda. When people ask me what I think of music piracy, I say, "As far as I know, when pirates attack they don't do it by playing instruments badly, they do it with arms. So it's not music 'piracy,' because piracy is attacking ships, and sharing is as far as you get from being the moral equivalent of attacking ships." Attacking ships is bad, sharing with other people is good, so we should firmly denounce that propaganda term "piracy" whenever we hear it.

People might have objected twenty years ago: "If we don't give up our freedom, if we don't let the publishers of these works control us, the works won't get made and that will be a horrible disaster." Now, looking at the free software community, and all the recipes that circulate, and reference works like Wikipedia—we are even starting to see free textbooks being published—we know that that fear is misguided.

There is no need to despair and give up our freedom thinking that otherwise the works won't get made. There are lots of ways to encourage them to get made if we want more—lots of ways that are consistent with and respect our freedom. In this category, they should all be free.

But what about the second category, of works that say what certain people thought, like memoirs, essays of opinion, scientific papers,[2] and various other things? To publish a modified version of somebody else's statement of what he thought is misrepresenting [that] somebody. That's not particularly a contribution to society.

Therefore it is workable and acceptable to have a somewhat reduced copyright system where all commercial use is covered by copyright, all modification is covered by copyright, but everyone is free to non-commercially redistribute exact copies.

That freedom is the minimum freedom we must establish for all published works, because the denial of that freedom is what creates the War on Sharing—what creates the vicious propaganda that sharing is theft, that sharing is like being a pirate and attacking ships. Absurdities, but absurdities backed by a

[2] 2015: I included scientific papers because I thought that publishing modified versions of someone else's paper would cause harm; however, publishing physics and math papers under the Creative Commons Attribution License on `arXiv.org` and many libre journals seems to have no problems. Thus, I subsequently concluded that scientific papers ought to be free.

lot of money that has corrupted our governments. We need to end the War on Sharing; we need to legalize sharing exact copies of any published work.

In the second category of works, that's all we need; we don't need to make them free. Therefore I think it's OK to have a reduced copyright system which covers commercial use and all modifications. And this will provide a revenue stream to the authors in more or less the same (usually inadequate) way as the present system. You've got to keep in mind [that] the present system, except for superstars, is usually totally inadequate.

What about works of art and entertainment? Here it took me a while to decide what to think about modifications.

You see, on one hand, a work of art can have an artistic integrity and modifying it could destroy that. Of course, copyright doesn't necessarily stop works from being butchered that way. Hollywood does it all the time. On the other hand, modifying the work can be a contribution to art. It makes possible the folk process which leads to things which are beautiful and rich.

Even if we look at named authors only: consider Shakespeare, who borrowed stories from other works only a few decades old, and did them in different ways, and made important works of literature. If today's copyright law had existed then, that would have been forbidden and those plays wouldn't have been written.

But eventually I realized that modifying a work of art can be a contribution to art, but it's not desperately urgent in most cases. If you had to wait ten years for the copyright to expire, you could wait that long. Not like the present-day copyright that makes you wait maybe 75 years, or 95 years. In Mexico you might have to wait almost 200 years in some cases, because copyright in Mexico expires a hundred years after the author dies. This is insane, but ten years, as I've proposed copyright should last, that people can wait.

So I propose the same partly reduced copyright that covers commercial use and modification, but everyone's got to be free to non-commercially redistribute exact copies. After ten years it goes into the public domain, and people can contribute to art by publishing their modified versions.

One other thing: if you're going to take little pieces out of a bunch of works and rearrange them into something totally different, that should just be legal, because the purpose of copyright is to promote art, not to obstruct art. It's stupid to apply copyright to using snippets like that—it's self-defeating. It's a kind of distortion that you'd only get when the government is under the control of the publishers of the existing successful works, and has totally lost sight of its intended purpose.

That's what I propose, and in particular, this means that sharing copies on the internet must be legal. Sharing is good. Sharing builds the bonds of society. To attack sharing is to attack society.

So any time the government proposes some new means to attack people who share, to stop them from sharing, we have to recognize that this is evil, not just because the means proposed almost invariably offend basic ideas of justice. But that's not a coincidence; the reason is because the purpose is evil. Sharing is good and the government should encourage sharing.

But copyright did after all have a useful purpose. Copyright as a means to carry out that purpose has a problem now, because it doesn't fit in with the technology we use. It interferes with all the vital freedoms for all the readers, listeners, viewers, and whatever, but the goal of promoting the arts is still desirable. So in addition to the partly reduced copyright system, which would continue to be a copyright system, I propose two other methods.

One [works via] taxes—distribute tax money directly to artists. This could be a special tax, perhaps on internet connectivity, or it could come from general revenue, because it won't be that much money in total, not if it's distributed in an efficient way. To distribute it efficiently to promote the arts means not in linear proportion to popularity. It should be based on popularity, because we don't want bureaucrats to have the discretion to decide which artists to support and which to ignore, but based on popularity does not imply linear proportion.

What I propose is measure the popularity of the various artists, which you could do through polling (samples) in which nobody is required to participate, and then take the cube root. The cube root looks like this: it means basically that [the payment] tapers off after a while.

If superstar A is a thousand times as popular as successful artist B, with this system A would get ten times as much money as B, not a thousand times.

Linearly would give A a thousand times as much as B, which means that if we wanted B to get enough to live on we're going to have to make A tremendously rich. This is wasteful use of the tax money—it shouldn't be done.

But if we make it taper off, then yes, each superstar will get handsomely more than an ordinary successful artist, but the total of all the superstars will be a small fraction of the [total] money. Most of the money will go to support a large number of fairly successful artists, fairly appreciated artists, fairly popular artists. Thus the system will use money a lot more efficiently than the existing system.

The existing system is regressive. It actually gives far, far more per record, for instance, to a superstar than to anybody else. The money is extremely badly used. The result is we'd actually be paying a lot less this way. I hope that's enough to mollify some of these people who have a knee-jerk hostile reaction to taxes—one that I don't share, because I believe in a welfare state.

I have another suggestion which is voluntary payments. Suppose every player had a button you could push to send a dollar to the artist who made the work you're currently playing or the last one you played. This money would be delivered anonymously to those artists. I think a lot of people would push that button fairly often.

For instance, all of us could afford to push that button once every day, and we wouldn't miss that much money. It's not that much money for us, I'm pretty sure. Of course, there are poor people who couldn't afford to push it ever, and it's OK if they don't. We don't need to squeeze money out of poor people to support the artists. There are enough people who are not poor to do the job just fine. I'm sure you're aware that a lot of people really love certain art and are really happy to support the artists.

An idea just came to me. The player could also give you a certificate of having supported so-and-so, and it could even count up how many times you had done it and give you a certificate that says, "I sent so much to these artists." There are various ways we could encourage people who want to do it.

For instance, we could have a PR campaign which is friendly and kind: "Have you sent a dollar to some artists today? Why not? It's only a dollar—you'll never miss it and don't you love what they're doing? Push the button!" It will make people feel good, and they'll think, "Yeah, I love what I just watched. I'll send a dollar."

This is already starting to work to some extent. There's a Canadian singer who used to be called Jane Siberry. She put her music on her web site and invited people to download it and pay whatever amount they wished. She reported getting an average of more than a dollar per copy, which is interesting because the major record companies charge just under a dollar per copy. By letting people decide whether and how much to pay, she got more—she got even more per visitor who was actually downloading something. But this might not even count whether there was an effect of bringing more people to come, and [thus] increasing the total number that this average was against.

So it can work, but it's a pain in the neck under present circumstances. You've got to have a credit card to do it, and that means you can't do it anonymously. And you've got to go find where you're going to pay, and the payment systems for small amounts, they're not very efficient, so the artists are only getting half of it. If we set up a good system for this, it would work far, far better.

So these are my two suggestions.

And in `mecenat-global.org`,[3] you can find another scheme that combines aspects of the two, which was invented by Francis Muguet and designed to fit in with existing legal systems better to make it easier to enact.

Be careful of proposals to "compensate the rights holders," because when they say "compensate," they're trying to presume that if you have appreciated a work, you now have a specific debt to somebody, and that you have to "compensate" that somebody. When they say "rights holders," it's supposed to make you think it's supporting artists while in fact it's going to the publishers—the same publishers who basically exploit all the artists (except the few that you've all heard of, who are so popular that they have clout).

We don't owe a debt; we have nobody that we have to "compensate." [But] supporting the arts is still a useful thing to do. That was the motivation for copyright back when copyright fit in with the technology of the day. Today copyright is a bad way to do it, but it's still good to do it other ways that respect our freedom.

---

[3] That page is no longer active; please see `https://stallman.org/mecenat/global-patronage.html` instead.

Demand that they change the two evil parts of the New Zealand Copyright Act. They shouldn't replace the three strikes punishment,[4] because sharing is good, and they've got to get rid of the censorship for the software to break DRM. Beware of ACTA—they're trying to negotiate a treaty between various countries, for all of these countries to attack their citizens, and we don't know how because they won't tell us.

[4] New Zealand had enacted a system of punishment without trial for internet users accused of copying; then, facing popular protest, the government did not implement it, and announced a plan to implement a modified unjust punishment system. The point here was that they should not proceed to implement a replacement—rather, they should have no such system. However, the words I used don't say this clearly.

The New Zealand government subsequently implemented the punishment scheme more or less as originally planned.

Part IV:
Software Patents:
Danger to Programmers

22 Software Patents and Literary Patents

When politicians consider the question of software patents, they are usually voting blind; not being programmers, they don't understand what software patents really do. They often think patents are similar to copyright law ("except for some details")—which is not the case. For instance, when I publicly asked Patrick Devedjian, then Minister for Industry in France, how France would vote on the issue of software patents, Devedjian responded with an impassioned defense of copyright law, praising Victor Hugo for his role in the adoption of copyright. (The misleading term "intellectual property" promotes this confusion—one of the reasons it should never be used.)

Those who imagine effects like those of copyright law cannot grasp the disastrous effects of software patents. We can use Victor Hugo as an example to illustrate the difference.

A novel and a modern complex program have certain points in common: each one is large, and implements many ideas in combination. So let's follow the analogy, and suppose that patent law had been applied to novels in the 1800s; suppose that states such as France had permitted the patenting of literary ideas. How would this have affected Victor Hugo's writing? How would the effects of literary patents compare with the effects of literary copyright?

Consider Victor Hugo's novel *Les Misérables*. Since he wrote it, the copyright belonged only to him. He did not have to fear that some stranger could sue him for copyright infringement and win. That was impossible, because copyright covers only the details of a work of authorship, not the ideas embodied in them, and it only restricts copying. Hugo had not copied *Les Misérables*, so he was not in danger from copyright.

Patents work differently. Patents cover ideas; each patent is a monopoly on practicing some idea, which is described in the patent itself. Here's one example of a hypothetical literary patent:

- Claim 1: a communication process that represents in the mind of a reader the concept of a character who has been in jail for a long time and becomes bitter towards society and humankind.
- Claim 2: a communication process according to claim 1, wherein said character subsequently finds moral redemption through the kindness of another.
- Claim 3: a communication process according to claims 1 and 2, wherein said character changes his name during the story.

This essay was originally published on `http://guardian.co.uk`, on 23 June 2005. It was then titled "Patent Absurdity" and focused on the proposed European software patent directive. This version is part of *Free Software, Free Society: Selected Essays of Richard M. Stallman*, 3rd ed. (Boston: GNU Press, 2015).

If such a patent had existed in 1862 when *Les Misérables* was published, the novel would have conflicted with all three claims, since all these things happened to Jean Valjean in the novel. Victor Hugo could have been sued, and if sued, he would have lost. The novel could have been prohibited—in effect, censored—by the patent holder.

Now consider this hypothetical literary patent:

- Claim 1: a communication process that represents in the mind of a reader the concept of a character who has been in jail for a long time and subsequently changes his name.

Les Misérables would have been prohibited by that patent too, because this description too fits the life story of Jean Valjean. And here's another hypothetical patent:

- Claim 1: a communication process that represents in the mind of a reader the concept of a character who finds moral redemption and then changes his name.

Jean Valjean would have been forbidden by this patent too.

All three patents would cover, and prohibit, the life story of this one character. They overlap, but they do not precisely duplicate each other, so they could all be valid simultaneously; all three patent holders could have sued Victor Hugo. Any one of them could have prohibited publication of *Les Misérables.*

This patent also could have been violated:

- Claim 1: a communication process that presents a character whose given name matches the last syllable of his family name.

through the name "Jean Valjean," but at least this patent would have been easy to avoid.

You might think that these ideas are so simple that no patent office would have issued them. We programmers are often amazed by the simplicity of the ideas that real software patents cover—for instance, the European Patent Office has issued a patent on the progress bar, and a patent on accepting payment via credit cards. These patents would be laughable if they were not so dangerous.

Other aspects of *Les Misérables* could also have run afoul of patents. For instance, there could have been a patent on a fictionalized portrayal of the Battle of Waterloo, or a patent on using Parisian slang in fiction. Two more lawsuits. In fact, there is no limit to the number of different patents that might have been applicable for suing the author of a work such as *Les Misérables.* All the patent holders would say they deserved a reward for the literary progress that their patented ideas represent, but these obstacles would not promote progress in literature, they would only obstruct it.

However, a very broad patent could have made all these issues irrelevant. Imagine a patent with broad claims like these:

- A communication process structured with narration that continues through many pages.
- A narration structure sometimes resembling a fugue or improvisation.
- Intrigue articulated around the confrontation of specific characters, each in turn setting traps for the others.
- Narration that presents many layers of society.
- Narration that shows the wheels of hidden conspiracy.

Who would the patent holders have been? They could have been other novelists, perhaps Dumas or Balzac, who had written such novels—but not necessarily. It isn't required to write a program to patent a software idea, so if our hypothetical literary patents follow the real patent system, these patent holders would not have had to write novels, or stories, or anything—except patent applications. Patent parasite companies, businesses that produce nothing except threats and lawsuits, are booming nowadays.

Given these broad patents, Victor Hugo would not have reached the point of asking what patents might get him sued for using the character of Jean Valjean, because he could not even have considered writing a novel of this kind.

This analogy can help nonprogrammers see what software patents do. Software patents cover features, such as defining abbreviations in a word processor, or natural order recalculation in a spreadsheet. Patents cover algorithms that programs need to use. Patents cover aspects of file formats, such as Microsoft's OOXML format. MPEG 2 video format is covered by 39 different US patents.

Just as one novel could run afoul of many different literary patents at once, one program can be prohibited by many different patents at once. It is so much work to identify all the patents that appear to apply to a large program that only one such study has been done. A 2004 study of Linux, the kernel of the GNU/Linux operating system, found 283 different US software patents that seemed to cover it. That is to say, each of these 283 different patents forbids some computational process found somewhere in the thousands of pages of source code of Linux. At the time, Linux was around 1 percent of the whole GNU/Linux system. How many patents might there be that a distributor of the whole system could be sued under?

The way to prevent software patents from bollixing software development is simple: don't authorize them. This ought to be easy, since most patent laws have provisions against software patents. They typically say that "software per se" cannot be patented. But patent offices around the world are trying to twist the words and issuing patents on the ideas implemented in programs. Unless this is blocked, the result will be to put all software developers in danger.

23 The Danger of Software Patents

> This is an unedited transcript of the talk presented by Richard Stallman on 8 October 2009 at Victoria University of Wellington, in Wellington, New Zealand.

I'm most known for starting the free software movement and leading development of the GNU operating system—although most of the people who use the system mistakenly believe it's Linux and think it was started by somebody else a decade later. But I'm not going to be speaking about any of that today. I'm here to talk about a legal danger to all software developers, distributors, and users: the danger of patents—on computational ideas, computational techniques, an idea for something you can do on a computer.

Now, to understand this issue, the first thing you need to realize is that patent law has nothing to do with copyright law—they're totally different. Whatever you learn about one of them, you can be sure it doesn't apply to the other.

So, for example, any time a person makes a statement about "intellectual property," that's spreading confusion, because it's lumping together not only these two laws but also at least a dozen others. They're all different, and the result is any statement which purports to be about "intellectual property" is pure confusion—either the person making the statement is confused, or the person is trying to confuse others. But either way, whether it's accidental or malicious, it's confusion.

Protect yourself from this confusion by rejecting any statement which makes use of that term. The only way to make thoughtful comments and think clear thoughts about any one of these laws is to distinguish it first from all the others, and talk or think about one particular law, so that we can understand what it actually does and then form conclusions about it. So I'll be talking about patent law, and what happens in those countries which have allowed patent law to restrict software.

So, what does a patent do? A patent is an explicit, government-issued monopoly on using a certain idea. In the patent there's a part called the claims, which describe exactly what you're not allowed to do (although they're written in a way you probably can't understand). It's a struggle to figure out what those prohibitions actually mean, and they may go on for many pages of fine print.

So the patent typically lasts for 20 years, which is a fairly long time in our field. Twenty years ago there was no World Wide Web—a tremendous amount of the use of computers goes on in an area which wasn't even possible to propose 20 years ago. So of course everything that people do on it is something that's new since 20 years ago—at least in some aspect it is new. So if patents had been

---

This transcript was originally published on `http://gnu.org`, in 2009. This version is part of *Free Software, Free Society: Selected Essays of Richard M. Stallman*, 3rd ed. (Boston: GNU Press, 2015).

applied for we'd be prohibited from doing all of it, and we may be prohibited from doing all of it in countries that have been foolish enough to have such a policy.

Most of the time, when people describe the function of the patent system, they have a vested interest in the system. They may be patent lawyers, or they may work in the Patent Office, or they may be in the patent office of a megacorporation, so they want you to like the system.

The Economist once referred to the patent system as "a time-consuming lottery." If you've ever seen publicity for a lottery, you understand how it works: they dwell on the very unlikely probability of winning, and they don't talk about the overwhelming likelihood of losing. In this way, they intentionally and systematically present a biased picture of what's likely to happen to you, without actually lying about any particular fact.

It's the same way for the publicity for the patent system: they talk about what it's like to walk down the street with a patent in your pocket—or first of all, what it's like to get a patent, then what it's like to have a patent in your pocket, and every so often you can pull it out and point it at somebody and say, "Give me your money."

To compensate for their bias, I'm going to describe it from the other side, the victim side—what it's like for people who want to develop or distribute or run software. You have to worry that any day someone might walk up to you and point a patent at you and say, "Give me your money."

If you want to develop software in a country that allows software patents, and you want to work with patent law, what will you have to do?

You could try to make a list of all the ideas that one might be able to find in the program that you're about to write, aside from the fact that you don't know that when you start writing the program. [But] even after you finish writing the program you wouldn't be able to make such a list.

The reason is. . . in the process you conceived of it in one particular way—you've got a mental structure to apply to your design. And because of that, it will block you from seeing other structures that somebody might use to understand the same program—because you're not coming to it fresh; you already designed it with one structure in mind. Someone else who sees it for the first time might see a different structure, which involves different ideas, and it would be hard for you to see what those other ideas are. But nonetheless they're implemented in your program, and those patents could prohibit your program, if those ideas are patented.

For instance, suppose there were graphical-idea patents and you wanted to draw a square. Well, you would realize that if there was a patent on a bottom edge, it would prohibit your square. You could put "bottom edge" on the list of all ideas implemented in your drawing. But you might not realize that somebody else with a patent on bottom corners could sue you easily also, because he could take your drawing and turn it by 45 degrees. And now your square is like this, and it has a bottom corner.

So you couldn't make a list of all the ideas which, if patented, could prohibit your program.

What you might try to do is find out all the ideas that are patented that might be in your program. Now you can't do that actually, because patent applications are kept secret for at least 18 months; and the result is the Patent Office could be considering now whether to issue a patent, and they won't tell you. And this is not just an academic, theoretical possibility.

For instance, in 1984 the Compress program was written, a program for compressing files using the data compression algorithm, and at that time there was no patent on that algorithm for compressing files. The author got the algorithm from an article in a journal. That was when we thought that the purpose of computer science journals was to publish algorithms so people could use them.

He wrote this program, he released it, and in 1985 a patent was issued on that algorithm. But the patent holder was cunning and didn't immediately go around telling people to stop using it. The patent holder figured, "Let's let everybody dig their grave deeper." A few years later they started threatening people; it became clear we couldn't use Compress, so I asked for people to suggest other algorithms we could use for compressing files.

And somebody wrote and said, "I developed another data compression algorithm that works better, I've written a program, I'd like to give it to you." So we got ready to release it, and a week before it was ready to be released, I read in *The New York Times'* weekly patent column, which I rarely saw—it's a couple of times a year I might see it—but just by luck I saw that someone had gotten a patent for "inventing a new method of compressing data." And so I said we had better look at this, and sure enough it covered the program we were about to release. But it could have been worse: the patent could have been issued a year later, or two years later, or three years later, or five years later.

Anyway, someone else came up with another, even better compression algorithm, which was used in the program gzip, and just about everybody who wanted to compress files switched to gzip, so it sounds like a happy ending. But you'll hear more later. It's not entirely so happy.

So, you can't find out about the patents that are being considered even though they may prohibit your work once they come out, but you can find out about the already issued patents. They're all published by the Patent Office. The problem is you can't read them all, because there are too many of them.

In the US I believe there are hundreds of thousands of software patents; keeping track of them would be a tremendous job. So you're going to have to search for relevant patents. And you'll find a lot of relevant patents, but you won't necessarily find them all.

For instance, in the 80s and 90s, there was a patent on "natural order recalculation" in spreadsheets. Somebody once asked me for a copy of it, so I looked in our computer file which lists the patent numbers. And then I pulled out the drawer to get the paper copy of this patent and xeroxed it and sent it to him. And when he got it, he said, "I think you sent me the wrong patent. This is something about compilers." So I thought maybe our file has the wrong number in it. I looked in it again, and sure enough it said, "A method for compiling formulas into object code." So I started to read it to see if it was indeed the wrong patent. I read the claims, and sure enough it was the natural order recalculation patent, but it didn't use those terms. It didn't use the term "spreadsheet." In fact, what the patent prohibited was dozens of different ways of implementing topological sort—all the ways they could think of. But I don't think it used the term "topological sort."

So if you were writing a spreadsheet and you tried to find relevant patents by searching, you might have found a lot of patents. But you wouldn't have found this one until you told somebody, "Oh, I'm working on a spreadsheet," and he said, "Oh, did you know those other companies that are making spreadsheets are getting sued?" Then you would have found out.

Well, you can't find all the patents by searching, but you can find a lot of them. And then you've got to figure out what they mean, which is hard, because patents are written in tortuous legal language which is very hard to understand the real meaning of. So you're going to have to spend a lot of time talking with an expensive lawyer explaining what you want to do in order to find out from the lawyer whether you're allowed to do it.

Even the patent holders often can't recognize just what their patents mean. For instance, there's somebody named Paul Heckel who released a program for displaying a lot of data on a small screen, and based on a couple of the ideas in that program he got a couple of patents.

I once tried to find a simple way to describe what claim 1 of one of those patents covered. I found that I couldn't find any simpler way of saying it than what was in the patent itself; and that sentence, I couldn't manage to keep it all in my mind at once, no matter how hard I tried.

And Heckel couldn't follow it either, because when he saw HyperCard, all he noticed was it was nothing like his program. It didn't occur to him that the way his patent was written it might prohibit HyperCard; but his lawyer had that idea, so he threatened Apple. And then he threatened Apple's customers, and eventually Apple made a settlement with him which is secret, so we don't know who really won. And this is just an illustration of how hard it is for anybody to understand what a patent does or doesn't prohibit.

In fact, I once gave this speech and Heckel was in the audience. And at this point he jumped up and said, "That's not true, I just didn't know the scope of my protection." And I said, "Yeah, that's what I said," at which point he sat down and that was the end of my experience being heckled by Heckel. If I had said no, he probably would have found a way to argue with me.

Anyway, after a long, expensive conversation with a lawyer, the lawyer will give you an answer like this:

> If you do something in this area, you're almost certain to lose a lawsuit; if you do something in this area, there's a considerable chance of losing a lawsuit; and if you really want to be safe you've got to stay out of this area. But there's a sizeable element of chance in the outcome of any lawsuit.

So now that you have clear, predictable rules for doing business, what are you actually going to do? Well, there are three things that you could do to deal with the issue of any particular patent. One is to avoid it, another is to get a license for it, and the third is to invalidate it. So I'll talk about these one by one.

First, there's the possibility of avoiding the patent, which means, don't implement what it prohibits. Of course, if it's hard to tell what it prohibits, it might be hard to tell what would suffice to avoid it.

A couple of years ago Kodak sued Sun [for] using a patent for something having to do with object-oriented programming, and Sun didn't think it was infringing that patent. But the court decided it was; and when other people look at that patent they haven't the faintest idea whether that decision was right or not. No one can tell what that patent does or doesn't cover, but Sun had to pay hundreds of millions of dollars because of violating a completely incomprehensible law.

Sometimes you can tell what you need to avoid, and sometimes what you need to avoid is an algorithm.

For instance, I saw a patent for something like the fast Fourier transform, but it ran twice as fast. Well, if the ordinary FFT is fast enough for your application then that's an easy way to avoid this other one. And most of the time that would work. Once in a while you might be trying to do something where it runs doing FFT all the time, and it's just barely fast enough using the faster algorithm. And then you can't avoid it, although maybe you could wait a couple of years for a faster computer. But that's going to be rare. Most of the time that patent will to be easy to avoid.

On the other hand, a patent on an algorithm may be impossible to avoid. Consider the LZW data compression algorithm. Well, as I explained, we found a better data compression algorithm, and everybody who wanted to compress files switched to the program gzip which used the better algorithm. And the reason is, if you just want to compress the file and uncompress it later, you can tell people to use this program to uncompress it; then you can use any program with any algorithm, and you only care how well it works.

But LZW is used for other things, too; for instance the PostScript language specifies operators for LZW compression and LZW uncompression. It's no use having another, better algorithm because it makes a different format of data. They're not interoperable. If you compress it with the gzip algorithm, you won't be able to uncompress it using LZW. So no matter how good your other algorithm is, and no matter what it is, it just doesn't enable you to implement PostScript according to the specs.

But I noticed that users rarely ask their printers to compress things. Generally the only thing they want their printers to do is to uncompress; and I also noticed that both of the patents on the LZW algorithm were written in such a way that if your system can only uncompress, it's not forbidden. These patents were written so that they covered compression, and they had other claims covering both compression and uncompression; but there was no claim covering only uncompression. So I realized that if we implement only the uncompression for LZW, we would be safe. And although it would not satisfy the specification, it would please the users sufficiently; it would do what they actually needed. So that's how we barely squeaked by avoiding the two patents.

Now there is GIF format, for images. That uses the LZW algorithm also. It didn't take long for people to define another image format, called PNG, which stands for "PNG's Not GIF." I think it uses the gzip algorithm. And we started saying to people, "Don't use GIF format, it's dangerous. Switch to PNG." And the users said, "Well, maybe some day, but the browsers don't implement it yet," and the browser developers said, "We may implement it someday, but there's not much demand from users."

Well, it's pretty obvious what's going on—GIF was a de facto standard. In effect, asking people to switch to a different format, instead of their de facto standard, is like asking everyone in New Zealand to speak Hungarian. People will say, "Well, yeah, I'll learn to speak it after everyone else does." And so we never succeeded in asking people to stop using GIF, even though one of those patent holders was going around to operators of web sites, threatening to sue them unless they could prove that all of the GIFs on the site were made with authorized, licensed software.

So GIF was a dangerous trap for a large part of our community. We thought we had an alternative to GIF format, namely JPEG, but then somebody said, "I was just looking through my portfolio of patents"—I think it was somebody that just bought patents and used them to threaten people—and he said, "and I found that one of them covers JPEG format."

Well, JPEG was not a de facto standard, it's an official standard, issued by a standards committee; and the committee had a lawyer too. Their lawyer said he didn't think that this patent actually covered JPEG format.

So who's right? Well, this patent holder sued a bunch of companies, and if there was a decision, it would have said who was right. But I haven't heard about a decision; I'm not sure if there ever was one. I think they settled, and the settlement is almost certainly secret, which means that it didn't tell us anything about who's right.

These are fairly lightweight cases: one patent on JPEG, two patents on the LZW algorithm used in GIF. Now you might wonder how come there are two patents on the same algorithm? It's not supposed to happen, but it did. And the reason is that the patent examiners can't possibly take the time to study every pair of things they might need to study and compare, because they're not allowed to take that much time. And because algorithms are just mathematics, there's no way you can narrow down which applications and patents you need to compare.

You see, in physical engineering fields, they can use the physical nature of what's going on to narrow things down. For instance, in chemical engineering, they can say, "What are the substances going in? What are the substances coming out?" If two different [patent] applications are different in that way, then they're not the same process so you don't need to worry. But the same math can be represented in ways that can look very different, and until you study them both together, you don't realize they're talking about the same thing. And, because of this, it's quite common to see the same thing get patented multiple times [in software].

Remember that program that was killed by a patent before we released it? Well, that algorithm got patented twice also. In one little field we've seen it happen in two cases that we ran into—the same algorithm being patented twice. Well, I think my explanation tells you why that happens.

But one or two patents is a lightweight case. What about MPEG2, the video format? I saw a list of over 70 patents covering that, and the negotiations to arrange a way for somebody to license all those patents took longer than developing the standard itself. The JPEG committee wanted to develop a follow-on standard, and they gave up. They said there were too many patents; there was no way to do it.

Sometimes it's a feature that's patented, and the only way to avoid that patent is not to implement that feature. For instance, the users of the word processor Xywrite once got a downgrade in the mail, which removed a feature. The feature was that you could define a list of abbreviations. For instance, if you define "exp" as an abbreviation for "experiment," then if you type "exp-space" or "exp-comma," the "exp" would change automatically to "experiment."

Then somebody who had a patent on this feature threatened them, and they concluded that the only thing they could do was to take the feature out. And so they sent all the users a downgrade.

But they also contacted me, because my Emacs editor had a feature like that starting from the late 70s. And it was described in the Emacs manual, so they thought I might be able to help them invalidate that patent. Well, I'm happy to know I've had at least one patentable idea in my life, but I'm unhappy that someone else patented it.

Fortunately, in fact, that patent was eventually invalidated, and partly on the strength of the fact that I had published using it earlier. But in the meantime they had had to remove this feature.

Now, to remove one or two features may not be a disaster. But when you have to remove 50 features, you could do it, but people are likely to say, "This program's no good; it's missing all the features I want." So it may not be a solution. And sometimes a patent is so broad that it wipes out an entire field, like the patent on public-key encryption, which in fact put public-key encryption basically off limits for about ten years.

So that's the option of avoiding the patent—often possible, but sometimes not, and there's a limit to how many patents you can avoid.

What about the next possibility, of getting a license for the patent?

Well, the patent holder may not offer you a license. It's entirely up to him. He could say, "I just want to shut you down." I once got a letter from somebody whose family business was making casino games, which were of course computerized, and he had been threatened by a patent holder who wanted to make his business shut down. He sent me the patent. Claim 1 was something like "a network with a multiplicity of computers, in which each computer supports a multiplicity of games, and allows a multiplicity of game sessions at the same time."

Now, I'm sure in the 1980s there was a university that set up a room with a network of workstations, and each workstation had some kind of windowing facility. All they had to do was to install multiple games and it would be possible to display multiple game sessions at once. This is so trivial and uninteresting that nobody would have bothered to publish an article about doing it. No one would have been interested in publishing an article about doing it, but it was worth patenting it. If it had occurred to you that you could get a monopoly on this trivial thing, then you could shut down your competitors with it.

But why does the Patent Office issue so many patents that seem absurd and trivial to us?

It's not because the patent examiners are stupid, it's because they're following a system, and the system has rules, and the rules lead to this result.

You see, if somebody has made a machine that does something once, and somebody else designs a machine that will do the same thing, but N times, for us that's a `for`-loop, but for the Patent Office that's an invention. If there are machines that can do A, and there are machines that can do B, and somebody designs a machine that can do A or B, for us that's an `if-then-else` statement, but for the Patent Office that's an invention. So they have very low standards, and they follow those standards; and the result is patents that look absurd and trivial to us. Whether they're legally valid I can't say. But every programmer who sees them laughs.

In any case, I was unable to suggest anything he could do to help himself, and he had to shut down his business. But most patent holders will offer you a license. It's likely to be rather expensive.

But there are some software developers that find it particularly easy to get licenses, most of the time. Those are the megacorporations. In any field the megacorporations generally own about half the patents, and they cross-license each other, and they can make anybody else cross-license if he's really producing anything. The result is that they end up painlessly with licenses for almost all the patents.

IBM wrote an article in its house magazine, *Think* magazine—I think it's issue 5, 1990—about the benefit IBM got from its almost 9,000 US patents at the time (now it's up to 45,000 or more). They said that one of the benefits was that they collected money, but the main benefit, which they said was perhaps an order of magnitude greater, was "getting access to the patents of others," namely cross-licensing.

What this means is since IBM, with so many patents, can make almost everybody give them a cross-license, IBM avoids almost all the grief that the patent system would have inflicted on anybody else. So that's why IBM wants software patents. That's why the megacorporations in general want software patents, because they know that by cross-licensing, they will have a sort of exclusive club on top of a mountain peak. And all the rest of us will be down here, and there's no way we can get up there. You know, if you're a genius, you might start up a small company and get some patents, but you'll never get into IBM's league, no matter what you do.

Now a lot of companies tell their employees, "Get us patents so we can defend ourselves" and they mean, "use them to try to get cross-licensing," but it just doesn't work well. It's not an effective strategy if you've got a small number of patents.

Suppose you've got three patents. One points there, one points there, and one points there, and somebody over there points a patent at you. Well, your three patents don't help you at all, because none of them points at him. On the other hand, sooner or later, somebody in the company is going to notice that this patent is actually pointing at some people, and [the company] could threaten them and squeeze money out of them—never mind that those people didn't attack this company.

So if your employer says to you, "We need some patents to defend ourselves, so help us get patents," I recommend this response:

> Boss, I trust you and I'm sure you would only use those patents to defend the company if it's attacked. But I don't know who's going to be the CEO of this company in five years. For all I know, it might get acquired by Microsoft. So I really can't trust the company's word to only use these patents for defense unless I get it in writing. Please put it in writing that any patents I provide for the company will only be used for self-defense and collective security, and not for repression, and then I'll be able to get patents for the company with a clean conscience.

It would be most interesting to raise this not just in private with your boss, but also on the company's discussion list.

The other thing that could happen is that the company could fail and its assets could be auctioned off, including the patents; and the patents will be bought by someone who means to use them to do something nasty.

This cross-licensing practice is very important to understand, because this is what punctures the argument of the software patent advocates who say that software patents are needed to protect the starving genius. They give you a scenario which is a series of unlikelihoods.

So let's look at it. According to this scenario, there's a brilliant designer of whatever, who's been working for years by himself in his attic coming up with a better way to do whatever it is. And now that it's ready, he wants to start a business and mass-produce this thing; and because his idea is so good his company will inevitably succeed— except for one thing: the big companies will compete with him and take all his market the away. And because of this, his business will almost certainly fail, and then he will starve.

Well, let's look at all the unlikely assumptions here.

First of all, that he comes up with this idea working by himself. That's not very likely. In a high-tech field, most progress is made by people working in a field, doing things and talking with people in the field. But I wouldn't say it's impossible, not that one thing by itself.

But anyway the next supposition is that he's going to start a business and that it's going to succeed. Well, just because he's a brilliant engineer doesn't mean that he's any good at running a business. Most new businesses fail; more than 95 percent of them, I think, fail within a few years. So that's probably what's going to happen to him, no matter what.

OK, let's assume that in addition to being a brilliant engineer who came up with something great by himself, he's also talented at running businesses. If he has a knack for running businesses, then maybe his business won't fail. After all, not all new businesses fail, there are a certain few that succeed. Well, if he understands business, then instead of trying to go head to head with large companies, he might try to do things that small companies are better at and have a better chance of succeeding. He might succeed. But let's suppose it fails anyway. If he's so brilliant and has a knack for running businesses, I'm sure he won't starve, because somebody will want to give him a job.

So a series of unlikelihoods—it's not a very plausible scenario. But let's look at it anyway.

Because where they go from there is to say the patent system will "protect" our starving genius, because he can get a patent on this technique. And then when IBM wants to compete with him, he says, "IBM, you can't compete with me, because I've got this patent," and IBM says, "Oh, no, not again!"

Well, here's what really happens.

IBM says, "Oh, how nice, you have a patent. Well, we have this patent, and this patent, and this patent, and this patent, and this patent, all of which cover other ideas implemented in your product, and if you think you can fight us on all those, we'll pull out some more. So let's sign a cross-license agreement, and that way nobody will get hurt." Now since we've assumed that our genius understands business, he's going to realize that he has no choice. He's going to sign the cross-license agreement, as just about everybody does when IBM demands it. And then this means that IBM will get "access" to his patent, meaning IBM would be free to compete with him just as if there were no patents, which means that the supposed benefit that they claim he would get by having this patent is not real. He won't get this benefit.

The patent might "protect" him from competition from you or me, but not from IBM—not from the very megacorporations which the scenario says are the threat to him. You know in advance that there's got to be a flaw in this reasoning when people who are lobbyists for megacorporations recommend a policy supposedly because it's going to protect their small competitors from them. If it really were going to do that, they wouldn't be in favor of it. But this explains why [software patents] won't do it.

Even IBM can't always do this, because there are companies that we refer to as patent trolls or patent parasites, and their only business is using patents to squeeze money out of people who really make something.

Patent lawyers tell us that it's really wonderful to have patents in your field, but they don't have patents in their field. There are no patents on how to send or write a threatening letter, no patents on how to file a lawsuit, and no patents on how to persuade a judge or jury, so even IBM can't make the patent trolls cross-license. But IBM figures, "Our competition will have to pay them too; this is just part of the cost of doing business, and we can live with it." IBM and the other megacorporations figure that the general dominion over all activity that they get from their patents is good for them, and paying off the trolls they can live with. So that's why they want software patents.

There are also certain software developers who find it particularly difficult to get a patent license, and those are the developers of free software. The reason is that the usual patent license has conditions we can't possibly fulfill, because usual patent licenses demand a payment per copy. But when software gives users the freedom to distribute and make more copies, we have no way to count the copies that exist.

If someone offered me a patent license for a payment of one-millionth of a dollar per copy, the total amount of money I'd have to pay maybe is in my pocket now. Maybe it's $50, but I don't know if it's $50, or $49, or what, because there's no way I can count the copies that people have made.

A patent holder doesn't have to demand a payment per copy; a patent holder could offer you a license for a single lump sum, but those lump sums tend to be big, like US$100,000.

And the reason that we've been able to develop so much freedom-respecting software is [that] we can develop software without money, but we can't pay a lot of money without money. If we're forced to pay for the privilege of writing software for the public, we won't be able to do it very much.

That's the possibility of getting a license for the patent. The other possibility is to invalidate the patent. If the country considers software patents to be basically valid, and allowed, the only question is whether that particular patent meets the criteria. It's only useful to go to court if you've got an argument to make that might prevail.

What would that argument be? You have to find evidence that, years ago, before the patent was applied for, people knew about the same idea. And you'd have to find things today that demonstrate that they knew about it publicly at that time. So the dice were cast years ago, and if they came up favorably for you, and if you can prove that fact today, then you have an argument to use to try to invalidate the patent. And it might work.

It might cost you a lot of money to go through this case, and as a result, a probably invalid patent is a very frightening weapon to be threatened with if you don't have a lot of money. There are people who can't afford to defend their rights—lots of them. The ones who can afford it are the exception.

These are the three things that you might be able to do about each patent that prohibits something in your program. The thing is, whether each one is possible depends on different details of the circumstances, so some of the time, none of them is possible; and when that happens, your project is dead.

But lawyers in most countries tell us, "Don't try to find the patents in advance," and the reason is that the penalty for infringement is bigger if you knew about the patent. So what they tell you is "Keep your eyes shut. Don't try to find out about the patents, just go blindly taking your design decisions, and hope."

And of course, with each single design decision, you probably don't step on a patent. Probably nothing happens to you. But there are so many steps you have to take to get across the minefield, it's very unlikely you will get through safely. And of course, the patent holders don't all show up at the same time, so you don't know how many there are going to be.

The patent holder of the natural order recalculation patent was demanding 5 percent of the gross sales of every spreadsheet. You could imagine paying for a few such licenses, but what happens when patent holder number 20 comes along, and wants you to pay out the last remaining 5 percent? And then what happens when patent holder number 21 comes along?

People in business say that this scenario is amusing but absurd, because your business would fail long before you got there. They told me that two or three such licenses would make your business fail. So you'd never get to 20. They show up one by one, so you never know how many more there are going to be.

Software patents are a mess. They're a mess for software developers, but in addition they're a restriction on every computer user because software patents restrict what you can do on your computer.

This is very different from patents, for instance, on automobile engines. These only restrict companies that make cars; they don't restrict you and me. But software patents do restrict you and me, and everybody who uses computers. So we can't think of them in purely economic terms; we can't judge this issue purely in economic terms. There's something more important at stake.

But even in economic terms, the system is self-defeating, because its purpose is supposed to be to promote progress. Supposedly by creating this artificial incentive for people to publish ideas, it's going to help the field progress. But all it does is the exact opposite, because the big job in software is not coming up with ideas, it's implementing thousands of ideas together in one program. And software patents obstruct that, so they're economically self-defeating.

And there's even economic research showing that this is so—showing how in a field with a lot of incremental innovation, a patent system can actually reduce investment in R&D. And of course, it also obstructs development in other ways. So even if we ignore the injustice of software patents, even if we were to look at it in the narrow economic terms that are usually proposed, it's still harmful.

People sometimes respond by saying that "People in other fields have been living with patents for decades, and they've gotten used to it, so why should you be an exception?"

Now, that question has an absurd assumption. It's like saying, "Other people get cancer, why shouldn't you?" I think every time someone doesn't get cancer, that's good, regardless of what happened to the others. That question is absurd because of its presupposition that somehow we all have a duty to suffer the harm done by patents.

But there is a sensible question buried inside it, and that sensible question is "What differences are there between various fields that might affect what is good or bad patent policy in those fields?"

There is an important basic difference between fields in regard to how many patents are likely to prohibit or cover parts of any one product.

Now we have a naive idea in our minds which I'm trying to get rid of, because it's not true. And it's that on any one product there is one patent, and that patent covers the overall design of that product. So if you design a new product, it can't be patented already, and you will have an opportunity to get "the patent" on that product.

That's not how things work. In the 1800s, maybe they did, but not now. In fact, fields fall on a spectrum of how many patents [there are] per product. The beginning of the spectrum is one, but no field is like that today; fields are at various places on this spectrum.

The field that's closest to that is pharmaceuticals. A few decades ago, there really was one patent per pharmaceutical, at least at any time, because the patent covered the entire chemical formula of that one particular substance. Back then, if you developed a new drug, you could be sure it wasn't already patented by somebody else and you could get the one patent on that drug.

But that's not how it works now. Now there are broader patents, so now you could develop a new drug, and you're not allowed to make it because somebody has a broader patent which covers it already.

And there might even be a few such patents covering your new drug simultaneously, but there won't be hundreds. The reason is, our ability to do biochemical engineering is so limited that nobody knows how to combine so many ideas to make something that's useful in medicine. If you can combine a couple of them you're doing pretty well at our level of knowledge. But other fields involve combining more ideas to make one thing.

At the other end of the spectrum is software, where we can combine more ideas into one usable design than anybody else, because our field is basically easier than all other fields. I'm presuming that the intelligence of people in our field is the same as that of people in physical engineering. It's not that we're fundamentally better than they are; it's that our field is fundamentally easier, because we're working with mathematics.

A program is made out of mathematical components, which have a definition, whereas physical objects don't have a definition. The matter does what it does, so through the perversity of matter, your design may not work the way it "should" have worked. And that's just tough. You can't say that the matter has a bug in it, and the physical universe should get fixed. [Whereas] we [programmers] can make a castle that rests on a mathematically thin line, and it stays up because nothing weighs anything.

There're so many complications you have to cope with in physical engineering that we don't have to worry about.

For instance, when I put an `if`-statement inside of a `while`-loop,

- I don't have to worry that if this `while`-loop repeats at the wrong rate, the `if`-statement might start to vibrate and it might resonate and crack;
- I don't have to worry that if it resonates much faster—you know, millions of times per second—that it might generate radio frequency signals that might induce wrong values in other parts of the program;
- I don't have to worry that corrosive fluids from the environment might seep in between the `if`-statement and the `while`-statement and start eating away at them until the signals don't pass anymore;
- I don't have to worry about how the heat generated by my `if`-statement is going to get out through the `while`-statement so that it doesn't make the `if`-statement burn out; and
- I don't have to worry about how I would take out the broken `if`-statement if it does crack, burn, or corrode, and replace it with another `if`-statement to make the program run again.

For that matter, I don't have to worry about how I'm going to insert the `if`-statement inside the `while`-statement every time I produce a copy of the program. I don't have to design a factory to make copies of my program, because there are various general commands that will make copies of anything.

If I want to make copies on CD, I just have to write a master; and there's one program I can [use to] make a master out of anything, write any data I want. I can make a master CD and write it and send it off to a factory, and they'll duplicate whatever I send them. I don't have to design a different factory for each thing I want to duplicate.

Very often with physical engineering you have to do that; you have to design products for manufacturability. Designing the factory may even be a bigger job than designing the product, and then you may have to spend millions of dollars to build the factory. So with all of this trouble, you're not going to be able to put together so many different ideas in one product and have it work.

A physical design with a million nonrepeating different design elements is a gigantic project. A program with a million different design elements, that's nothing. It's a few hundred thousand lines of code, and a few people will write that in a few years, so it's not a big deal. So the result is that the patent system weighs proportionately heavier on us than it does on people in any other field who are being held back by the perversity of matter.

A lawyer did a study of one particular large program, namely the kernel Linux, which is used together with the GNU operating system that I launched. This was five years ago now; he found 283 different US patents, each of which appeared to prohibit some computation done somewhere in the code of Linux. At the time I saw an article saying that Linux was 0.25 percent of the whole system. So by multiplying 300 by 400 we can estimate the number of patents that would prohibit something in the whole system as being around 100,000. This is a very rough estimate only, and no more accurate information is available, since trying to figure it out would be a gigantic task.

to combine them with lots of well-known ideas. He could put a few new ideas into a composition together with a lot of old and uncontroversial ideas. And the result was a piece that was controversial, but not so much so that people couldn't get used to it.

To us, Beethoven's music doesn't sound controversial; I'm told it was, when it was new. But because he combined his new ideas with a lot of known ideas, he was able to give people a chance to stretch a certain amount. And they could, which is why to us those ideas sound just fine. But nobody, not even a Beethoven, is such a genius that he could reinvent music from zero, not using any of the well-known ideas, and make something that people would want to listen to. And nobody is such a genius he could reinvent computing from zero, not using any of the well-known ideas, and make something that people want to use.

When the technological context changes so frequently, you end up with a situation where what was done 20 years ago is totally inadequate. Twenty years ago there was no World Wide Web. So, sure, people did a lot of things with computers back then, but what they want to do today are things that work with the World Wide Web. And you can't do that using only the ideas that were known 20 years ago. And I presume that the technological context will continue to change, creating fresh opportunities for somebody to get patents that give the shaft to the whole field.

Big companies can even do this themselves. For instance, a few years ago Microsoft decided to make a phony open standard for documents and to get it approved as a standard by corrupting the International Standards Organization, which they did. But they designed it using something that Microsoft had patented. Microsoft is big enough that it can start with a patent, design a format or protocol to use that patented idea (whether it's helpful or not), in such a way that there's no way to be compatible unless you use that same idea too. And then Microsoft can make that a de facto standard with or without help from corrupted standards bodies. Just by its weight it can push people into using that format, and that basically means that they get a stranglehold over the whole world. So we need to show the politicians what's really going on here. We need to show them why this is bad.

Now I've heard it said that the reason New Zealand is considering software patents is that one large company wants to be given some monopolies. To restrict everyone in the country so that one company will make more money is the absolute opposite of statesmanship.

24 Giving the Software Field Protection from Patents

Patents threaten every software developer, and the patent wars we have long feared have broken out. Software developers and software users—which, in our society, is most people—need software to be free of patents.

The patents that threaten us are often called "software patents," but that term is misleading. Such patents are not about any specific program. Rather, each patent describes some practical idea, and says that anyone carrying out the idea can be sued. So it is clearer to call them "computational idea patents."

The US patent system doesn't label patents to say this one's a "software patent" and that one isn't. Software developers are the ones who make a distinction between the patents that threaten us—those that cover ideas that can be implemented in software—and the rest. For example, if the patented idea is the shape of a physical structure or a chemical reaction, no program can implement that idea; that patent doesn't threaten the software field. But if the idea that's patented is a computation, that patent's barrel points at software developers and users.

This is not to say that computational idea patents prohibit only software. These ideas can also be implemented in hardware—and many of them have been. Each patent typically covers both hardware *and* software implementations of the idea.

The Special Problem of Software

Still, software is where computational idea patents cause a special problem. In software, it's easy to implement thousands of ideas together in one program. If 10 percent are patented, that means hundreds of patents threaten it.

When Dan Ravicher of the Public Patent Foundation studied one large program (Linux, which is the kernel of the GNU/Linux operating system) in 2004, he found 283 US patents that appeared to cover computing ideas implemented in the source code of that program. That same year, a magazine estimated that Linux was .25 percent of the whole GNU/Linux system. Multiplying 300

See also my article "Patent Reform Is Not Enough," at `http://gnu.org/philosophy/patent-reform-is-not-enough.html`.

A version of this article was first published on the *Wired* web site, as "Let's Limit the Effect of Software Patents, Since We Can't Eliminate Them" (*Wired*, 1 November 2012, `http://wired.com/opinion/2012/11/richard-stallman-software-patents/`). It was published on `http://gnu.org` in 2012. This version is part of *Free Software, Free Society: Selected Essays of Richard M. Stallman*, 3rd ed. (Boston: GNU Press, 2015).

by 400 we get the order-of-magnitude estimate that the system as a whole was *threatened by around 100,000 patents.*

If half of those patents were eliminated as "bad quality"—mistakes of the patent system, that is—it would not really change things. Whether 100,000 patents or 50,000, it's the same disaster. This is why it's a mistake to limit our criticism of software patents to just "patent trolls" or "bad quality" patents. The worst patent aggressor today is Apple, which isn't a "troll" by the usual definition; I don't know whether Apple's patents are "good quality," but the better the patent's "quality" the more dangerous its threat.

We need to fix the whole problem, not just part of it.

The usual suggestions for correcting this problem legislatively involve changing the criteria for granting patents—for instance, to ban issuance of patents on computational practices and systems to perform them. This approach has two drawbacks.

First, patent lawyers are clever at reformulating patents to fit whatever rules may apply; they transform any attempt at limiting the substance of patents into a requirement of mere form. For instance, many US computational idea patents describe a system including an arithmetic unit, an instruction sequencer, a memory, plus controls to carry out a particular computation. This is a peculiar way of describing a computer running a program that does a certain computation; it was designed to make the patent application satisfy criteria that the US patent system was believed for a time to require.

Second, the US already has many thousands of computational idea patents, and changing the criteria to prevent issuing more would not get rid of the existing ones. We would have to wait almost 20 years for the problem to be entirely corrected through the expiration of these patents. We could envision legislating the abolition of these existing patents, but that is probably unconstitutional. (The Supreme Court has perversely insisted that Congress can extend private privileges at the expense of the public's rights but that it can't go in the other direction.)

A Different Approach: Limit Effect, Not Patentability

My suggestion is to change the *effect* of patents. We should legislate that developing, distributing, or running a program on generally used computing hardware does not constitute patent infringement. This approach has several advantages:

- It does not require classifying patents or patent applications as "software" or "not software."
- It provides developers and users with protection from both existing and potential future computational idea patents.
- Patent lawyers cannot defeat the intended effect by writing applications differently.

This approach doesn't entirely invalidate existing computational idea patents, because they would continue to apply to implementations using special-purpose hardware. This is an advantage because it eliminates an argument against the legal validity of the plan. The US passed a law some years ago shielding surgeons from patent lawsuits, so that even if surgical procedures are patented, surgeons are safe. That provides a precedent for this solution.

Software developers and software users need protection from patents. This is the only legislative solution that would provide full protection for all. We could then go back to competing or cooperating. . . without the fear that some stranger will wipe away our work.

Part V:
Free Software Licensing

Now this lawyer did not publish the list of patents, because that would have endangered the developers of Linux the kernel, putting them in a position where the penalties if they were sued would be greater. He didn't want to hurt them; he wanted to demonstrate how bad this problem is, of patent gridlock.

Programmers can understand this immediately, but politicians usually don't know much about programming; they usually imagine that patents are basically much like copyrights, only somehow stronger. They imagine that since software developers are not endangered by the copyrights on their work, that they won't be endangered by the patents on their work either. They imagine that, since when you write a program you have the copyright, [therefore likewise] if you write a program you have the patents also. This is false—so how do we give them a clue what patents would really do? What they really do in countries like the US?

I find it's useful to make an analogy between software and symphonies. Here's why it's a good analogy.

A program or symphony combines many ideas. A symphony combines many musical ideas. But you can't just pick a bunch of ideas and say "Here's my combination of ideas, do you like it?" Because in order to make them work you have to implement them all. You can't just pick musical ideas and list them and say, "Hey, how do you like this combination?" You can't hear that [list]. You have to write notes which implement all these ideas together.

The hard task, the thing most of us wouldn't be any good at, is writing all these notes to make the whole thing sound good. Sure, lots of us could pick musical ideas out of a list, but we wouldn't know how to write a good-sounding symphony to implement those ideas. Only some of us have that talent. That's the thing that limits you. I could probably invent a few musical ideas, but I wouldn't know how to use them to any effect.

So imagine that it's the 1700s, and the governments of Europe decide that they want to promote the progress of symphonic music by establishing a system of musical idea patents, so that any musical idea described in words could be patented.

For instance, using a particular sequence of notes as a motif could be patented, or a chord progression could be patented, or a rhythmic pattern could be patented, or using certain instruments by themselves could be patented, or a format of repetitions in a movement could be patented. Any sort of musical idea that could be described in words would have been patentable.

Now imagine that it's 1800 and you're Beethoven, and you want to write a symphony. You're going to find it's much harder to write a symphony you don't get sued for than to write one that sounds good, because you have to thread your way around all the patents that exist. If you complained about this, the patent holders would say, "Oh, Beethoven, you're just jealous because we had these ideas first. Why don't you go and think of some ideas of your own?"

Now Beethoven had ideas of his own. The reason he's considered a great composer is because of all of the new ideas that he had, and he actually used. And he knew how to use them in such a way that they would work, which was

25 Introduction to the Licenses

Written by Brett Smith and Richard Stallman.

This part contains the text of the latest versions of the primary GNU licenses: the GNU General Public License (GNU GPL), the GNU Lesser General Public License (LGPL), and the GNU Free Documentation License (FDL). Though they are legal documents, they belong in this book of essays because they are concrete expressions of the ideals of free software.

Software development for the GNU operating system began in 1984. Once Richard Stallman had parts of the GNU system that were worth releasing, he needed a license to release them under. Some free software licenses already existed; these gave users permission to modify and redistribute the software, but they also allowed using the code in proprietary versions and proprietary programs. Using those licenses, GNU would have failed to achieve its goal of delivering freedom to all users, because middlemen would have converted the GNU code into proprietary software.

So Stallman devised a license to assure every user the freedom to modify and redistribute the software. It granted these permissions under one key condition: whoever distributed the software must pass along the authorization to modify and redistribute that same software, along with the source code making it practical to do so. Stallman coined the term "copyleft" (see "What Is Copyleft?" on p. 184) to describe this key twist of using the legal power of copyright to ensure freedom for all users.

GNU copyleft licenses were first developed for software, and later for related areas such as software documentation. In them, the principles of the free software movement, explained throughout the essays in this book, take practical form. Each of their successive revisions has had to wrestle with free software's legal and practical obstacles and offers numerous illustrations of how free software ideals are codified into legal terms.

The Origins of the GPL

The first version of the GNU General Public License was published in 1989—but Stallman had been releasing software under copyleft licenses as part of the GNU Project since as early as 1985. Prior to 1989, each published GNU program had been covered by a license specifically tailored for it. Instead of a single GNU General Public License, there was a GNU CC General Public License, a GDB General Public License, and so on. These licenses were identical except for minor differences: for instance, terms about displaying license notices to users were different for different programs and, unless it covered a program that was

---

This essay is published in *Free Software, Free Society: Selected Essays of Richard M. Stallman*, 3rd ed. (Boston: GNU Press, 2015).

just one source file, each license contained the name of the program it applied to.

By 1989, Stallman had had enough experience with different GNU packages under slightly different licenses to conclude that it was crucial to unify them into one license that would cover all these packages. He worked with Jerry Cohen, an attorney at Perkins Smith & Cohen LLP, to collect concepts from all the different licenses written up to that point, and bring them together into one license. It was thus that on 1 February 1989 the GNU General Public License was born.

The first version of the license sought to ensure two results: first, that all derived works of the software would be released under the same license and, second, that everyone who received the software would have a chance to get the source code. These requirements implement a strong copyleft by blocking the three main ways of making programs proprietary: with copyright, with end-user license agreements, and by not distributing source code.

In comparison to the program-specific licenses that had preceded it, GPL version 1 featured few substantial changes—the GPL was evolutionary, not revolutionary—but it made a big practical difference. Previously, developers who had wanted to copyleft a program had needed to tailor one of the existing licenses to that program. Many had not bothered. With the release of the GPL, those developers had a license they could use out of the box to provide all of their users with freedom to share and change the software. It was a powerful tool.

Version 2

After the 1981 US Supreme Court decision in *Diamond v. Diehr,* the US Patent and Trademark Office began issuing patents for software. Software patents threaten free software and proprietary software alike (see part IV in this book), and Stallman realized that they could subvert the copyleft in the GNU GPL.

By selectively issuing patent licenses, patent holders can arbitrarily control how the software under them is distributed or modified. A patent holder can give one party permission to resell the program, another permission to develop and use a modified version at her company, and a third permission to do all the activities that the GPL itself allows. They can demand whatever they wish in exchange for these permissions. They have this power over any software that implements the patented idea, whether or not they have modified or distributed it themselves. This power threatens free software because third parties with patents can impose restrictions on free software users and developers.

If patent holders don't distribute or modify software, then a software license based on copyright like the GPL can't control their activities: they haven't done anything that requires permission under the license. But the software license can stop each of the program's distributors from entering limiting agreements with the patent holder. Enter GPL version 2: a new section in the license (sec. 7) explicitly says that if parties are subject to other legal agreements—such as a patent license—that contradict the GPL's terms, then the licensee must refrain from distributing the software at all. As a result, any party that wants to distribute or modify the software, and also obtain a patent license, must ensure that the terms of that license are consistent with all of the GPL's conditions: recipients of the software must receive it under the same terms, with no additional restrictions, and have the means to get the source code.

This new section protected the integrity of the distribution system for GPL-covered software. A fundamental principle of the license is that every licensee, from the most humble individual to the largest corporation, has the exact same rights to share and change the software. Patent holders who do not distribute the software themselves and selectively issues patent licenses could potentially interfere with this goal, splitting licensees into different groups however they see fit. Section 7 of GPL version 2 prevents this abuse.

The LGPL

The GPL worked well for the programming tools, utilities, and games that were released by the GNU Project in the early years; however, Stallman recognized that releasing the recently developed GNU C Library the same way could backfire. Aside from some extensions, the GNU C Library was to be a compatible replacement for the Unix C Library, so any C program would be able link with either one. If proprietary C programs were not allowed to use the GNU C Library, they would simply use the Unix library. Being strict in this case would gain nothing.

Stallman decided to compromise with a modified copyleft: one that would protect the freedom of the library itself, but not that of the programs that use it. This idea was implemented in a license originally called the GNU Library General Public License, first published as version 2.0, in June 1991. The original LGPL stated Conditions like the GPL's—with an important exception: if someone else's program used the library only by referring to it as a library, that program's source could be distributed under license terms of the author's choosing. However, the executable made by combining the program and the library had to come with a copy of the LGPL and source code for the library, and provide some mechanism for users who have modified the library to update the executable to use their modified library.

How does a developer use the work as a library in order to take advantage of the special set of conditions provided by LGPLv2? Think of a computer program as a series of instructions for doing a particular job: compiling or linking the program with a library provides the programmer with a means to say, "When the program gets to this point, get further instructions from the library, and come back here when those are done." Libraries are commonly used in software development because they make the effort less repetitive and less error prone: programmers don't have to reinvent the wheel—and perhaps introduce bugs in the process—every time they want to accomplish a particular task. Because libraries are so widely created and used, developers have the means to readily take advantage of the LGPL's additional permissions.

Version 2.0 of the license worked as intended: in some situations, proprietary software developers chose to use an LGPL-covered library over a proprietary alternative, and users received the freedom to share and change that library. This did not produce an "ideal" outcome—where the user had complete control over the entire program—but in these cases the GPL would not have achieved that ideal outcome either. The LGPL assured the users some freedom where they would have otherwise had none.

The name "Library GPL" led some free software developers to assume all libraries ought on principle to be licensed this way, but that was not the intent—when a free library has no proprietary competitor, releasing it under the GNU GPL can benefit free software. To avoid this unintended message, Stallman renamed this license to the Lesser General Public License, and incremented the version number to 2.1 to reflect the relatively minor changes in the text: the license sported a new preamble, a few wording clarifications, and allowed programs to make their calls to the library through special system facilities for shared libraries where those are available. The Lesser General Public License version 2.1 was released in February 1999.

The FDL

At the turn of the century, free software was growing much faster than it had been previously; the documentation, however, was not keeping pace. Stallman was concerned about this failure and wrote about it in "Free Software Needs Free Documentation" (p. 40).

While there are some similarities between software and documentation—they are both works that are meant for practical use—there are important differences in the ways they can be used. The GPL and the LGPL were not suitable for manuals.

For some time, GNU packages had been using an untitled, simple, ad hoc copyleft license for each manual. Since each manual's license was different, text could not be copied from one manual to another. So Stallman wrote the GNU Free Documentation License, a copyleft license designed primarily for software documentation and other practical written works.

The FDL was first published in March 2000. The principles of the copyleft remain the same: everyone who receives a copy of the work should be able to modify and redistribute it. Where the FDL differs from the software licenses is in the details of its implementation: conditions about how to attribute the work and provide "source code"—an editable version of the document—are different.

Version 3

During the 1990s, as free software became more popular, the GPL emerged as the clear copyleft license of choice for the community, and was adopted by the majority of free software projects; at the same time, however, proprietary developers had come up with methods of effectively denying users the freedoms that the GPL was meant to protect, without actually violating the GPL. In addition, there were other practices that the GPL did not handle conveniently. To deal with these issues called for an updated version of the license.

Around 2002, Stallman and others at the Free Software Foundation began discussing how to update the GPL, and the LGPL along with it. The FSF established a public review process, run with help from attorneys at the Software Freedom Law Center, to catch possible problems before actually releasing the new licenses. Committees of advisors from the community studied issues raised by public comments and reported the various positions and arguments to Stallman, who decided what policy to adopt; then he wrote license text with advice and suggestions from the attorneys. The importance of the changes made are explained in "Why Upgrade to GPLv3" (p. 204).

Version 3 used new terminology to promote uniform interpretations in different jurisdictions, and modified some requirements to fit new practices in the free software community. Beyond that, it introduced several new conditions to strengthen the copyleft and thereby the free software community as a whole. For instance, it

- blocked distributors from restricting users by building hardware that rejects the users' modified versions ("tivoization");
- allowed code to carry limited additional requirements, for compatibility with some other popular free software licenses;
- and strengthened patent requirements by providing clear terms to handle patent cross-licenses, which are common arrangements between large patent-holding companies.

Both GPLv3 and LGPLv3 included terms to address all of these issues, and were finally released on 29 June 2007. These licenses are the state of the art in copyleft, going farther than any other software license to protect users' freedom and bring about a world in harmony with the ideals expressed in this book.

26 How to Choose a License for Your Own Work

Introduction

People often ask us what license we recommend they use for their project. We've written about this publicly before, but the information has been scattered around between different essays, FAQ entries, and license commentaries. This article collects all that information into a single source, to make it easier for people to follow and refer back to.

These recommendations are for works designed to do practical jobs. Those include software, documentation, and some other things. Works of art, and works that state a point of view, are different issues; the GNU Project has no general stand about how they should be released, except that they should all be usable without nonfree software (in particular, without DRM[1]). However, you might want to follow these recommendations for art works that go with a particular program.

The recommendations apply to licensing a work that you create—whether that's a modification of an existing work, or a new original work. They do not address the issue of combining existing material under different licenses. If you're looking for help with that, please check our GPL FAQ.[2]

After you see what we recommend here, if you'd like advice, you can write to `licensing@gnu.org`. Note that it will probably take a few weeks for the licensing team to get back to you; if you get no response in a month, please write again.

Contributing to an Existing Project

When you contribute to an existing project, you should usually release your modified versions under the same license as the original work. It's good to cooperate with the project's maintainers, and using a different license for your modifications often makes that cooperation very difficult. You should only do that when there is a strong reason to justify it.

One case where using a different license can be justified is when you make major changes to a work under a noncopyleft license. If the version you've

[1] See our campaign against Digital Restrictions Management, at `DefectiveByDesign.org`.
[2] At `http://gnu.org/licenses/gpl-faq.html`.

This essay was first published on `http://gnu.org`, in 2011. This version of it is part of *Free Software, Free Society: Selected Essays of Richard M. Stallman*, 3rd ed. (Boston: GNU Press, 2015).

created is considerably more useful than the original, then it's worth copylefting your work, for all the same reasons we normally recommend copyleft. If you are in this situation, please follow the recommendations below for licensing a new project.

If you choose to release your contributions under a different license for whatever reason, you must make sure that the original license allows use of the material under your chosen license. For honesty's sake, show explicitly which parts of the work are under which license.

Software

We recommend different licenses for different projects, depending mostly on the software's purpose. In general, we recommend using the strongest copyleft license that doesn't interfere with that purpose. Our essay "What is Copyleft?" (p. 184) explains the concept of copyleft in more detail, and why it is generally the best licensing strategy.

For most programs, we recommend that you use the most recent version of the GNU General Public License (GPL) (p. 191) for your project. Its strong copyleft is appropriate for all kinds of software, and includes numerous protections for users' freedom.

Now for the exceptions.

Small Programs

It is not worth the trouble to use copyleft for most small programs. We use 300 lines as our benchmark: when a software package's source code is shorter than that, the benefits provided by copyleft are usually too small to justify the inconvenience of making sure a copy of the license always accompanies the software.

For those programs, we recommend the Apache License 2.0.[3] This is a pushover (noncopyleft) software license that has terms to prevent contributors and distributors from suing for patent infringement. This doesn't make the software immune to threats from patents (a software license can't do that), but it does prevent patent holders from setting up a "bait and switch" where they release the software under free terms then require recipients to agree to nonfree terms in a patent license.

Among the lax pushover licenses, Apache 2.0 is best; so if you are going to use a lax pushover license, whatever the reason, we recommend using that one.

---

[3] See `http://apache.org/licenses/LICENSE-2.0` for the full text of the license.

Libraries

For libraries, we distinguish three kind of cases.

Some libraries implement free standards that are competing against restricted standards, such as Ogg Vorbis (which competes against MP3 audio) and WebM (which competes against MPEG-4 video). For these projects, widespread use of the code is vital for advancing the cause of free software, and does more good than a copyleft on the project's code would do.

In these special situations, we recommend the Apache License 2.0.

For all other libraries, we recommend some kind of copyleft. If developers are already using an established alternative library released under a nonfree license or a lax pushover license, then we recommend using the GNU Lesser General Public License (LGPL) (p. 207).

Unlike the first case, where the library implements an ethically superior standard, here adoption for its own sake will not accomplish any special objective goal, so there's no reason to avoid copyleft entirely. However, if you require developers who use your library to release their whole programs under copyleft, they'll simply use one of the alternatives available, and that won't advance our cause either. The Lesser GPL was designed to fill the middle ground between these cases, allowing proprietary software developers to use the covered library, but providing a weak copyleft that gives users freedom regarding the library code itself.

For libraries that provide specialized facilities, and which do not face entrenched noncopylefted or nonfree competition, we recommend using the plain GNU GPL. For the reasons why, read "Why You Shouldn't Use the Lesser GPL for Your Next Library," at `http://gnu.org/licenses/why-not-lgpl.html`.

Server Software

If it is likely that others will make improved versions of your program to run on servers and not distribute their versions to anyone else, and you're concerned that this will put your released version at a disadvantage, we recommend the GNU Affero General Public License (AGPL).[4] The AGPL's terms are almost identical to the GPL's; the sole substantive difference is that it has an extra condition to ensure that people who use the software over a network will be able to get the source code for it.

The AGPL's requirement doesn't address the problems that can arise *for users* when they entrust their computing or their data to someone else's server. For instance, it won't stop Service as a Software Substitute (SaaSS) from denying users' freedom[5]—but most servers don't do SaaSS. For more about these issues, read "Why the Affero GPL," at `http://gnu.org/licenses/why-affero-gpl.html`.

---

[4] See `http://gnu.org/licenses/agpl.html` for the full text of the license.

[5] See "Who Does That Server Really Serve?" for more on the issue of SaaSS.

Documentation

We recommend the GNU Free Documentation License (p. 210) for tutorials, reference manuals and other large works of documentation. It's a strong copyleft license for educational works, initially written for software manuals, and includes terms which specifically address common issues that arise when those works are distributed or modified.

For short, secondary documentation works, such as a reference card, it is better to use the GNU all-permissive license,[6] since a copy of the GFDL could hardly fit in a reference card. Don't use CC-BY, since it is incompatible with the GFDL.

For man pages, we recommend the GFDL if the page is long, and the GNU all-permissive license if it is short.

Some documentation includes software source code. For instance, a manual for a programming language might include examples for readers to follow. You should both include these in the manual under the FDL's terms, and release them under another license that's appropriate for software. Doing so helps make it easy to use the code in other projects. We recommend that you dedicate small pieces of code to the public domain using CC0,[7] and distribute larger pieces under the same license that the associated software project uses.

Other Data for Programs

This section discusses all other works for practical use that you might include with software. To give you some examples, this includes icons and other functional or useful graphics, fonts, and geographic data. You can also follow them for art, though we wouldn't criticize if you don't.

If you are creating these works specifically for use with a software project, we generally recommend that you release your work under the same license as the software. There is no problem in doing so with the licenses we have recommended: GPLv3, LGPLv3, AGPLv3, and GPLv2 can all be applied to any kind of work—not just software—that is copyrightable and has a clear preferred form for modification. Using the same license as the software will help make compliance easier for distributors, and avoids any doubt about potential compatibility issues. Using a different free license may be appropriate if it provides some specific practical benefit, like better cooperation with other free projects.

If your work is not being created for use with a particular software project, or if it wouldn't be appropriate to use the same license as the project, then we only recommend that you choose a copyleft license that's appropriate for your work. We have some of these listed on our license list.[8] If no license seems especially appropriate, the Creative Commons Attribution-ShareAlike[9] license is a copyleft that can be used for many different kinds of works.

---

[6] See `http://gnu.org/licenses/license-list.html#GNUAllPermissive`.

[7] See `http://creativecommons.org/about/cc0` for more on the license.

[8] See `http://gnu.org/licenses/license-list.html#OtherLicenses`.

[9] See `http://gnu.org/licenses/license-list.html#ccbysa` for more on using this license.

27 The X Window System Trap

To copyleft or not to copyleft? That is one of the major controversies in the free software community. The idea of copyleft is that we should fight fire with fire—that we should use copyright to make sure our code stays free. The GNU General Public License (GNU GPL) is one example of a copyleft license.

Some free software developers prefer noncopyleft distribution. Noncopyleft licenses such as the XFree86 and BSD licenses are based on the idea of never saying no to anyone—not even to someone who seeks to use your work as the basis for restricting other people. Noncopyleft licensing does nothing wrong, but it misses the opportunity to actively protect our freedom to change and redistribute software. For that, we need copyleft.

For many years, the X Consortium was the chief opponent of copyleft. It exerted both moral suasion and pressure to discourage free software developers from copylefting their programs. It used moral suasion by suggesting that it is not nice to say no. It used pressure through its rule that copylefted software could not be in the X Distribution.

Why did the X Consortium adopt this policy? It had to do with their conception of success. The X Consortium defined success as popularity—specifically, getting computer companies to use the X Window System. This definition put the computer companies in the driver's seat: whatever they wanted, the X Consortium had to help them get it.

Computer companies normally distribute proprietary software. They wanted free software developers to donate their work for such use. If they had asked for this directly, people would have laughed. But the X Consortium, fronting for them, could present this request as an unselfish one. "Join us in donating our work to proprietary software developers," they said, suggesting that this is a noble form of self-sacrifice. "Join us in achieving popularity," they said, suggesting that it was not even a sacrifice.

But self-sacrifice is not the issue: tossing away the defense that copyleft provides, which protects the freedom of the whole community, is sacrificing more than yourself. Those who granted the X Consortium's request entrusted the community's future to the goodwill of the X Consortium.

This trust was misplaced. In its last year, the X Consortium made a plan to restrict the forthcoming X11R6.4 release so that it would not be free software. They decided to start saying no, not only to proprietary software developers, but to our community as well.

This essay was originally published on `http://gnu.org`, in 1998. This version is part of *Free Software, Free Society: Selected Essays of Richard M. Stallman*, 3rd ed. (Boston: GNU Press, 2015).

There is an irony here. If you said yes when the X Consortium asked you not to use copyleft, you put the X Consortium in a position to license and restrict its version of your program, along with the code for the core of X.

The X Consortium did not carry out this plan. Instead it closed down and transferred X development to the Open Group, whose staff are now carrying out a similar plan. To give them credit, when I asked them to release X11R6.4 under the GNU GPL in parallel with their planned restrictive license, they were willing to consider the idea. (They were firmly against staying with the old X11 distribution terms.) Before they said yes or no to this proposal, it had already failed for another reason: the XFree86 group followed the X Consortium's old policy, and will not accept copylefted software.

In September 1998, several months after X11R6.4 was released with nonfree distribution terms, the Open Group reversed its decision and rereleased it under the same noncopyleft free software license that was used for X11R6.3. Thus, the Open Group therefore eventually did what was right, but that does not alter the general issue.

Even if the X Consortium and the Open Group had never planned to restrict X, someone else could have done it. Noncopylefted software is vulnerable from all directions; it lets anyone make a nonfree version dominant, if he will invest sufficient resources to add significantly important features using proprietary code. Users who choose software based on technical characteristics, rather than on freedom, could easily be lured to the nonfree version for short-term convenience.

The X Consortium and Open Group can no longer exert moral suasion by saying that it is wrong to say no. This will make it easier to decide to copyleft your X-related software.

When you work on the core of X, on programs such as the X server, Xlib, and Xt, there is a practical reason not to use copyleft. The X.org group does an important job for the community in maintaining these programs, and the benefit of copylefting our changes would be less than the harm done by a fork in development. So it is better to work with them, and not copyleft our changes on these programs. Likewise for utilities such as `xset` and `xrdb`, which are close to the core of X and do not need major improvements. At least we know that the X.org group has a firm commitment to developing these programs as free software.

The issue is different for programs outside the core of X: applications, window managers, and additional libraries and widgets. There is no reason not to copyleft them, and we should copyleft them.

In case anyone feels the pressure exerted by the criteria for inclusion in the X distributions, the GNU Project will undertake to publicize copylefted packages that work with X. If you would like to copyleft something, and you worry that its omission from the X distribution will impede its popularity, please ask us to help.

At the same time, it is better if we do not feel too much need for popularity. When a businessman tempts you with "more popularity," he may try to convince you that his use of your program is crucial to its success. Don't believe it! If your program is good, it will find many users anyway; you don't need to feel desperate for any particular users, and you will be stronger if you do not. You can get an indescribable sense of joy and freedom by responding, "Take it or leave it—that's no skin off my back." Often the businessman will turn around and accept the program with copyleft, once you call the bluff.

Friends, free software developers, don't repeat old mistakes! If we do not copyleft our software, we put its future at the mercy of anyone equipped with more resources than scruples. With copyleft, we can defend freedom, not just for ourselves, but for our whole community.

28 Programs Must Not Limit the Freedom to Run Them

Free software means software controlled by its users, rather than the reverse. Specifically, it means the software comes with four essential freedoms that software users deserve.[1] At the head of the list is freedom zero, the freedom to run the program as you wish, in order to do what you wish.

Some developers propose to place usage restrictions in software licenses to ban using the program for certain purposes, but that would be a disastrous path. This article explains why freedom zero must not be limited. Conditions to limit the use of a program would achieve little of their aims, but could wreck the free software community.

First of all, let's be clear what freedom zero means. It means that the distribution of the software does not restrict how you use it. This doesn't make you exempt from laws. For instance, fraud is a crime in the US—a law which I think is right and proper. Whatever the free software license says, using a free program to carry out your fraud won't shield you from prosecution.

A license condition against fraud would be superfluous in a country where fraud is a crime. But why not a condition against using it for torture, a practice that states frequently condone when carried out by the "security forces"?

A condition against torture would not work, because enforcement of any free software license is done through the state. A state that wants to carry out torture will ignore the license. When victims of US torture try suing the US government, courts dismiss the cases on the grounds that their treatment is a national security secret. If a software developer tried to sue the US government for using a program for torture against the conditions of its license, that suit would be dismissed too. In general, states are clever at making legal excuses for whatever terrible things they want to do. Businesses with powerful lobbies can do it too.

What if the condition were against some specialized private activity? For instance, PETA proposed a license that would forbid use of the software to cause pain to animals with a spinal column. Or there might be a condition against using a certain program to make or publish drawings of Mohammad. Or against its use in experiments with embryonic stem cells. Or against using it to make unauthorized copies of musical recordings.

It is not clear these would be enforcible. Free software licenses are based on copyright law, and trying to impose usage conditions that way is stretching what

[1] See "What Is Free Software?" (p. 3) for the full definition of free software.

This essay was originally published on `http://gnu.org`, in 2012. This version is part of *Free Software, Free Society: Selected Essays of Richard M. Stallman*, 3rd ed. (Boston: GNU Press, 2015).

copyright law permits, stretching it in a dangerous way. Would you like books to carry license conditions about how you can use the information in them?

What if such conditions are legally enforcible—would that be good?

The fact is, people have very different ethical ideas about the activities that might be done using software. I happen to think those four unusual activities are legitimate and should not be forbidden. In particular I support the use of software for medical experiments on animals, and for processing meat. I defend the human rights of animal right activists but I don't agree with them; I would not want PETA to get its way in restricting the use of software.

Since I am not a pacifist, I would also disagree with a "no military use" provision. I condemn wars of aggression but I don't condemn fighting back. In fact, I have supported efforts to convince various armies to switch to free software, since they can check it for back doors and surveillance features that could imperil national security.

Since I am not against business in general, I would oppose a restriction against commercial use. A system that we could use only for recreation, hobbies and school is off limits to much of what we do with computers.

I've stated some of my views about other political issues, about activities that are or aren't unjust. Your views might differ, and that's precisely the point. If we accepted programs with usage restrictions as part of a free operating system such as GNU, people would come up with lots of different usage restrictions. There would be programs banned for use in meat processing, programs banned only for pigs, programs banned only for cows, and programs limited to kosher foods. Someone who hates spinach might write a program allowing use for processing any vegetable except spinach, while a Popeye fan might allow use only for spinach. There would be music programs allowed only for rap music, and others allowed only for classical music.

The result would be a system that you could not count on for any purpose. For each task you wish to do, you'd have to check lots of licenses to see which parts of your system are off limits for that task.

How would users respond to that? I think most of them would use proprietary systems. Allowing any usage restrictions whatsoever in free software would mainly push users towards nonfree software. Trying to stop users from doing something through usage restrictions in free software is as ineffective as pushing on an object through a long, soft, straight piece of spaghetti.

It is worse than ineffective; it is wrong too, because software developers should not exercise such power over what users do. Imagine selling pens with conditions about what you can write with them; that would be noisome, and we should not stand for it. Likewise for general software. If you make something that is generally useful, like a pen, people will use it to write all sorts of things, even horrible things such as orders to torture a dissident; but you must not have the power to control people's activities through their pens. It is the same for a text editor, compiler or kernel.

You do have an opportunity to determine what your software can be used for: when you decide what functionality to implement. You can write programs that lend themselves mainly to uses you think are positive, and you have no obligation to write any features that might lend themselves to activities you disapprove of.

The conclusion is clear: a program must not restrict what jobs its users do with it. Freedom 0 must be complete. We need to stop torture, but we can't do it through software licenses. The proper job of software licenses is to establish and protect users' freedom.

29 What Is Copyleft?

Copyleft is a general method for making a program (or other work) free, and requiring all modified and extended versions of the program to be free as well.

The simplest way to make a program free software is to put it in the public domain, uncopyrighted. This allows people to share the program and their improvements, if they are so minded. But it also allows uncooperative people to convert the program into proprietary software. They can make changes, many or few, and distribute the result as a proprietary product. People who receive the program in that modified form do not have the freedom that the original author gave them; the middleman has stripped it away.

In the GNU Project, our aim is to give *all* users the freedom to redistribute and change GNU software. If middlemen could strip off the freedom, we might have many users, but those users would not have freedom. So instead of putting GNU software in the public domain, we "copyleft" it. Copyleft says that anyone who redistributes the software, with or without changes, must pass along the freedom to further copy and change it. Copyleft guarantees that every user has freedom.

Copyleft also provides an incentive for other programmers to add to free software. Important free programs such as the GNU C++ compiler exist only because of this.

Copyleft also helps programmers who want to contribute improvements to free software get permission to do so. These programmers often work for companies or universities that would do almost anything to get more money. A programmer may want to contribute her changes to the community, but her employer may want to turn the changes into a proprietary software product.

When we explain to the employer that it is illegal to distribute the improved version except as free software, the employer usually decides to release it as free software rather than throw it away.

To copyleft a program, we first state that it is copyrighted; then we add distribution terms, which are a legal instrument that gives everyone the rights to use, modify, and redistribute the program's code, *or any program derived from it,* but only if the distribution terms are unchanged. Thus, the code and the freedoms become legally inseparable.

Proprietary software developers use copyright to take away the users' freedom; we use copyright to guarantee their freedom. That's why we reverse the name, changing "copyright" into "copyleft."

Copyleft is a way of using of the copyright on the program. It doesn't mean abandoning the copyright; in fact, doing so would make copyleft impossible.

This essay was originally published on `http://gnu.org`, in 1996. This version is part of *Free Software, Free Society: Selected Essays of Richard M. Stallman*, 3rd ed. (Boston: GNU Press, 2015).

The "left" in "copyleft" is not a reference to the verb "to leave"—only to the direction which is the inverse of "right."

Copyleft is a general concept, and you can't use a general concept directly; you can only use a specific implementation of the concept. In the GNU Project, the specific distribution terms that we use for most software are contained in the GNU General Public License (p. 191). The GNU General Public License is often called the GNU GPL for short. There is also a Frequently Asked Questions page about the GNU GPL, at `http://gnu.org/licenses/gpl-faq.html`. You can also read about why the FSF gets copyright assignments from contributors, at `http://gnu.org/copyleft/why-assign.html`.

An alternate form of copyleft, the GNU Affero General Public License (AGPL), is designed for programs that are likely to be used on servers. It ensures that modified versions used to implement services available to the public are released as source code to the public.

An alternate form of copyleft, the GNU Lesser General Public License (LGPL) (p. 207), applies to a few (but not all) GNU libraries. To learn more about properly using the LGPL, please read the article "Why You Shouldn't Use the Lesser GPL for Your Next Library," available at `http://gnu.org/philosophy/why-not-lgpl.html`.

The GNU Free Documentation License (FDL) (p. 210) is a form of copyleft intended for use on a manual, textbook or other document to assure everyone the effective freedom to copy and redistribute it, with or without modifications, either commercially or noncommercially.

The appropriate license is included in many manuals and in each GNU source code distribution.

All these licenses are designed so that you can easily apply them to your own works, assuming you are the copyright holder. You don't have to modify the license to do this, just include a copy of the license in the work, and add notices in the source files that refer properly to the license.

Using the same distribution terms for many different programs makes it easy to copy code between various different programs. When they all have the same distribution terms, there is no problem. The Lesser GPL, version 2, includes a provision that lets you alter the distribution terms to the ordinary GPL, so that you can copy code into another program covered by the GPL. Version 3 of the Lesser GPL is built as an exception added to GPL version 3, making the compatibility automatic.

If you would like to copyleft your program with the GNU GPL or the GNU LGPL, please see the license instructions page, at `http://gnu.org/copyleft/gpl-howto.html`, for advice. Please note that you must use the entire text of the license you choose. Each is an integral whole, and partial copies are not permitted.

If you would like to copyleft your manual with the GNU FDL, please see the instructions at the end of the FDL text (p. 218), and the GFDL instructions page, at `http://gnu.org/copyleft/fdl-howto.html`. Again, partial copies are not permitted.

It is a legal mistake to use a backwards C in a circle instead of a copyright symbol. Copyleft is based legally on copyright, so the work should have a copyright notice. A copyright notice requires either the copyright symbol (a C in a circle) or the word "Copyright."

A backwards C in a circle has no special legal significance, so it doesn't make a copyright notice. It may be amusing in book covers, posters, and such, but be careful how you represent it in a web page!

30 Why Copyleft?

> When it comes to defending the freedom of others, to lie down and do nothing is an act of weakness, not humility.

In the GNU Project we usually recommend people use copyleft[1] licenses like GNU GPL, rather than permissive noncopyleft free software licenses. We don't argue harshly against the noncopyleft licenses—in fact, we occasionally recommend them in special circumstances—but the advocates of those licenses show a pattern of arguing harshly against the GPL.

In one such argument, a person stated that his use of one of the BSD licenses was an "act of humility": "I ask nothing of those who use my code, except to credit me." It is rather a stretch to describe a legal demand for credit as "humility," but there is a deeper point to be considered here.

Humility is abnegating your own self interest, but you and the one who uses your code are not the only ones affected by your choice of which free software license to use for your code. Someone who uses your code in a nonfree program is trying to deny freedom to others, and if you let him do it, you're failing to defend their freedom. When it comes to defending the freedom of others, to lie down and do nothing is an act of weakness, not humility.

Releasing your code under one of the BSD licenses, or some other permissive noncopyleft license, is not doing wrong; the program is still free software, and still a contribution to our community. But it is weak, and in most cases it is not the best way to promote users' freedom to share and change software.

[1] See "What Is Copyleft?" (p. 184).

This essay was originally published on `http://gnu.org`, in 2003. This version is part of *Free Software, Free Society: Selected Essays of Richard M. Stallman*, 3rd ed. (Boston: GNU Press, 2015).

31 Copyleft: Pragmatic Idealism

Every decision a person makes stems from the person's values and goals. People can have many different goals and values; fame, profit, love, survival, fun, and freedom, are just some of the goals that a good person might have. When the goal is a matter of principle, we call that idealism.

My work on free software is motivated by an idealistic goal: spreading freedom and cooperation. I want to encourage free software to spread, replacing proprietary software that forbids cooperation, and thus make our society better.[1]

That's the basic reason why the GNU General Public License is written the way it is—as a copyleft. All code added to a GPL-covered program must be free software, even if it is put in a separate file. I make my code available for use in free software, and not for use in proprietary software, in order to encourage other people who write software to make it free as well. I figure that since proprietary software developers use copyright to stop us from sharing, we cooperators can use copyright to give other cooperators an advantage of their own: they can use our code.

Not everyone who uses the GNU GPL has this goal. Many years ago, a friend of mine was asked to rerelease a copylefted program under noncopyleft terms, and he responded more or less like this: "Sometimes I work on free software, and sometimes I work on proprietary software—but when I work on proprietary software, I expect to get *paid*."

He was willing to share his work with a community that shares software, but saw no reason to give a handout to a business making products that would be off-limits to our community. His goal was different from mine, but he decided that the GNU GPL was useful for his goal too.

If you want to accomplish something in the world, idealism is not enough—you need to choose a method that works to achieve the goal. In other words, you need to be "pragmatic." Is the GPL pragmatic? Let's look at its results.

Consider GNU C++. Why do we have a free C++ compiler? Only because the GNU GPL said it had to be free. GNU C++ was developed by an industry consortium, MCC, starting from the GNU C compiler. MCC normally makes its work as proprietary as can be. But they made the C++ front end free software, because the GNU GPL said that was the only way they could release it. The C++ front end included many new files, but since they were meant to be linked with GCC, the GPL did apply to them. The benefit to our community is evident.

[1] See "Why Copyleft?" (p. 187).

This version of this essay is part of *Free Software, Free Society: Selected Essays of Richard M. Stallman*, 3rd ed. (Boston: GNU Press, 2015).

Consider GNU Objective C. NeXT initially wanted to make this front end proprietary; they proposed to release it as `.o` files, and let users link them with the rest of GCC, thinking this might be a way around the GPL's requirements. But our lawyer said that this would not evade the requirements, that it was not allowed. And so they made the Objective C front end free software.

Those examples happened years ago, but the GNU GPL continues to bring us more free software.

Many GNU libraries are covered by the GNU Lesser General Public License, but not all. One GNU library which is covered by the ordinary GNU GPL is Readline, which implements command-line editing. I once found out about a nonfree program which was designed to use Readline, and told the developer this was not allowed. He could have taken command-line editing out of the program, but what he actually did was rerelease it under the GPL. Now it is free software.

The programmers who write improvements to GCC (or Emacs, or Bash, or Linux, or any GPL-covered program) are often employed by companies or universities. When the programmer wants to return his improvements to the community, and see his code in the next release, the boss may say, "Hold on there—your code belongs to us! We don't want to share it; we have decided to turn your improved version into a proprietary software product."

Here the GNU GPL comes to the rescue. The programmer shows the boss that this proprietary software product would be copyright infringement, and the boss realizes that he has only two choices: release the new code as free software, or not at all. Almost always he lets the programmer do as he intended all along, and the code goes into the next release.

The GNU GPL is not Mr. Nice Guy. It says no to some of the things that people sometimes want to do. There are users who say that this is a bad thing—that the GPL "excludes" some proprietary software developers who "need to be brought into the free software community."

But we are not excluding them from our community; they are choosing not to enter. Their decision to make software proprietary is a decision to stay out of our community. Being in our community means joining in cooperation with us; we cannot "bring them into our community" if they don't want to join.

What we *can* do is offer them an inducement to join. The GNU GPL is designed to make an inducement from our existing software: "If you will make your software free, you can use this code." Of course, it won't win 'em all, but it wins some of the time.

Proprietary software development does not contribute to our community, but its developers often want handouts from us. Free software users can offer free software developers strokes for the ego—recognition and gratitude—but it can be very tempting when a business tells you, "Just let us put your package in our proprietary program, and your program will be used by many thousands of people!" The temptation can be powerful, but in the long run we are all better off if we resist it.

The temptation and pressure are harder to recognize when they come indirectly, through free software organizations that have adopted a policy of catering to proprietary software. The X Consortium (and its successor, the Open Group) offers an example: funded by companies that made proprietary software, they strived for a decade to persuade programmers not to use copyleft. When the Open Group tried to make X11R6.4 nonfree software,[2] those of us who had resisted that pressure were glad that we did.

In September 1998, several months after X11R6.4 was released with nonfree distribution terms, the Open Group reversed its decision and rereleased it under the same noncopyleft free software license that was used for X11R6.3. Thank you, Open Group—but this subsequent reversal does not invalidate the conclusions we draw from the fact that adding the restrictions was *possible.*

Pragmatically speaking, thinking about greater long-term goals will strengthen your will to resist this pressure. If you focus your mind on the freedom and community that you can build by staying firm, you will find the strength to do it. "Stand for something, or you will fall for anything."

And if cynics ridicule freedom, ridicule community. . . if "hard-nosed realists" say that profit is the only ideal. . . just ignore them, and use copyleft all the same.

---

[2] For more on this, see "The X Window System Trap" (p. 178).

32 The GNU General Public License

Version 3, 29 June 2007

Preamble

The GNU General Public License is a free, copyleft license for software and other kinds of works.

The licenses for most software and other practical works are designed to take away your freedom to share and change the works. By contrast, the GNU General Public License is intended to guarantee your freedom to share and change all versions of a program—to make sure it remains free software for all its users. We, the Free Software Foundation, use the GNU General Public License for most of our software; it applies also to any other work released this way by its authors. You can apply it to your programs, too.

When we speak of free software, we are referring to freedom, not price. Our General Public Licenses are designed to make sure that you have the freedom to distribute copies of free software (and charge for them if you wish), that you receive source code or can get it if you want it, that you can change the software or use pieces of it in new free programs, and that you know you can do these things.

To protect your rights, we need to prevent others from denying you these rights or asking you to surrender the rights. Therefore, you have certain responsibilities if you distribute copies of the software, or if you modify it: responsibilities to respect the freedom of others.

For example, if you distribute copies of such a program, whether gratis or for a fee, you must pass on to the recipients the same freedoms that you received. You must make sure that they, too, receive or can get the source code. And you must show them these terms so they know their rights.

Developers that use the GNU GPL protect your rights with two steps: (1) assert copyright on the software, and (2) offer you this License giving you legal permission to copy, distribute and/or modify it.

For the developers' and authors' protection, the GPL clearly explains that there is no warranty for this free software. For both users' and authors' sake, the GPL requires that modified versions be marked as changed, so that their problems will not be attributed erroneously to authors of previous versions.

Some devices are designed to deny users access to install or run modified versions of the software inside them, although the manufacturer can do so. This is fundamentally incompatible with the aim of protecting users' freedom to change the software. The systematic pattern of such abuse occurs in the area of products for individuals to use, which is precisely where it is most unacceptable. Therefore, we have designed this version of the GPL to prohibit the practice for those products. If such problems arise substantially in other domains, we stand ready to extend this provision to those domains in future versions of the GPL, as needed to protect the freedom of users.

Finally, every program is threatened constantly by software patents. States should not allow patents to restrict development and use of software on general-purpose computers, but in those that do, we wish to avoid the special danger that patents applied to a free program could make it effectively proprietary. To prevent this, the GPL assures that patents cannot be used to render the program non-free.

The precise terms and conditions for copying, distribution and modification follow.

TERMS AND CONDITIONS

0. **Definitions.**

   "This License" refers to version 3 of the GNU General Public License.

   "Copyright" also means copyright-like laws that apply to other kinds of works, such as semiconductor masks.

   "The Program" refers to any copyrightable work licensed under this License. Each licensee is addressed as "you". "Licensees" and "recipients" may be individuals or organizations.

   To "modify" a work means to copy from or adapt all or part of the work in a fashion requiring copyright permission, other than the making of an exact copy. The resulting work is called a "modified version" of the earlier work or a work "based on" the earlier work.

   A "covered work" means either the unmodified Program or a work based on the Program.

   To "propagate" a work means to do anything with it that, without permission, would make you directly or secondarily liable for infringement under applicable copyright law, except executing it on a computer or modifying a private copy. Propagation includes copying, distribution (with or without modification), making available to the public, and in some countries other activities as well.

   To "convey" a work means any kind of propagation that enables other parties to make or receive copies. Mere interaction with a user through a computer network, with no transfer of a copy, is not conveying.

   An interactive user interface displays "Appropriate Legal Notices" to the extent that it includes a convenient and prominently visible feature that (1) displays an appropriate copyright notice, and (2) tells the user that there is no warranty for the work (except to the extent that warranties are provided), that licensees may convey the work under this License, and how to view a copy of this License. If the interface presents a list of user commands or options, such as a menu, a prominent item in the list meets this criterion.

1. **Source Code.**

   The "source code" for a work means the preferred form of the work for making modifications to it. "Object code" means any non-source form of a work.

   A "Standard Interface" means an interface that either is an official standard defined by a recognized standards body, or, in the case of interfaces specified for a particular programming language, one that is widely used among developers working in that language.

   The "System Libraries" of an executable work include anything, other than the work as a whole, that (a) is included in the normal form of packaging a Major Component, but which is not part of that Major Component, and (b) serves only to enable use of the work with that Major Component, or to implement a Standard Interface for which an implementation is available to the public in source code form. A "Major Component", in this context, means a major essential component (kernel, window system, and so on) of the specific operating system (if any) on which the executable work runs, or a compiler used to produce the work, or an object code interpreter used to run it.

   The "Corresponding Source" for a work in object code form means all the source code needed to generate, install, and (for an executable work) run the object code and to modify the work, including scripts to control those activities. However, it does not include the work's System Libraries, or general-purpose tools or generally available free programs which are used unmodified in performing those activities but which are not part of the work. For example, Corresponding Source includes interface definition files associated with source files for the work, and the source code for shared libraries and dynamically linked subprograms that the work is specifically designed to require, such as by intimate data communication or control flow between those subprograms and other parts of the work.

   The Corresponding Source need not include anything that users can regenerate automatically from other parts of the Corresponding Source.

   The Corresponding Source for a work in source code form is that same work.

2. **Basic Permissions.**

   All rights granted under this License are granted for the term of copyright on the Program, and are irrevocable provided the stated conditions are met. This License explicitly affirms your unlimited permission to run the unmodified Program. The output from running a covered work is covered by this License only if the output, given its content, constitutes a covered work. This License acknowledges your rights of fair use or other equivalent, as provided by copyright law.

You may make, run and propagate covered works that you do not convey, without conditions so long as your license otherwise remains in force. You may convey covered works to others for the sole purpose of having them make modifications exclusively for you, or provide you with facilities for running those works, provided that you comply with the terms of this License in conveying all material for which you do not control copyright. Those thus making or running the covered works for you must do so exclusively on your behalf, under your direction and control, on terms that prohibit them from making any copies of your copyrighted material outside their relationship with you.

Conveying under any other circumstances is permitted solely under the conditions stated below. Sublicensing is not allowed; section 10 makes it unnecessary.

3. **Protecting Users' Legal Rights From Anti-Circumvention Law.**

   No covered work shall be deemed part of an effective technological measure under any applicable law fulfilling obligations under article 11 of the WIPO copyright treaty adopted on 20 December 1996, or similar laws prohibiting or restricting circumvention of such measures.

   When you convey a covered work, you waive any legal power to forbid circumvention of technological measures to the extent such circumvention is effected by exercising rights under this License with respect to the covered work, and you disclaim any intention to limit operation or modification of the work as a means of enforcing, against the work's users, your or third parties' legal rights to forbid circumvention of technological measures.

4. **Conveying Verbatim Copies.**

   You may convey verbatim copies of the Program's source code as you receive it, in any medium, provided that you conspicuously and appropriately publish on each copy an appropriate copyright notice; keep intact all notices stating that this License and any non-permissive terms added in accord with section 7 apply to the code; keep intact all notices of the absence of any warranty; and give all recipients a copy of this License along with the Program.

   You may charge any price or no price for each copy that you convey, and you may offer support or warranty protection for a fee.

5. **Conveying Modified Source Versions.**

   You may convey a work based on the Program, or the modifications to produce it from the Program, in the form of source code under the terms of section 4, provided that you also meet all of these conditions:

   a. The work must carry prominent notices stating that you modified it, and giving a relevant date.

b. The work must carry prominent notices stating that it is released under this License and any conditions added under section 7. This requirement modifies the requirement in section 4 to "keep intact all notices".

c. You must license the entire work, as a whole, under this License to anyone who comes into possession of a copy. This License will therefore apply, along with any applicable section 7 additional terms, to the whole of the work, and all its parts, regardless of how they are packaged. This License gives no permission to license the work in any other way, but it does not invalidate such permission if you have separately received it.

d. If the work has interactive user interfaces, each must display Appropriate Legal Notices; however, if the Program has interactive interfaces that do not display Appropriate Legal Notices, your work need not make them do so.

A compilation of a covered work with other separate and independent works, which are not by their nature extensions of the covered work, and which are not combined with it such as to form a larger program, in or on a volume of a storage or distribution medium, is called an "aggregate" if the compilation and its resulting copyright are not used to limit the access or legal rights of the compilation's users beyond what the individual works permit. Inclusion of a covered work in an aggregate does not cause this License to apply to the other parts of the aggregate.

6. **Conveying Non-Source Forms.**

You may convey a covered work in object code form under the terms of sections 4 and 5, provided that you also convey the machine-readable Corresponding Source under the terms of this License, in one of these ways:

a. Convey the object code in, or embodied in, a physical product (including a physical distribution medium), accompanied by the Corresponding Source fixed on a durable physical medium customarily used for software interchange.

b. Convey the object code in, or embodied in, a physical product (including a physical distribution medium), accompanied by a written offer, valid for at least three years and valid for as long as you offer spare parts or customer support for that product model, to give anyone who possesses the object code either (1) a copy of the Corresponding Source for all the software in the product that is covered by this License, on a durable physical medium customarily used for software interchange, for a price no more than your reasonable cost of physically performing this conveying of source, or (2) access to copy the Corresponding Source from a network server at no charge.

c. Convey individual copies of the object code with a copy of the written offer to provide the Corresponding Source. This alternative is allowed only occasionally and noncommercially, and only if you received the object code with such an offer, in accord with subsection 6b.

d. Convey the object code by offering access from a designated place (gratis or for a charge), and offer equivalent access to the Corresponding Source in the same way through the same place at no further charge. You need not require recipients to copy the Corresponding Source along with the object code. If the place to copy the object code is a network server, the Corresponding Source may be on a different server (operated by you or a third party) that supports equivalent copying facilities, provided you maintain clear directions next to the object code saying where to find the Corresponding Source. Regardless of what server hosts the Corresponding Source, you remain obligated to ensure that it is available for as long as needed to satisfy these requirements.

e. Convey the object code using peer-to-peer transmission, provided you inform other peers where the object code and Corresponding Source of the work are being offered to the general public at no charge under subsection 6d.

A separable portion of the object code, whose source code is excluded from the Corresponding Source as a System Library, need not be included in conveying the object code work.

A "User Product" is either (1) a "consumer product", which means any tangible personal property which is normally used for personal, family, or household purposes, or (2) anything designed or sold for incorporation into a dwelling. In determining whether a product is a consumer product, doubtful cases shall be resolved in favor of coverage. For a particular product received by a particular user, "normally used" refers to a typical or common use of that class of product, regardless of the status of the particular user or of the way in which the particular user actually uses, or expects or is expected to use, the product. A product is a consumer product regardless of whether the product has substantial commercial, industrial or non-consumer uses, unless such uses represent the only significant mode of use of the product.

"Installation Information" for a User Product means any methods, procedures, authorization keys, or other information required to install and execute modified versions of a covered work in that User Product from a modified version of its Corresponding Source. The information must suffice to ensure that the continued functioning of the modified object code is in no case prevented or interfered with solely because modification has been made.

If you convey an object code work under this section in, or with, or specifically for use in, a User Product, and the conveying occurs as part of a transaction in which the right of possession and use of the User Product is transferred to the recipient in perpetuity or for a fixed term (regardless of how the transaction is characterized), the Corresponding Source conveyed under this section must be accompanied by the Installation Information. But this requirement does not apply if neither you nor any third party retains the ability to install modified object code on the User Product (for example, the work has been installed in ROM).

The requirement to provide Installation Information does not include a requirement to continue to provide support service, warranty, or updates for a work that has been modified or installed by the recipient, or for the User Product in which it has been modified or installed. Access to a network may be denied when the modification itself materially and adversely affects the operation of the network or violates the rules and protocols for communication across the network.

Corresponding Source conveyed, and Installation Information provided, in accord with this section must be in a format that is publicly documented (and with an implementation available to the public in source code form), and must require no special password or key for unpacking, reading or copying.

7. **Additional Terms.**

"Additional permissions" are terms that supplement the terms of this License by making exceptions from one or more of its conditions. Additional permissions that are applicable to the entire Program shall be treated as though they were included in this License, to the extent that they are valid under applicable law. If additional permissions apply only to part of the Program, that part may be used separately under those permissions, but the entire Program remains governed by this License without regard to the additional permissions.

When you convey a copy of a covered work, you may at your option remove any additional permissions from that copy, or from any part of it. (Additional permissions may be written to require their own removal in certain cases when you modify the work.) You may place additional permissions on material, added by you to a covered work, for which you have or can give appropriate copyright permission.

Notwithstanding any other provision of this License, for material you add to a covered work, you may (if authorized by the copyright holders of that material) supplement the terms of this License with terms:

a. Disclaiming warranty or limiting liability differently from the terms of sections 15 and 16 of this License; or
b. Requiring preservation of specified reasonable legal notices or author attributions in that material or in the Appropriate Legal Notices displayed by works containing it; or

c. Prohibiting misrepresentation of the origin of that material, or requiring that modified versions of such material be marked in reasonable ways as different from the original version; or

d. Limiting the use for publicity purposes of names of licensors or authors of the material; or

e. Declining to grant rights under trademark law for use of some trade names, trademarks, or service marks; or

f. Requiring indemnification of licensors and authors of that material by anyone who conveys the material (or modified versions of it) with contractual assumptions of liability to the recipient, for any liability that these contractual assumptions directly impose on those licensors and authors.

All other non-permissive additional terms are considered "further restrictions" within the meaning of section 10. If the Program as you received it, or any part of it, contains a notice stating that it is governed by this License along with a term that is a further restriction, you may remove that term. If a license document contains a further restriction but permits relicensing or conveying under this License, you may add to a covered work material governed by the terms of that license document, provided that the further restriction does not survive such relicensing or conveying.

If you add terms to a covered work in accord with this section, you must place, in the relevant source files, a statement of the additional terms that apply to those files, or a notice indicating where to find the applicable terms.

Additional terms, permissive or non-permissive, may be stated in the form of a separately written license, or stated as exceptions; the above requirements apply either way.

8. **Termination.**

You may not propagate or modify a covered work except as expressly provided under this License. Any attempt otherwise to propagate or modify it is void, and will automatically terminate your rights under this License (including any patent licenses granted under the third paragraph of section 11).

However, if you cease all violation of this License, then your license from a particular copyright holder is reinstated (a) provisionally, unless and until the copyright holder explicitly and finally terminates your license, and (b) permanently, if the copyright holder fails to notify you of the violation by some reasonable means prior to 60 days after the cessation.

Moreover, your license from a particular copyright holder is reinstated permanently if the copyright holder notifies you of the violation by some reasonable means, this is the first time you have received notice of violation of this License (for any work) from that copyright holder, and you cure the violation prior to 30 days after your receipt of the notice.

Termination of your rights under this section does not terminate the licenses of parties who have received copies or rights from you under this License. If your rights have been terminated and not permanently reinstated, you do not qualify to receive new licenses for the same material under section 10.

9. **Acceptance Not Required for Having Copies.**

   You are not required to accept this License in order to receive or run a copy of the Program. Ancillary propagation of a covered work occurring solely as a consequence of using peer-to-peer transmission to receive a copy likewise does not require acceptance. However, nothing other than this License grants you permission to propagate or modify any covered work. These actions infringe copyright if you do not accept this License. Therefore, by modifying or propagating a covered work, you indicate your acceptance of this License to do so.

10. **Automatic Licensing of Downstream Recipients.**

    Each time you convey a covered work, the recipient automatically receives a license from the original licensors, to run, modify and propagate that work, subject to this License. You are not responsible for enforcing compliance by third parties with this License.

    An "entity transaction" is a transaction transferring control of an organization, or substantially all assets of one, or subdividing an organization, or merging organizations. If propagation of a covered work results from an entity transaction, each party to that transaction who receives a copy of the work also receives whatever licenses to the work the party's predecessor in interest had or could give under the previous paragraph, plus a right to possession of the Corresponding Source of the work from the predecessor in interest, if the predecessor has it or can get it with reasonable efforts.

    You may not impose any further restrictions on the exercise of the rights granted or affirmed under this License. For example, you may not impose a license fee, royalty, or other charge for exercise of rights granted under this License, and you may not initiate litigation (including a cross-claim or counterclaim in a lawsuit) alleging that any patent claim is infringed by making, using, selling, offering for sale, or importing the Program or any portion of it.

11. **Patents.**

    A "contributor" is a copyright holder who authorizes use under this License of the Program or a work on which the Program is based. The work thus licensed is called the contributor's "contributor version".

    A contributor's "essential patent claims" are all patent claims owned or controlled by the contributor, whether already acquired or hereafter acquired, that would be infringed by some manner, permitted by this License, of making, using, or selling its contributor version, but do not include claims that would be infringed only as a consequence of further modification of the contributor version. For purposes of this definition, "control" includes the right to grant patent sublicenses in a manner consistent with the requirements of this License.

Each contributor grants you a non-exclusive, worldwide, royalty-free patent license under the contributor's essential patent claims, to make, use, sell, offer for sale, import and otherwise run, modify and propagate the contents of its contributor version.

In the following three paragraphs, a "patent license" is any express agreement or commitment, however denominated, not to enforce a patent (such as an express permission to practice a patent or covenant not to sue for patent infringement). To "grant" such a patent license to a party means to make such an agreement or commitment not to enforce a patent against the party.

If you convey a covered work, knowingly relying on a patent license, and the Corresponding Source of the work is not available for anyone to copy, free of charge and under the terms of this License, through a publicly available network server or other readily accessible means, then you must either (1) cause the Corresponding Source to be so available, or (2) arrange to deprive yourself of the benefit of the patent license for this particular work, or (3) arrange, in a manner consistent with the requirements of this License, to extend the patent license to downstream recipients. "Knowingly relying" means you have actual knowledge that, but for the patent license, your conveying the covered work in a country, or your recipient's use of the covered work in a country, would infringe one or more identifiable patents in that country that you have reason to believe are valid.

If, pursuant to or in connection with a single transaction or arrangement, you convey, or propagate by procuring conveyance of, a covered work, and grant a patent license to some of the parties receiving the covered work authorizing them to use, propagate, modify or convey a specific copy of the covered work, then the patent license you grant is automatically extended to all recipients of the covered work and works based on it.

A patent license is "discriminatory" if it does not include within the scope of its coverage, prohibits the exercise of, or is conditioned on the non-exercise of one or more of the rights that are specifically granted under this License. You may not convey a covered work if you are a party to an arrangement with a third party that is in the business of distributing software, under which you make payment to the third party based on the extent of your activity of conveying the work, and under which the third party grants, to any of the parties who would receive the covered work from you, a discriminatory patent license (a) in connection with copies of the covered work conveyed by you (or copies made from those copies), or (b) primarily for and in connection with specific products or compilations that contain the covered work, unless you entered into that arrangement, or that patent license was granted, prior to 28 March 2007.

Nothing in this License shall be construed as excluding or limiting any implied license or other defenses to infringement that may otherwise be available to you under applicable patent law.

12. **No Surrender of Others' Freedom.**

    If conditions are imposed on you (whether by court order, agreement or otherwise) that contradict the conditions of this License, they do not excuse you from the conditions of this License. If you cannot convey a covered work so as to satisfy simultaneously your obligations under this License and any other pertinent obligations, then as a consequence you may not convey it at all. For example, if you agree to terms that obligate you to collect a royalty for further conveying from those to whom you convey the Program, the only way you could satisfy both those terms and this License would be to refrain entirely from conveying the Program.

13. **Use with the GNU Affero General Public License.**

    Notwithstanding any other provision of this License, you have permission to link or combine any covered work with a work licensed under version 3 of the GNU Affero General Public License into a single combined work, and to convey the resulting work. The terms of this License will continue to apply to the part which is the covered work, but the special requirements of the GNU Affero General Public License, section 13, concerning interaction through a network will apply to the combination as such.

14. **Revised Versions of this License.**

    The Free Software Foundation may publish revised and/or new versions of the GNU General Public License from time to time. Such new versions will be similar in spirit to the present version, but may differ in detail to address new problems or concerns.

    Each version is given a distinguishing version number. If the Program specifies that a certain numbered version of the GNU General Public License "or any later version" applies to it, you have the option of following the terms and conditions either of that numbered version or of any later version published by the Free Software Foundation. If the Program does not specify a version number of the GNU General Public License, you may choose any version ever published by the Free Software Foundation.

    If the Program specifies that a proxy can decide which future versions of the GNU General Public License can be used, that proxy's public statement of acceptance of a version permanently authorizes you to choose that version for the Program.

    Later license versions may give you additional or different permissions. However, no additional obligations are imposed on any author or copyright holder as a result of your choosing to follow a later version.

15. **Disclaimer of Warranty.**

    THERE IS NO WARRANTY FOR THE PROGRAM, TO THE EXTENT PERMITTED BY APPLICABLE LAW. EXCEPT WHEN OTHERWISE STATED IN WRITING THE COPYRIGHT HOLDERS AND/OR OTHER PARTIES PROVIDE THE PROGRAM "AS IS" WITHOUT WARRANTY OF ANY KIND, EITHER EXPRESSED OR IMPLIED, INCLUDING, BUT NOT LIMITED TO, THE IMPLIED WARRANTIES OF MERCHANTABILITY AND FITNESS FOR A PARTICULAR PURPOSE. THE ENTIRE RISK AS TO THE QUALITY AND PERFORMANCE OF THE PROGRAM IS WITH YOU. SHOULD THE PROGRAM PROVE DEFECTIVE, YOU ASSUME THE COST OF ALL NECESSARY SERVICING, REPAIR OR CORRECTION.

16. **Limitation of Liability.**

    IN NO EVENT UNLESS REQUIRED BY APPLICABLE LAW OR AGREED TO IN WRITING WILL ANY COPYRIGHT HOLDER, OR ANY OTHER PARTY WHO MODIFIES AND/OR CONVEYS THE PROGRAM AS PERMITTED ABOVE, BE LIABLE TO YOU FOR DAMAGES, INCLUDING ANY GENERAL, SPECIAL, INCIDENTAL OR CONSEQUENTIAL DAMAGES ARISING OUT OF THE USE OR INABILITY TO USE THE PROGRAM (INCLUDING BUT NOT LIMITED TO LOSS OF DATA OR DATA BEING RENDERED INACCURATE OR LOSSES SUSTAINED BY YOU OR THIRD PARTIES OR A FAILURE OF THE PROGRAM TO OPERATE WITH ANY OTHER PROGRAMS), EVEN IF SUCH HOLDER OR OTHER PARTY HAS BEEN ADVISED OF THE POSSIBILITY OF SUCH DAMAGES.

17. **Interpretation of Sections 15 and 16.**

    If the disclaimer of warranty and limitation of liability provided above cannot be given local legal effect according to their terms, reviewing courts shall apply local law that most closely approximates an absolute waiver of all civil liability in connection with the Program, unless a warranty or assumption of liability accompanies a copy of the Program in return for a fee.

END OF TERMS AND CONDITIONS

How to Apply These Terms to Your New Programs

If you develop a new program, and you want it to be of the greatest possible use to the public, the best way to achieve this is to make it free software which everyone can redistribute and change under these terms.

To do so, attach the following notices to the program. It is safest to attach them to the start of each source file to most effectively state the exclusion of warranty; and each file should have at least the "copyright" line and a pointer to where the full notice is found.

```
one line to give the program's name and a brief idea of what it does.
Copyright (C) year name of author

This program is free software: you can redistribute it and/or modify
it under the terms of the GNU General Public License as published by
the Free Software Foundation, either version 3 of the License, or (at
your option) any later version.

This program is distributed in the hope that it will be useful, but
WITHOUT ANY WARRANTY; without even the implied warranty of
MERCHANTABILITY or FITNESS FOR A PARTICULAR PURPOSE.  See the GNU
General Public License for more details.

You should have received a copy of the GNU General Public License
along with this program.  If not, see http://www.gnu.org/licenses/.
```

Also add information on how to contact you by electronic and paper mail.

If the program does terminal interaction, make it output a short notice like this when it starts in an interactive mode:

```
program Copyright (C) year name of author
This program comes with ABSOLUTELY NO WARRANTY;
for details type 'show w'.  This is free software,
and you are welcome to redistribute it under
certain conditions; type 'show c' for details.
```

The hypothetical commands '`show w`' and '`show c`' should show the appropriate parts of the General Public License. Of course, your program's commands might be different; for a GUI interface, you would use an "about box".

You should also get your employer (if you work as a programmer) or school, if any, to sign a "copyright disclaimer" for the program, if necessary. For more information on this, and how to apply and follow the GNU GPL, see `http://www.gnu.org/licenses/`.

The GNU General Public License does not permit incorporating your program into proprietary programs. If your program is a subroutine library, you may consider it more useful to permit linking proprietary applications with the library. If this is what you want to do, use the GNU Lesser General Public License instead of this License. But first, please read `http://www.gnu.org/philosophy/why-not-lgpl.html`.

33 Why Upgrade to GPLv3

Version 3 of the GNU General Public License (GNU GPL) has been released, enabling free software packages to upgrade from GPL version 2. This article explains why upgrading the license is important.

First of all, it is important to note that upgrading is a choice. GPL version 2 will remain a valid license, and no disaster will happen if some programs remain under GPLv2 while others advance to GPLv3. These two licenses are incompatible, but that isn't a fundamental problem.

When we say that GPLv2 and GPLv3 are incompatible, it means there is no legal way to combine code under GPLv2 with code under GPLv3 in a single program. This is because both GPLv2 and GPLv3 are copyleft licenses: each of them says, "If you include code under this license in a larger program, the larger program must be under this license too." There is no way to make them compatible. We could add a GPLv2-compatibility clause to GPLv3, but it wouldn't do the job, because GPLv2 would need a similar clause.

Fortunately, license incompatibility matters only when you want to link, merge or combine code from two different programs into a single program. There is no problem in having GPLv3-covered and GPLv2-covered programs side by side in an operating system. For instance, the TeX license and the Apache license are incompatible with GPLv2, but that doesn't stop us from running TeX and Apache in the same system with Linux, Bash and GCC. This is because they are all separate programs. Likewise, if Bash and GCC move to GPLv3, while Linux remains under GPLv2, there is no conflict.

Keeping a program under GPLv2 won't create problems. The reason to migrate is because of the existing problems that GPLv3 will address.

One major danger that GPLv3 will block is tivoization. Tivoization means certain "appliances" (which have computers inside) contain GPL-covered software that you can't effectively change, because the appliance shuts down if it detects modified software. The usual motive for tivoization is that the software has features the manufacturer knows people will want to change, and aims to stop people from changing them. The manufacturers of these computers take advantage of the freedom that free software provides, but they don't let you do likewise.

Some argue that competition between appliances in a free market should suffice to keep nasty features to a low level. Perhaps competition alone would avoid arbitrary, pointless misfeatures like "Must shut down between 1pm and 5pm every Tuesday," but even so, a choice of masters isn't freedom. Freedom

This essay was originally published on `http://gnu.org`, in 2007. This version is part of *Free Software, Free Society: Selected Essays of Richard M. Stallman*, 3rd ed. (Boston: GNU Press, 2015).

means *you* control what your software does, not merely that you can beg or threaten someone else who decides for you.

In the crucial area of Digital Restrictions Management (DRM)—nasty features designed to restrict your use of the data in your computer—competition is no help, because relevant competition is forbidden. Under the Digital Millennium Copyright Act and similar laws, it is illegal, in the US and many other countries, to distribute DVD players unless they restrict the user according to the official rules of the DVD conspiracy (its web site is `http://www.dvdcca.org/`, but the rules do not seem to be published there). The public can't reject DRM by buying non-DRM players because none are available. No matter how many products you can choose from, they all have equivalent digital handcuffs.

GPLv3 ensures you are free to remove the handcuffs. It doesn't forbid DRM, or any kind of feature. It places no limits on the substantive functionality you can add to a program, or remove from it. Rather, it makes sure that you are just as free to remove nasty features as the distributor of your copy was to add them. Tivoization is the way they deny you that freedom; to protect your freedom, GPLv3 forbids tivoization.

The ban on tivoization applies to any product whose use by consumers is to be expected, even occasionally. GPLv3 tolerates tivoization only for products that are almost exclusively meant for businesses and organizations.

Another threat that GPLv3 resists is that of patent deals like the Novell-Microsoft pact. Microsoft wants to use its thousands of patents to make users pay Microsoft for the privilege of running GNU/Linux, and made this pact to try to achieve that. The deal offers rather limited protection from Microsoft patents to Novell's customers.

Microsoft made a few mistakes in the Novell-Microsoft deal, and GPLv3 is designed to turn them against Microsoft, extending that limited patent protection to the whole community. In order to take advantage of this protection, programs need to use GPLv3.

Microsoft's lawyers are not stupid, and next time they may manage to avoid those mistakes. GPLv3 therefore says they don't get a "next time." Releasing a program under GPL version 3 protects it from Microsoft's future attempts to make redistributors collect Microsoft royalties from the program's users.

GPLv3 also provides users with explicit patent protection from the program's contributors and redistributors. With GPLv2, users rely on an implicit patent license to make sure that the company which provided them a copy won't sue them, or the people they redistribute copies to, for patent infringement.

The explicit patent license in GPLv3 does not go as far as we might have liked. Ideally, we would make everyone who redistributes GPL-covered code give up all software patents, along with everyone who does not redistribute GPL-covered code, because there should be no software patents. Software patents are a vicious and absurd system that puts all software developers in danger of being sued by companies they have never heard of, as well as by all the megacorporations in the field. Large programs typically combine thousands of ideas, so it is no surprise if they implement ideas covered by hundreds of patents. Megacorporations collect thousands of patents, and use those patents to bully smaller developers. Patents already obstruct free software development.

The only way to make software development safe is to abolish software patents, and we aim to achieve this some day. But we cannot do this through a software license. Any program, free or not, can be killed by a software patent in the hands of an unrelated party, and the program's license cannot prevent that. Only court decisions or changes in patent law can make software development safe from patents. If we tried to do this with GPLv3, it would fail.

Therefore, GPLv3 seeks to limit and channel the danger. In particular, we have tried to save free software from a fate worse than death: to be made effectively proprietary, through patents. The explicit patent license of GPLv3 makes sure companies that use the GPL to give users the four freedoms cannot turn around and use their patents to tell some users, "That doesn't include you." It also stops them from colluding with other patent holders to do this.

Further advantages of GPLv3 include better internationalization, gentler termination, support for BitTorrent, and compatibility with the Apache license. All in all, plenty of reason to upgrade.

Change is unlikely to cease once GPLv3 is released. If new threats to users' freedom develop, we will have to develop GPL version 4. It is important to make sure that programs will have no trouble upgrading to GPLv4 if and when we write one.

One way to do this is to release a program under "GPL version 3 or any later version." Another way is for all the contributors to a program to state a proxy who can decide on upgrading to future GPL versions. The third way is for all the contributors to assign copyright to one designated copyright holder, who will be in a position to upgrade the license version. One way or another, programs should provide this flexibility for future GPL versions.

34 The GNU Lesser General Public License

Version 3, 29 June 2007

This version of the GNU Lesser General Public License incorporates the terms and conditions of version 3 of the GNU General Public License, supplemented by the additional permissions listed below.

0. **Additional Definitions.**

   As used herein, "this License" refers to version 3 of the GNU Lesser General Public License, and the "GNU GPL" refers to version 3 of the GNU General Public License.

   "The Library" refers to a covered work governed by this License, other than an Application or a Combined Work as defined below.

   An "Application" is any work that makes use of an interface provided by the Library, but which is not otherwise based on the Library. Defining a subclass of a class defined by the Library is deemed a mode of using an interface provided by the Library.

   A "Combined Work" is a work produced by combining or linking an Application with the Library. The particular version of the Library with which the Combined Work was made is also called the "Linked Version".

   The "Minimal Corresponding Source" for a Combined Work means the Corresponding Source for the Combined Work, excluding any source code for portions of the Combined Work that, considered in isolation, are based on the Application, and not on the Linked Version.

   The "Corresponding Application Code" for a Combined Work means the object code and/or source code for the Application, including any data and utility programs needed for reproducing the Combined Work from the Application, but excluding the System Libraries of the Combined Work.

1. **Exception to Section 3 of the GNU GPL.**

   You may convey a covered work under sections 3 and 4 of this License without being bound by section 3 of the GNU GPL.

2. **Conveying Modified Versions.**

   If you modify a copy of the Library, and, in your modifications, a facility refers to a function or data to be supplied by an Application that uses the facility (other than as an argument passed when the facility is invoked), then you may convey a copy of the modified version:

a. under this License, provided that you make a good faith effort to ensure that, in the event an Application does not supply the function or data, the facility still operates, and performs whatever part of its purpose remains meaningful, or
b. under the GNU GPL, with none of the additional permissions of this License applicable to that copy.

3. **Object Code Incorporating Material from Library Header Files.**

   The object code form of an Application may incorporate material from a header file that is part of the Library. You may convey such object code under terms of your choice, provided that, if the incorporated material is not limited to numerical parameters, data structure layouts and accessors, or small macros, inline functions and templates (ten or fewer lines in length), you do both of the following:

   a. Give prominent notice with each copy of the object code that the Library is used in it and that the Library and its use are covered by this License.
   b. Accompany the object code with a copy of the GNU GPL and this license document.

4. **Combined Works.**

   You may convey a Combined Work under terms of your choice that, taken together, effectively do not restrict modification of the portions of the Library contained in the Combined Work and reverse engineering for debugging such modifications, if you also do each of the following:

   a. Give prominent notice with each copy of the Combined Work that the Library is used in it and that the Library and its use are covered by this License.
   b. Accompany the Combined Work with a copy of the GNU GPL and this license document.
   c. For a Combined Work that displays copyright notices during execution, include the copyright notice for the Library among these notices, as well as a reference directing the user to the copies of the GNU GPL and this license document.
   d. Do one of the following:

      0. Convey the Minimal Corresponding Source under the terms of this License, and the Corresponding Application Code in a form suitable for, and under terms that permit, the user to recombine or relink the Application with a modified version of the Linked Version to produce a modified Combined Work, in the manner specified by section 6 of the GNU GPL for conveying Corresponding Source.

1. Use a suitable shared library mechanism for linking with the Library. A suitable mechanism is one that (a) uses at run time a copy of the Library already present on the user's computer system, and (b) will operate properly with a modified version of the Library that is interface-compatible with the Linked Version.

e. Provide Installation Information, but only if you would otherwise be required to provide such information under section 6 of the GNU GPL, and only to the extent that such information is necessary to install and execute a modified version of the Combined Work produced by recombining or relinking the Application with a modified version of the Linked Version. (If you use option 4d0, the Installation Information must accompany the Minimal Corresponding Source and Corresponding Application Code. If you use option 4d1, you must provide the Installation Information in the manner specified by section 6 of the GNU GPL for conveying Corresponding Source.)

5. **Combined Libraries.**

   You may place library facilities that are a work based on the Library side by side in a single library together with other library facilities that are not Applications and are not covered by this License, and convey such a combined library under terms of your choice, if you do both of the following:

   a. Accompany the combined library with a copy of the same work based on the Library, uncombined with any other library facilities, conveyed under the terms of this License.

   b. Give prominent notice with the combined library that part of it is a work based on the Library, and explaining where to find the accompanying uncombined form of the same work.

6. **Revised Versions of the GNU Lesser General Public License.**

   The Free Software Foundation may publish revised and/or new versions of the GNU Lesser General Public License from time to time. Such new versions will be similar in spirit to the present version, but may differ in detail to address new problems or concerns.

   Each version is given a distinguishing version number. If the Library as you received it specifies that a certain numbered version of the GNU Lesser General Public License "or any later version" applies to it, you have the option of following the terms and conditions either of that published version or of any later version published by the Free Software Foundation. If the Library as you received it does not specify a version number of the GNU Lesser General Public License, you may choose any version of the GNU Lesser General Public License ever published by the Free Software Foundation.

   If the Library as you received it specifies that a proxy can decide whether future versions of the GNU Lesser General Public License shall apply, that proxy's public statement of acceptance of any version is permanent authorization for you to choose that version for the Library.

35 GNU Free Documentation License

Version 1.3, 3 November 2008

0. **PREAMBLE**

The purpose of this License is to make a manual, textbook, or other functional and useful document *free* in the sense of freedom: to assure everyone the effective freedom to copy and redistribute it, with or without modifying it, either commercially or noncommercially. Secondarily, this License preserves for the author and publisher a way to get credit for their work, while not being considered responsible for modifications made by others.

This License is a kind of "copyleft", which means that derivative works of the document must themselves be free in the same sense. It complements the GNU General Public License, which is a copyleft license designed for free software.

We have designed this License in order to use it for manuals for free software, because free software needs free documentation: a free program should come with manuals providing the same freedoms that the software does. But this License is not limited to software manuals; it can be used for any textual work, regardless of subject matter or whether it is published as a printed book. We recommend this License principally for works whose purpose is instruction or reference.

1. **APPLICABILITY AND DEFINITIONS**

This License applies to any manual or other work, in any medium, that contains a notice placed by the copyright holder saying it can be distributed under the terms of this License. Such a notice grants a world-wide, royalty-free license, unlimited in duration, to use that work under the conditions stated herein. The "Document", below, refers to any such manual or work. Any member of the public is a licensee, and is addressed as "you". You accept the license if you copy, modify or distribute the work in a way requiring permission under copyright law.

A "Modified Version" of the Document means any work containing the Document or a portion of it, either copied verbatim, or with modifications and/or translated into another language.

A "Secondary Section" is a named appendix or a front-matter section of the Document that deals exclusively with the relationship of the publishers or authors of the Document to the Document's overall subject (or to related matters) and contains nothing that could fall directly within that overall subject. (Thus, if the Document is in part a textbook of mathematics, a

Secondary Section may not explain any mathematics.) The relationship could be a matter of historical connection with the subject or with related matters, or of legal, commercial, philosophical, ethical or political position regarding them.

The "Invariant Sections" are certain Secondary Sections whose titles are designated, as being those of Invariant Sections, in the notice that says that the Document is released under this License. If a section does not fit the above definition of Secondary then it is not allowed to be designated as Invariant. The Document may contain zero Invariant Sections. If the Document does not identify any Invariant Sections then there are none.

The "Cover Texts" are certain short passages of text that are listed, as Front-Cover Texts or Back-Cover Texts, in the notice that says that the Document is released under this License. A Front-Cover Text may be at most 5 words, and a Back-Cover Text may be at most 25 words.

A "Transparent" copy of the Document means a machine-readable copy, represented in a format whose specification is available to the general public, that is suitable for revising the document straightforwardly with generic text editors or (for images composed of pixels) generic paint programs or (for drawings) some widely available drawing editor, and that is suitable for input to text formatters or for automatic translation to a variety of formats suitable for input to text formatters. A copy made in an otherwise Transparent file format whose markup, or absence of markup, has been arranged to thwart or discourage subsequent modification by readers is not Transparent. An image format is not Transparent if used for any substantial amount of text. A copy that is not "Transparent" is called "Opaque".

Examples of suitable formats for Transparent copies include plain ASCII without markup, Texinfo input format, LaTeX input format, SGML or XML using a publicly available DTD, and standard-conforming simple HTML, PostScript or PDF designed for human modification. Examples of transparent image formats include PNG, XCF and JPG. Opaque formats include proprietary formats that can be read and edited only by proprietary word processors, SGML or XML for which the DTD and/or processing tools are not generally available, and the machine-generated HTML, PostScript or PDF produced by some word processors for output purposes only.

The "Title Page" means, for a printed book, the title page itself, plus such following pages as are needed to hold, legibly, the material this License requires to appear in the title page. For works in formats which do not have any title page as such, "Title Page" means the text near the most prominent appearance of the work's title, preceding the beginning of the body of the text.

The "publisher" means any person or entity that distributes copies of the Document to the public.

A section "Entitled XYZ" means a named subunit of the Document whose title either is precisely XYZ or contains XYZ in parentheses following text that translates XYZ in another language. (Here XYZ stands for a specific section name mentioned below, such as "Acknowledgements", "Dedications", "Endorsements", or "History".) To "Preserve the Title" of such a section when you modify the Document means that it remains a section "Entitled XYZ" according to this definition.

The Document may include Warranty Disclaimers next to the notice which states that this License applies to the Document. These Warranty Disclaimers are considered to be included by reference in this License, but only as regards disclaiming warranties: any other implication that these Warranty Disclaimers may have is void and has no effect on the meaning of this License.

2. **VERBATIM COPYING**

   You may copy and distribute the Document in any medium, either commercially or noncommercially, provided that this License, the copyright notices, and the license notice saying this License applies to the Document are reproduced in all copies, and that you add no other conditions whatsoever to those of this License. You may not use technical measures to obstruct or control the reading or further copying of the copies you make or distribute. However, you may accept compensation in exchange for copies. If you distribute a large enough number of copies you must also follow the conditions in section 3.

   You may also lend copies, under the same conditions stated above, and you may publicly display copies.

3. **COPYING IN QUANTITY**

   If you publish printed copies (or copies in media that commonly have printed covers) of the Document, numbering more than 100, and the Document's license notice requires Cover Texts, you must enclose the copies in covers that carry, clearly and legibly, all these Cover Texts: Front-Cover Texts on the front cover, and Back-Cover Texts on the back cover. Both covers must also clearly and legibly identify you as the publisher of these copies. The front cover must present the full title with all words of the title equally prominent and visible. You may add other material on the covers in addition. Copying with changes limited to the covers, as long as they preserve the title of the Document and satisfy these conditions, can be treated as verbatim copying in other respects.

   If the required texts for either cover are too voluminous to fit legibly, you should put the first ones listed (as many as fit reasonably) on the actual cover, and continue the rest onto adjacent pages.

   If you publish or distribute Opaque copies of the Document numbering more than 100, you must either include a machine-readable Transparent copy along with each Opaque copy, or state in or with each Opaque copy a computer-network location from which the general network-using public has access to download using public-standard network protocols a complete Transparent copy of the Document, free of added material. If you use the latter option, you must take reasonably prudent steps, when you begin distribution of Opaque copies in quantity, to ensure that this Transparent copy will remain thus accessible at the stated location until at least one year after the last time you distribute an Opaque copy (directly or through your agents or retailers) of that edition to the public.

It is requested, but not required, that you contact the authors of the Document well before redistributing any large number of copies, to give them a chance to provide you with an updated version of the Document.

4. **MODIFICATIONS**

You may copy and distribute a Modified Version of the Document under the conditions of sections 2 and 3 above, provided that you release the Modified Version under precisely this License, with the Modified Version filling the role of the Document, thus licensing distribution and modification of the Modified Version to whoever possesses a copy of it. In addition, you must do these things in the Modified Version:

A. Use in the Title Page (and on the covers, if any) a title distinct from that of the Document, and from those of previous versions (which should, if there were any, be listed in the History section of the Document). You may use the same title as a previous version if the original publisher of that version gives permission.

B. List on the Title Page, as authors, one or more persons or entities responsible for authorship of the modifications in the Modified Version, together with at least five of the principal authors of the Document (all of its principal authors, if it has fewer than five), unless they release you from this requirement.

C. State on the Title page the name of the publisher of the Modified Version, as the publisher.

D. Preserve all the copyright notices of the Document.

E. Add an appropriate copyright notice for your modifications adjacent to the other copyright notices.

F. Include, immediately after the copyright notices, a license notice giving the public permission to use the Modified Version under the terms of this License, in the form shown in the Addendum below.

G. Preserve in that license notice the full lists of Invariant Sections and required Cover Texts given in the Document's license notice.

H. Include an unaltered copy of this License.

I. Preserve the section Entitled "History", Preserve its Title, and add to it an item stating at least the title, year, new authors, and publisher of the Modified Version as given on the Title Page. If there is no section Entitled "History" in the Document, create one stating the title, year, authors, and publisher of the Document as given on its Title Page, then add an item describing the Modified Version as stated in the previous sentence.

J. Preserve the network location, if any, given in the Document for public access to a Transparent copy of the Document, and likewise the network locations given in the Document for previous versions it was based on. These may be placed in the "History" section. You may omit a network location for a work that was published at least four years before the Document itself, or if the original publisher of the version it refers to gives permission.

K. For any section Entitled "Acknowledgements" or "Dedications", Preserve the Title of the section, and preserve in the section all the substance and tone of each of the contributor acknowledgements and/or dedications given therein.

L. Preserve all the Invariant Sections of the Document, unaltered in their text and in their titles. Section numbers or the equivalent are not considered part of the section titles.

M. Delete any section Entitled "Endorsements". Such a section may not be included in the Modified Version.

N. Do not retitle any existing section to be Entitled "Endorsements" or to conflict in title with any Invariant Section.

O. Preserve any Warranty Disclaimers.

If the Modified Version includes new front-matter sections or appendices that qualify as Secondary Sections and contain no material copied from the Document, you may at your option designate some or all of these sections as invariant. To do this, add their titles to the list of Invariant Sections in the Modified Version's license notice. These titles must be distinct from any other section titles.

You may add a section Entitled "Endorsements", provided it contains nothing but endorsements of your Modified Version by various parties—for example, statements of peer review or that the text has been approved by an organization as the authoritative definition of a standard.

You may add a passage of up to five words as a Front-Cover Text, and a passage of up to 25 words as a Back-Cover Text, to the end of the list of Cover Texts in the Modified Version. Only one passage of Front-Cover Text and one of Back-Cover Text may be added by (or through arrangements made by) any one entity. If the Document already includes a cover text for the same cover, previously added by you or by arrangement made by the same entity you are acting on behalf of, you may not add another; but you may replace the old one, on explicit permission from the previous publisher that added the old one.

The author(s) and publisher(s) of the Document do not by this License give permission to use their names for publicity for or to assert or imply endorsement of any Modified Version.

5. **COMBINING DOCUMENTS**

   You may combine the Document with other documents released under this License, under the terms defined in section 4 above for modified versions, provided that you include in the combination all of the Invariant Sections of all of the original documents, unmodified, and list them all as Invariant Sections of your combined work in its license notice, and that you preserve all their Warranty Disclaimers.

   The combined work need only contain one copy of this License, and multiple identical Invariant Sections may be replaced with a single copy. If there are multiple Invariant Sections with the same name but different contents, make the title of each such section unique by adding at the end of it, in parentheses, the name of the original author or publisher of that section if known, or else a unique number. Make the same adjustment to the section titles in the list of Invariant Sections in the license notice of the combined work.

   In the combination, you must combine any sections Entitled "History" in the various original documents, forming one section Entitled "History"; likewise combine any sections Entitled "Acknowledgements", and any sections Entitled "Dedications". You must delete all sections Entitled "Endorsements."

6. **COLLECTIONS OF DOCUMENTS**

   You may make a collection consisting of the Document and other documents released under this License, and replace the individual copies of this License in the various documents with a single copy that is included in the collection, provided that you follow the rules of this License for verbatim copying of each of the documents in all other respects.

   You may extract a single document from such a collection, and distribute it individually under this License, provided you insert a copy of this License into the extracted document, and follow this License in all other respects regarding verbatim copying of that document.

7. **AGGREGATION WITH INDEPENDENT WORKS**

   A compilation of the Document or its derivatives with other separate and independent documents or works, in or on a volume of a storage or distribution medium, is called an "aggregate" if the copyright resulting from the compilation is not used to limit the legal rights of the compilation's users beyond what the individual works permit. When the Document is included in an aggregate, this License does not apply to the other works in the aggregate which are not themselves derivative works of the Document.

   If the Cover Text requirement of section 3 is applicable to these copies of the Document, then if the Document is less than one half of the entire aggregate, the Document's Cover Texts may be placed on covers that bracket the Document within the aggregate, or the electronic equivalent of covers if the Document is in electronic form. Otherwise they must appear on printed covers that bracket the whole aggregate.

8. **TRANSLATION**

   Translation is considered a kind of modification, so you may distribute translations of the Document under the terms of section 4. Replacing Invariant Sections with translations requires special permission from their copyright holders, but you may include translations of some or all Invariant Sections in addition to the original versions of these Invariant Sections. You may include a translation of this License, and all the license notices in the Document, and any Warranty Disclaimers, provided that you also include the original English version of this License and the original versions of those notices and disclaimers. In case of a disagreement between the translation and the original version of this License or a notice or disclaimer, the original version will prevail.

   If a section in the Document is Entitled "Acknowledgements", "Dedications", or "History", the requirement (section 4) to Preserve its Title (section 1) will typically require changing the actual title.

9. **TERMINATION**

   You may not copy, modify, sublicense, or distribute the Document except as expressly provided under this License. Any attempt otherwise to copy, modify, sublicense, or distribute it is void, and will automatically terminate your rights under this License.

   However, if you cease all violation of this License, then your license from a particular copyright holder is reinstated (a) provisionally, unless and until the copyright holder explicitly and finally terminates your license, and (b) permanently, if the copyright holder fails to notify you of the violation by some reasonable means prior to 60 days after the cessation.

   Moreover, your license from a particular copyright holder is reinstated permanently if the copyright holder notifies you of the violation by some reasonable means, this is the first time you have received notice of violation of this License (for any work) from that copyright holder, and you cure the violation prior to 30 days after your receipt of the notice.

   Termination of your rights under this section does not terminate the licenses of parties who have received copies or rights from you under this License. If your rights have been terminated and not permanently reinstated, receipt of a copy of some or all of the same material does not give you any rights to use it.

10. **FUTURE REVISIONS OF THIS LICENSE**

    The Free Software Foundation may publish new, revised versions of the GNU Free Documentation License from time to time. Such new versions will be similar in spirit to the present version, but may differ in detail to address new problems or concerns. See `http://www.gnu.org/copyleft/`.

    Each version of the License is given a distinguishing version number. If the Document specifies that a particular numbered version of this License "or any later version" applies to it, you have the option of following the terms and conditions either of that specified version or of any later version that has been published (not as a draft) by the Free Software Foundation. If the Document does not specify a version number of this License, you may choose any version ever published (not as a draft) by the Free Software Foundation. If the Document specifies that a proxy can decide which future versions of this License can be used, that proxy's public statement of acceptance of a version permanently authorizes you to choose that version for the Document.

11. **RELICENSING**

"Massive Multiauthor Collaboration Site" (or "MMC Site") means any World Wide Web server that publishes copyrightable works and also provides prominent facilities for anybody to edit those works. A public wiki that anybody can edit is an example of such a server. A "Massive Multiauthor Collaboration" (or "MMC") contained in the site means any set of copyrightable works thus published on the MMC site.

"CC-BY-SA" means the Creative Commons Attribution-Share Alike 3.0 license published by Creative Commons Corporation, a not-for-profit corporation with a principal place of business in San Francisco, California, as well as future copyleft versions of that license published by that same organization.

"Incorporate" means to publish or republish a Document, in whole or in part, as part of another Document.

An MMC is "eligible for relicensing" if it is licensed under this License, and if all works that were first published under this License somewhere other than this MMC, and subsequently incorporated in whole or in part into the MMC, (1) had no cover texts or invariant sections, and (2) were thus incorporated prior to November 1, 2008.

The operator of an MMC Site may republish an MMC contained in the site under CC-BY-SA on the same site at any time before August 1, 2009, provided the MMC is eligible for relicensing.

ADDENDUM: How to use this License for your documents

To use this License in a document you have written, include a copy of the License in the document and put the following copyright and license notices just after the title page:

```
Copyright (C)  year  your name.
Permission is granted to copy, distribute and/or modify this document
under the terms of the GNU Free Documentation License, Version 1.3 or
any later version published by the Free Software Foundation; with
no Invariant Sections, no Front-Cover Texts, and no Back-Cover Texts.
A copy of the license is included in the section entitled
``GNU Free Documentation License''.
```

If you have Invariant Sections, Front-Cover Texts and Back-Cover Texts, replace the "with...Texts." line with this:

```
with the Invariant Sections being list their titles, with
the Front-Cover Texts being list, and with the Back-Cover Texts
being list.
```

If you have Invariant Sections without Cover Texts, or some other combination of the three, merge those two alternatives to suit the situation.

If your document contains nontrivial examples of program code, we recommend releasing these examples in parallel under your choice of free software license, such as the GNU General Public License, to permit their use in free software.

36 On Selling Exceptions to the GNU GPL

> The practice of selling license exceptions became a hot topic when I co-signed Knowledge Ecology International's letter warning that Oracle's purchase of MySQL (plus the rest of Sun) might not be good for MySQL.
> As the following article explains, my feelings about selling license exceptions are mixed. Clearly it is possible to develop powerful and complex software packages under the GNU GPL without selling exceptions, and we do this. MySQL can be developed this way too. However, selling exceptions has been used by MySQL developers. Who should decide whether to continue this? I don't think it is wise to give major decisions about a free software project to a large proprietary competitor, which might naturally prefer that the project develop less rather than more.
> One thing that makes no sense at all is the idea of changing the license of MySQL to something noncopyleft. That would eliminate the possibility of selling exceptions, but allow all sorts of proprietary modified versions. Wherever MySQL should go, it isn't there.

When I co-signed the letter objecting to Oracle's planned purchase of MySQL[1] (along with the rest of Sun), some free software supporters were surprised that I approved of the practice of selling license exceptions which the MySQL developers have used. They expected me to condemn the practice outright. This article explains what I think of the practice, and why.

Selling exceptions means that the copyright holder of the code releases it to the public under a free software license, then lets customers pay for permission to use the same code under different terms, for instance allowing its inclusion in proprietary applications.

We must distinguish the practice of selling exceptions from something crucially different: purely proprietary extensions or versions of a free program. These two activities, even if practiced simultaneously by one company, are different issues. In selling exceptions, the same code that the exception applies to is available to the general public as free software. An extension or a modified version that is only available under a proprietary license is proprietary software, pure and simple, and no better than any other proprietary software. This article is concerned with cases that involve strictly and only the sale of exceptions.

I've considered selling exceptions acceptable since the 1990s, and on occasion I've suggested it to companies. Sometimes this approach has made it possible for important programs to become free software.

---

[1] James Love and Malini Aisola (Knowledge Ecology International), Richard Stallman (FSF), Jim Killock (Open Rights Group), letter to Neelie Kroes (Commissioner for Competition, European Commission), 19 October 2009, `http://keionline.org/sites/default/files/ec_letter_mysql_oct19.pdf`.

This version of this essay is part of *Free Software, Free Society: Selected Essays of Richard M. Stallman*, 3rd ed. (Boston: GNU Press, 2015).

The KDE desktop was developed in the 90s based on the Qt library. Qt was proprietary software, and TrollTech charged for permission to embed it in proprietary applications. TrollTech allowed gratis use of Qt in free applications, but this did not make it free/libre software. Completely free operating systems therefore could not include Qt, so they could not use KDE either.

In 1998, the management of TrollTech recognized that they could make Qt free software and continue charging for permission to embed it in proprietary software. I do not recall whether the suggestion came from me, but I certainly was happy to see the change, which made it possible to use Qt and thus KDE in the free software world.

Initially, they used their own license, the Q Public License (QPL)—quite restrictive as free software licenses go, and incompatible with the GNU GPL. Later they switched to the GNU GPL; I think I had explained to them that it would work for the purpose.

Selling exceptions depends fundamentally on using a copyleft license, such as the GNU GPL, for the free software release. A copyleft license permits embedding in a larger program only if the whole combined program is released under that license; this is how it ensures extended versions will also be free. Thus, users that want to make the combined program proprietary need special permission. Only the copyright holder can grant that, and selling exceptions is one style of doing so. Someone else, who received the code under the GNU GPL or another copyleft license, cannot grant an exception.

When I first heard of the practice of selling exceptions, I asked myself whether the practice is ethical. If someone buys an exception to embed a program in a larger proprietary program, he's doing something wrong (namely, making proprietary software). Does it follow that the developer that sold the exception is doing something wrong too?

If that implication is valid, it would also apply to releasing the same program under a noncopyleft free software license, such as the X11 license. That also permits such embedding. So either we have to conclude that it's wrong to release anything under the X11 license—a conclusion I find unacceptably extreme—or reject this implication. Using a noncopyleft license is weak, and usually an inferior choice, but it's not wrong.

In other words, selling exceptions permits limited embedding of the code in proprietary software, but the X11 license goes even further, permitting unlimited use of the code (and modified versions of it) in proprietary software. If this doesn't make the X11 license unacceptable, it doesn't make selling exceptions unacceptable.

There are three reasons why the FSF doesn't practice selling exceptions. One is that it doesn't lead to the FSF's goal: assuring freedom for each user of our software. That's what we wrote the GNU GPL for, and the way to achieve this most thoroughly is to release under GPL version 3-or-later and not allow embedding in proprietary software. Selling exceptions wouldn't achieve this, just as release under the X11 license wouldn't. So normally we don't do either of those things. We release under the GPL only.

Another reason we release only under the GPL is so as not to permit proprietary extensions that would present practical advantages over our free programs. Users for whom freedom is not a value might choose those nonfree versions rather than the free programs they are based on—and lose their freedom. We don't want to encourage that.

But there are occasional cases where, for specific reasons of strategy, we decide that using a more permissive license on a certain program is better for the cause of freedom. In those cases, we release the program to everyone under that permissive license.

This is because of another ethical principle that the FSF follows: to treat all users the same. An idealistic campaign for freedom should not discriminate, so the FSF is committed to giving the same license to all users. The FSF never sells exceptions; whatever license or licenses we release a program under, that is available to everyone.

But we need not insist that companies follow that principle. I consider selling exceptions an acceptable thing for a company to do, and I will suggest it where appropriate as a way to get programs freed.

Part VI:
Traps and Challenges

37 Can You Trust Your Computer?

Who should your computer take its orders from? Most people think their computers should obey them, not obey someone else. With a plan they call "trusted computing," large media corporations (including the movie companies and record companies), together with computer companies such as Microsoft and Intel, are planning to make your computer obey them instead of you. (Microsoft's version of this scheme is called Palladium.) Proprietary programs have included malicious features before, but this plan would make it universal.

Proprietary software means, fundamentally, that you don't control what it does; you can't study the source code, or change it. It's not surprising that clever businessmen find ways to use their control to put you at a disadvantage. Microsoft has done this several times: one version of Windows was designed to report to Microsoft all the software on your hard disk; a recent "security" upgrade in Windows Media Player required users to agree to new restrictions. But Microsoft is not alone: the KaZaa music-sharing software is designed so that KaZaa's business partner can rent out the use of your computer to its clients. These malicious features are often secret, but even once you know about them it is hard to remove them, since you don't have the source code.

In the past, these were isolated incidents. "Trusted computing" would make the practice pervasive. "Treacherous computing" is a more appropriate name, because the plan is designed to make sure your computer will systematically disobey you. In fact, it is designed to stop your computer from functioning as a general-purpose computer. Every operation may require explicit permission.

The technical idea underlying treacherous computing is that the computer includes a digital encryption and signature device, and the keys are kept secret from you. Proprietary programs will use this device to control which other programs you can run, which documents or data you can access, and what programs you can pass them to. These programs will continually download new authorization rules through the internet, and impose those rules automatically on your work. If you don't allow your computer to obtain the new rules periodically from the internet, some capabilities will automatically cease to function.

Of course, Hollywood and the record companies plan to use treacherous computing for Digital Restrictions Management (DRM), so that downloaded videos and music can be played only on one specified computer. Sharing will be entirely impossible, at least using the authorized files that you would get from those companies. You, the public, ought to have both the freedom and the ability to share these things. (I expect that someone will find a way to produce unencrypted

This essay was first published on http://gnu.org, in 2002. This version is part of *Free Software, Free Society: Selected Essays of Richard M. Stallman*, 3rd ed. (Boston: GNU Press, 2015).

versions, and to upload and share them, so DRM will not entirely succeed, but that is no excuse for the system.)

Making sharing impossible is bad enough, but it gets worse. There are plans to use the same facility for email and documents—resulting in email that disappears in two weeks, or documents that can only be read on the computers in one company.

Imagine if you get an email from your boss telling you to do something that you think is risky; a month later, when it backfires, you can't use the email to show that the decision was not yours. "Getting it in writing" doesn't protect you when the order is written in disappearing ink.

Imagine if you get an email from your boss stating a policy that is illegal or morally outrageous, such as to shred your company's audit documents, or to allow a dangerous threat to your country to move forward unchecked. Today you can send this to a reporter and expose the activity. With treacherous computing, the reporter won't be able to read the document; her computer will refuse to obey her. Treacherous computing becomes a paradise for corruption.

Word processors such as Microsoft Word could use treacherous computing when they save your documents, to make sure no competing word processors can read them. Today we must figure out the secrets of Word format by laborious experiments in order to make free word processors read Word documents. If Word encrypts documents using treacherous computing when saving them, the free software community won't have a chance of developing software to read them—and if we could, such programs might even be forbidden by the Digital Millennium Copyright Act.

Programs that use treacherous computing will continually download new authorization rules through the internet, and impose those rules automatically on your work. If Microsoft, or the US government, does not like what you said in a document you wrote, they could post new instructions telling all computers to refuse to let anyone read that document. Each computer would obey when it downloads the new instructions. Your writing would be subject to 1984-style retroactive erasure. You might be unable to read it yourself.

You might think you can find out what nasty things a treacherous-computing application does, study how painful they are, and decide whether to accept them. Even if you can find this out, it would be foolish to accept the deal, but you can't even expect the deal to stand still. Once you come to depend on using the program, you are hooked and they know it; then they can change the deal. Some applications will automatically download upgrades that will do something different—and they won't give you a choice about whether to upgrade.

Today you can avoid being restricted by proprietary software by not using it. If you run GNU/Linux or another free operating system, and if you avoid installing proprietary applications on it, then you are in charge of what your computer does. If a free program has a malicious feature, other developers in the community will take it out, and you can use the corrected version. You can also run free application programs and tools on nonfree operating systems; this falls short of fully giving you freedom, but many users do it.

Treacherous computing puts the existence of free operating systems and free applications at risk, because you may not be able to run them at all. Some versions of treacherous computing would require the operating system to be specifically authorized by a particular company. Free operating systems could not be installed. Some versions of treacherous computing would require every program to be specifically authorized by the operating system developer. You could not run free applications on such a system. If you did figure out how, and told someone, that could be a crime.

There are proposals already for US laws that would require all computers to support treacherous computing, and to prohibit connecting old computers to the internet. The CBDTPA (we call it the Consume But Don't Try Programming Act) is one of them. But even if they don't legally force you to switch to treacherous computing, the pressure to accept it may be enormous. Today people often use Word format for communication, although this causes several sorts of problems.[1] If only a treacherous-computing machine can read the latest Word documents, many people will switch to it, if they view the situation only in terms of individual action (take it or leave it). To oppose treacherous computing,[2] we must join together and confront the situation as a collective choice.

To block treacherous computing will require large numbers of citizens to organize. We need your help! Please support `DefectiveByDesign.org`, the FSF's campaign against Digital Restrictions Management.

Postscripts

1. The computer security field uses the term "trusted computing" in a different way—beware of confusion between the two meanings.
2. The GNU Project distributes the GNU Privacy Guard, a program that implements public-key encryption and digital signatures, which you can use to send secure and private email. It is useful to explore how GPG differs from treacherous computing, and see what makes one helpful and the other so dangerous.

   When someone uses GPG to send you an encrypted document, and you use GPG to decode it, the result is an unencrypted document that you can read, forward, copy, and even reencrypt to send it securely to someone else. A treacherous-computing application would let you read the words on the screen, but would not let you produce an unencrypted document that you could use in other ways. GPG, a free software package, makes security features available to the users; *they* use *it*. Treacherous computing is designed to impose restrictions on the users; *it* uses *them*.

---

[1] See my article "We Can Put an End to Word Attachments," at `http://gnu.org/philosophy/no-word-attachments.html`, for a description of the problems Word documents cause and a number of suggestions on how to tackle them.

[2] For further information, see the "'Trusted Computing' Frequently Asked Questions," at `http://www.cl.cam.ac.uk/users/rja14/tcpa-faq.html`.

3. The supporters of treacherous computing focus their discourse on its beneficial uses. What they say is often correct, just not important.

   Like most hardware, treacherous-computing hardware can be used for purposes which are not harmful. But these features can be implemented in other ways, without treacherous-computing hardware. The principal difference that treacherous computing makes for users is the nasty consequence: rigging your computer to work against you.

   What they say is true, and what I say is true. Put them together and what do you get? Treacherous computing is a plan to take away our freedom, while offering minor benefits to distract us from what we would lose.

4. Microsoft presents Palladium as a security measure, and claims that it will protect against viruses, but this claim is evidently false. A presentation by Microsoft Research in October 2002 stated that one of the specifications of Palladium is that existing operating systems and applications will continue to run; therefore, viruses will continue to be able to do all the things that they can do today.

   When Microsoft employees speak of "security" in connection with Palladium, they do not mean what we normally mean by that word: protecting your machine from things you do not want. They mean protecting your copies of data on your machine from access by you in ways others do not want. A slide in the presentation listed several types of secrets Palladium could be used to keep, including "third party secrets" and "user secrets"—but it put "user secrets" in quotation marks, recognizing that this is somewhat of an absurdity in the context of Palladium.

   The presentation made frequent use of other terms that we frequently associate with the context of security, such as "attack," "malicious code," "spoofing," as well as "trusted." None of them means what it normally means. "Attack" doesn't mean someone trying to hurt you, it means you trying to copy music. "Malicious code" means code installed by you to do what someone else doesn't want your machine to do. "Spoofing" doesn't mean someone's fooling you, it means your fooling Palladium. And so on.

5. A previous statement by the Palladium developers stated the basic premise that whoever developed or collected information should have total control of how you use it. This would represent a revolutionary overturn of past ideas of ethics and of the legal system, and create an unprecedented system of control. The specific problems of these systems are no accident; they result from the basic goal. It is the goal we must reject.

6. As of 2015, treacherous computing has been implemented for PCs in the form of the "Trusted Platform Module"; however, for practical reasons, the TPM has proved a total failure for the goal of providing a platform for remote attestation to verify Digital Restrictions Management. Thus, companies implement DRM using other methods. At present, "Trusted Platform Modules" are not being used for DRM at all, and there are reasons to think that it will not be feasible to use them for DRM. Ironically,

this means that the only current uses of the "Trusted Platform Modules" are the innocent secondary uses—for instance, to verify that no one has surreptitiously changed the system in a computer.

Therefore, we conclude that the "Trusted Platform Modules" available for PCs are not dangerous, and there is no reason not to include one in a computer or support it in system software.

This does not mean that everything is rosy. Other hardware systems for blocking the owner of a computer from changing the software in it are in use in some ARM PCs as well as processors in portable phones, cars, TVs and other devices, and these are fully as bad as we expected.

This also does not mean that remote attestation is harmless. If ever a device succeeds in implementing that, it will be a grave threat to users' freedom. The current "Trusted Platform Module" is harmless only because it failed in the attempt to make remote attestation feasible. We must not presume that all future attempts will fail too.

38 The JavaScript Trap

You may be running nonfree programs on your computer every day without realizing it—through your web browser.

In the free software community, the idea that nonfree programs mistreat their users is familiar. Some of us refuse entirely to install proprietary software, and many others consider nonfreedom a strike against the program. Many users are aware that this issue applies to the plug-ins that browsers offer to install, since they can be free or nonfree.

But browsers run other nonfree programs which they don't ask you about or even tell you about—programs that web pages contain or link to. These programs are most often written in JavaScript, though other languages are also used.

JavaScript (officially called ECMAScript, but few use that name) was once used for minor frills in web pages, such as cute but inessential navigation and display features. It was acceptable to consider these as mere extensions of HTML markup, rather than as true software; they did not constitute a significant issue.

Many sites still use JavaScript that way, but some use it for major programs that do large jobs. For instance, Google Docs downloads into your machine a JavaScript program which measures half a megabyte, in a compacted form that we could call Obfuscript because it has no comments and hardly any whitespace, and the method names are one letter long. The source code of a program is the preferred form for modifying it; the compacted code is not source code, and the real source code of this program is not available to the user.

Browsers don't normally tell you when they load JavaScript programs. Most browsers have a way to turn off JavaScript entirely, but none of them can check for JavaScript programs that are nontrivial and nonfree. Even if you're aware of this issue, it would take you considerable trouble to identify and then block those programs. However, even in the free software community most users are not aware of this issue; the browsers' silence tends to conceal it.

It is possible to release a JavaScript program as free software, by distributing the source code under a free software license. But even if the program's source is available, there is no easy way to run your modified version instead of the original. Current free browsers do not offer a facility to run your own modified version instead of the one delivered in the page. The effect is comparable to tivoization, although not quite so hard to overcome.

JavaScript is not the only language web sites use for programs sent to the user. Flash supports programming through an extended variant of JavaScript.

This essay was first published on `http://gnu.org`, in 2009. This version is part of *Free Software, Free Society: Selected Essays of Richard M. Stallman*, 3rd ed. (Boston: GNU Press, 2015).

We will need to study the issue of Flash to make suitable recommendations. Silverlight seems likely to create a problem similar to Flash, except worse, since Microsoft uses it as a platform for nonfree codecs. A free replacement for Silverlight does not do the job for the free world unless it normally comes with free replacement codecs.

Java applets also run in the browser, and raise similar issues. In general, any sort of applet system poses this sort of problem. Having a free execution environment for an applet only brings us far enough to encounter the problem.

A strong movement has developed that calls for web sites to communicate only through formats and protocols that are free (some say "open"); that is to say, whose documentation is published and which anyone is free to implement. With the presence of programs in web pages, that criterion is necessary, but not sufficient. JavaScript itself, as a format, is free, and use of JavaScript in a web site is not necessarily bad. However, as we've seen above, it also isn't necessarily OK. When the site transmits a program to the user, it is not enough for the program to be written in a documented and unencumbered language; that program must be free, too. "Only free programs transmitted to the user" must become part of the criterion for proper behavior by web sites.

Silently loading and running nonfree programs is one among several issues raised by "web applications." The term "web application" was designed to disregard the fundamental distinction between software delivered to users and software running on the server. It can refer to a specialized client program running in a browser; it can refer to specialized server software; it can refer to a specialized client program that works hand in hand with specialized server software. The client and server sides raise different ethical issues, even if they are so closely integrated that they arguably form parts of a single program. This article addresses only the issue of the client-side software. We are addressing the server issue separately.

In practical terms, how can we deal with the problem of nonfree JavaScript programs in web sites? The first step is to avoid running it.

What do we mean by "nontrivial"? It is a matter of degree, so this is a matter of designing a simple criterion that gives good results, rather than finding the one correct answer.

Our tentative policy is to consider a JavaScript program nontrivial if:

- it makes an AJAX request or is loaded along with scripts that make an AJAX request,
- it loads external scripts dynamically or is loaded along with scripts that do,
- it defines functions or methods and either loads an external script (from html) or is loaded as one,
- it uses dynamic JavaScript constructs that are difficult to analyze without interpreting the program, or is loaded along with scripts that use such constructs. These constructs are:

Thank you to Matt Lee and John Resig for their help in defining our proposed criterion, and to David Parunakian for helping to make me aware of the problem.

- using the eval function,
- calling methods with the square bracket notation,
- using any other construct than a string literal with certain methods (Obj.write, Obj.createElement,...).

How do we tell whether the JavaScript code is free? At the end of this article we propose a convention by which a nontrivial JavaScript program in a web page can state the URL where its source code is located, and can state its license too, using stylized comments.

Finally, we need to change free browsers to detect and block nontrivial nonfree JavaScript in web pages. The program LibreJS detects nonfree, nontrivial JavaScript in pages you visit, and blocks it.[1] LibreJS is an add-on for IceCat and IceWeasel (and Firefox).

Browser users also need a convenient facility to specify JavaScript code to use *instead* of the JavaScript in a certain page. (The specified code might be total replacement, or a modified version of the free JavaScript program in that page.) Greasemonkey comes close to being able to do this, but not quite, since it doesn't guarantee to modify the JavaScript code in a page before that program starts to execute. Using a local proxy works, but is too inconvenient now to be a real solution. We need to construct a solution that is reliable and convenient, as well as sites for sharing changes. The GNU Project would like to recommend sites which are dedicated to free changes only.

These features will make it possible for a JavaScript program included in a web page to be free in a real and practical sense. JavaScript will no longer be a particular obstacle to our freedom—no more than C and Java are now. We will be able to reject and even replace the nonfree nontrivial JavaScript programs, just as we reject and replace nonfree packages that are offered for installation in the usual way. Our campaign for web sites to free their JavaScript can then begin.

In the mean time, there's one case where it is acceptable to run a nonfree JavaScript program: to send a complaint to the web site operators saying they should free or remove the JavaScript code in the site. Please don't hesitate to enable JavaScript temporarily to do that—but remember to disable it again afterwards.

---

[1] The LibreJS project (`http://gnu.org/software/librejs/`) is in need of JavaScript programmers. If you have the necessary skills, please help us maintain this valuable browser extension.

Appendix A: A Convention for Releasing Free JavaScript Programs

For references to corresponding source code, we recommend

```
// @source:
```

followed by the URL. This satisfies the GNU GPL's requirement to distribute source code. If the source is on a different site, you must take care to handle that properly. Source code is necessary for the program to be free.

To indicate the license of the JavaScript code embedded in a page, we recommend putting the license notice between two notes of this form:

```
@licstart  The following is the entire license notice for the
JavaScript code in this page.
...
@licend  The above is the entire license notice
for the JavaScript code in this page.
```

Of course, all of this should be contained in a multiline comment.

The GNU GPL, like many other free software licenses, requires distribution of a copy of the license with both source and binary forms of the program. However, the GNU GPL is long enough that including it in a page with a JavaScript program can be inconvenient. You can remove that requirement, for code that you have the copyright on, with a license notice like this:

```
Copyright (C) YYYY  Developer

The JavaScript code in this page is free software: you can
redistribute it and/or modify it under the terms of the GNU
General Public License (GNU GPL) as published by the Free Software
Foundation, either version 3 of the License, or (at your option)
any later version.  The code is distributed WITHOUT ANY WARRANTY;
without even the implied warranty of MERCHANTABILITY or FITNESS
FOR A PARTICULAR PURPOSE.  See the GNU GPL for more details.

As additional permission under GNU GPL version 3 section 7, you
may distribute non-source (e.g., minimized or compacted) forms of
that code without the copy of the GNU GPL normally required by
section 4, provided you include this license notice and a URL
through which recipients can access the Corresponding Source.
```

I thank Jaffar Rumith for bringing this issue to my attention.

Appendix B: Publishing Free JavaScript Programs As a Webmaster

If you're a webmaster deploying free JavaScript software on your site, clearly and consistently publishing information about those files' licenses and source code helps your visitors make sure that they're running free software, and help you comply with license conditions.

One method of stating the licenses is the one described above in Appendix A. A second method, JavaScript license web labels, can be more convenient for libraries of minified JavaScript code, especially when you didn't write them.

39 Releasing Free Software If You Work at a University

In the free software movement, we believe computer users should have the freedom to change and redistribute the software that they use. The "free" in "free software" refers to freedom: it means users have the freedom to run, modify and redistribute the software. Free software contributes to human knowledge, while nonfree software does not. Universities should therefore encourage free software for the sake of advancing human knowledge, just as they should encourage scientists and other scholars to publish their work.

Alas, many university administrators have a grasping attitude towards software (and towards science); they see programs as opportunities for income, not as opportunities to contribute to human knowledge. Free software developers have been coping with this tendency for almost 20 years.

When I started developing the GNU operating system, in 1984, my first step was to quit my job at MIT. I did this specifically so that the MIT licensing office would be unable to interfere with releasing GNU as free software. I had planned an approach for licensing the programs in GNU that would ensure that all modified versions must be free software as well—an approach that developed into the GNU General Public License (GNU GPL)—and I did not want to have to beg the MIT administration to let me use it.

Over the years, university affiliates have often come to the Free Software Foundation for advice on how to cope with administrators who see software only as something to sell. One good method, applicable even for specifically funded projects, is to base your work on an existing program that was released under the GNU GPL. Then you can tell the administrators, "We're not allowed to release the modified version except under the GNU GPL—any other way would be copyright infringement." After the dollar signs fade from their eyes, they will usually consent to releasing it as free software.

You can also ask your funding sponsor for help. When a group at NYU developed the GNU Ada Compiler, with funding from the US Air Force, the contract explicitly called for donating the resulting code to the Free Software Foundation. Work out the arrangement with the sponsor first, then politely show the university administration that it is not open to renegotiation. They would rather have a contract to develop free software than no contract at all, so they will most likely go along.

Whatever you do, raise the issue early—well before the program is half finished. At this point, the university still needs you, so you can play hardball:

This essay was originally published on http://gnu.org, in 2002. This version is part of *Free Software, Free Society: Selected Essays of Richard M. Stallman*, 3rd ed. (Boston: GNU Press, 2015).

tell the administration you will finish the program, make it usable, if they agree in writing to make it free software (and agree to your choice of free software license). Otherwise you will work on it only enough to write a paper about it, and never make a version good enough to release. When the administrators know their choice is to have a free software package that brings credit to the university or nothing at all, they will usually choose the former.

The FSF may be able to persuade your university to accept the GNU General Public License, or to accept GPL version 3. If you can't do it alone, please give us the chance to help. Send mail to `licensing@fsf.org`, and put "urgent" in the Subject field.

Not all universities have grasping policies. The University of Texas has a policy that makes it easy to release software developed there as free software under the GNU General Public License. Univates in Brazil, and the International Institute of Information Technology in Hyderabad, India, both have policies in favor of releasing software under the GPL. By developing faculty support first, you may be able to institute such a policy at your university. Present the issue as one of principle: does the university have a mission to advance human knowledge, or is its sole purpose to perpetuate itself?

In persuading the university, it helps to approach the issue with determination and based on an ethical perspective, as we do in the free software movement. To treat the public ethically, the software should be free—as in freedom—for the whole public.

Many developers of free software profess narrowly practical reasons for doing so: they advocate allowing others to share and change software as an expedient for making software powerful and reliable. If those values motivate you to develop free software, well and good, and thank you for your contribution. But those values do not give you a good footing to stand firm when university administrators pressure or tempt you to make the program nonfree.

For instance, they may argue that "We could make it even more powerful and reliable with all the money we can get." This claim may or may not come true in the end, but it is hard to disprove in advance. They may suggest a license to offer copies "free of charge, for academic use only," which would tell the general public they don't deserve freedom, and argue that this will obtain the cooperation of academia, which is all (they say) you need.

If you start from values of convenience alone, it is hard to make a good case for rejecting these dead-end proposals, but you can do it easily if you base your stand on ethical and political values. What good is it to make a program powerful and reliable at the expense of users' freedom? Shouldn't freedom apply outside academia as well as within it? The answers are obvious if freedom and community are among your goals. Free software respects the users' freedom, while nonfree software negates it.

Nothing strengthens your resolve like knowing that the community's freedom depends, in one instance, on you.

40 Nonfree DRM'd Games on GNU/Linux: Good or Bad?

A well known company, Valve, that distributes nonfree computer games with Digital Restrictions Management, recently announced it would distribute these games for GNU/Linux. What good and bad effects can this have?

I suppose that availability of popular nonfree programs on GNU/Linux can boost adoption of the system. However, the aim of GNU goes beyond "success"; its purpose is to bring freedom to the users.[1] Thus, the larger question is how this development affects users' freedom.

The problem with these games is not that they are commercial.[2] (We see nothing wrong with that.) It is not that the developers sell copies;[3] that's not wrong either. The problem is that the games contain software that is not free (free in the sense of freedom, of course).[4]

Nonfree game programs (like other nonfree programs) are unethical because they deny freedom to their users. (Game art is a different issue, because it isn't software.) If you want freedom, one requisite for it is not having or running nonfree programs on your computer. That much is clear.

However, if you're going to use these games, you're better off using them on GNU/Linux rather than on Microsoft Windows. At least you avoid the harm to your freedom that Windows would do.[5]

Thus, in direct practical terms, this development can do both harm and good. It might encourage GNU/Linux users to install these games, and it might encourage users of the games to replace Windows with GNU/Linux. My guess is that the direct good effect will be bigger than the direct harm. But there is also an indirect effect: what does the use of these games teach people in our community?

Any GNU/Linux distro that comes with software to offer these games will teach users that the point is not freedom. Nonfree software in GNU/Linux distros[6] already works against the goal of freedom. Adding these games to a distro would augment that effect.

---

[1] See "Free Software Is Even More Important Now" (p. 28) for more on this.
[2] See p. 91 for an explanation of the confusion the term "commercial" can create.
[3] See "Selling Free Software" (p. 43) for more on this issue.
[4] See p. 3 for the full definition of free software.
[5] See our campaign at `http://upgradefromwindows8.org/` for more on this issue.
[6] See `http://gnu.org/distros/common-distros.html` for an explanation of why we don't endorse certain (often popular) distributions.

This version of this essay is part of *Free Software, Free Society: Selected Essays of Richard M. Stallman*, 3rd ed. (Boston: GNU Press, 2015).

Free software is a matter of freedom, not price. A free game need not be gratis. It is feasible to develop free games commercially, while respecting your freedom to change the software you use. Since the art in the game is not software, it does not need to be free. There is in fact free game software developed by companies, as well as free games developed noncommercially by volunteers. Crowdfunding development will only get easier.

But if we suppose that it is *not feasible* in the current situation to develop a certain kind of free game—what would follow then? There's no good in writing it as a nonfree game. To have freedom in your computing, requires rejecting nonfree software, pure and simple. You as a freedom-lover won't use the nonfree game if it exists, so you won't lose anything if it does not exist.

If you want to promote the cause of freedom in computing, please take care not to talk about the availability of these games on GNU/Linux as support for our cause. Instead you could tell people about the LibreGameWiki[7] that attempts to catalog free games, the FreeGameDev Forums,[8] and the LibrePlanet Gaming Collective's free gaming night.[9]

---

[7] See https://libregamewiki.org/Main_Page.

[8] See http://forum.freegamedev.net/index.php.

[9] See http://libreplanet.org/wiki/Group:LibrePlanet_Gaming_Collective.

41 The Danger of E-Books

In an age where business dominates our governments and writes our laws, every technological advance offers business an opportunity to impose new restrictions on the public. Technologies that could have empowered us are used to chain us instead.

With printed books,

- You can buy one with cash, anonymously.
- Then you own it.
- You are not required to sign a license that restricts your use of it.
- The format is known, and no proprietary technology is needed to read the book.
- You can give, lend or sell the book to another.
- You can, physically, scan and copy the book, and it's sometimes lawful under copyright.
- Nobody has the power to destroy your book.

Contrast that with Amazon e-books (fairly typical):

- Amazon requires users to identify themselves to get an e-book.
- In some countries, including the US, Amazon says the user cannot own the e-book.
- Amazon requires the user to accept a restrictive license on use of the e-book.
- The format is secret, and only proprietary user-restricting software can read it at all.
- An ersatz "lending" is allowed for some books, for a limited time, but only by specifying by name another user of the same system. No giving or selling.
- To copy the e-book is impossible due to Digital Restrictions Management[1] in the player and prohibited by the license, which is more restrictive than copyright law.
- Amazon can remotely delete the e-book using a back door. It used this back door in 2009 to delete thousands of copies of George Orwell's *1984*.

Even one of these infringements makes e-books a step backward from printed books. We must reject e-books until they respect our freedom.

[1] See "The Right to Read" (p. 107) for more on this.

This version of this essay is part of *Free Software, Free Society: Selected Essays of Richard M. Stallman*, 3rd ed. (Boston: GNU Press, 2015).

The e-book companies say denying our traditional freedoms is necessary to continue to pay authors. The current copyright system supports those companies handsomely and most authors badly. We can support authors better in other ways that don't require curtailing our freedom, and even legalize sharing. Two methods I've suggested are:

- To distribute tax funds to authors based on the cube root of each author's popularity.[2]
- To design players so users can send authors anonymous voluntary payments.

E-books need not attack our freedom (Project Gutenberg's e-books don't), but they will if companies get to decide. It's up to us to stop them.

Join the fight: sign up at `http://DefectiveByDesign.org/ebooks.html`.

[2] See both "Copyright vs. Community in the Age of Computer Networks" (p. 127) and my 2012 open letter to the President of the Brazilian Senate, Senator José Sarney, at `https://stallman.org/articles/internet-sharing-license.en.html`, for more on this.

42 E-books Must Increase Our Freedom, Not Decrease It

I love *The Jehovah Contract,* and I'd like everyone else to love it too. I have lent it out at least six times over the years. Printed books let us do that.

I couldn't do that with most commercial e-books. It's "not allowed." And if I tried to disobey, the software in e-readers has malicious features called Digital Restrictions Management (DRM, for short) to restrict reading, so it simply won't work. The e-books are encrypted so that only proprietary software with malicious functionality can display them.

Many other habits that we readers are accustomed to are "not allowed" for e-books. With the Amazon "Kindle" (for which "Swindle"[1] is a more fitting name), to take one example, users can't buy a book anonymously with cash. "Kindle" books are typically available from Amazon only, and Amazon makes users identify themselves. Thus, Amazon knows exactly which books each user has read. In a country such as the UK, where you can be prosecuted for possessing a forbidden book,[2] this is more than hypothetically Orwellian.

Furthermore, you can't sell the e-book after you read it (if Amazon has its way, the used book stores where I have passed many an afternoon will be history). You can't give it to a friend either, because according to Amazon you never really owned it. Amazon requires users to sign an end-user license agreement (EULA) which says so.

You can't even be sure it will still be in your machine tomorrow. People reading *1984* in the "Kindle" had an Orwellian experience: their e-books vanished right before their eyes, as Amazon used a malicious software feature called a "back door" to remotely delete them (virtual book-burning; is that what "Kindle" means?). But don't worry; Amazon promised never to do this again, except by order of the state.

---

[1] See "Why Call It the Swindle?" (p. 87) for more on this.

[2] Ben Quinn, "Man in London Charged with Terrorism Offences over Al-Qaida Document," 4 April 2012, `http://www.theguardian.com/world/2012/apr/04/al-qaida-terrorism`.

See also "The Danger of E-Books" (p. 238), and please consider joining our mailing about the dangers of e-books, at `http://defectivebydesign.org/ebooks.html`.

This essay was originally published on `http://guardian.co.uk`, on 17 April 2012, as "Technology Should Help Us Share, Not Constrain Us," with some surprise editing. This version incorporates parts of that editing while restoring parts of the original text and is part of *Free Software, Free Society: Selected Essays of Richard M. Stallman,* 3rd ed. (Boston: GNU Press, 2015).

With software, either the users control the program (making such software Libre or Free[3]) or the program controls its users (non-Libre). Amazon's e-book policies imitate the distribution policies of non-Libre software, but that's not the only relationship between the two. The malicious software features described above[4] are imposed on users via software that's not Libre. If a Libre program had malicious features like those, some users skilled at programming would remove them, then provide the corrected version to all the other users. Users can't change non-Libre software, which makes it an ideal instrument for exercising power over the public.[5]

Any one of these encroachments on our freedom is reason aplenty to say no. If these policies were limited to Amazon, we'd bypass them, but the other e-book dealers' policies are roughly similar.

What worries me most is the prospect of losing the option of printed books. *The Guardian* has announced "digital-only reads": in other words, books available only at the price of freedom. I will not read any book at that price. Five years from now, will unauthorized copies be the only ethically acceptable copies for most books?

It doesn't have to be that way. With anonymous payment on the internet, paying for downloads of non-DRM non-EULA e-books would respect our freedom. Physical stores could sell such e-books for cash, like digital music on CDs—still available even though the music industry is aggressively pushing DRM-restrictive services such as Spotify. Physical CD stores face the burden of an expensive inventory, but physical e-book stores could write copies onto your USB memory stick, the only inventory being memory sticks to sell if you need.

The reason publishers give for their restrictive e-books practices is to stop people from sharing copies. They say this is for the sake of the authors; but even if it did serve the authors' interests (which for quite famous authors it may), it could not justify DRM, EULAs or the Digital Economy Act which persecutes readers for sharing. In practice, the copyright system does a bad job of supporting authors aside from the most popular ones. Other authors' principal interest is to be better known, so sharing their work benefits them as well as readers. Why not switch to a system that does the job better and is compatible with sharing?

A tax on memories and internet connectivity, along the general lines of what most EU countries do, could do the job well if three points are got right. The money should be collected by the state and distributed according to law, not given to a private collecting society; it should be divided among all authors, and we mustn't let companies take any of it from them; and the distribution of money should be based on a sliding scale, not in linear proportion to popularity.

---

[3] See "What Is Free Software?" (p. 3) for the full definition of free software.

[4] See `http://gnu.org/proprietary/proprietary.html` for an evolving list of these threats.

[5] See my articles "Free Software Is Even More Important Now" (p. 28) and "The Problem Is Software Controlled by Its Developer," at `http://gnu.org/philosophy/the-root-of-this-problem.html`, for more on this issue.

I suggest using the cube root of each author's popularity: if A is eight times as popular as B, A gets twice B's amount (not eight times B's amount). This would support many fairly popular writers adequately instead of making a few stars richer.

Another system is to give each e-reader a button to send some small sum (perhaps 25 pence in the UK) to the author.

Sharing is good, and with digital technology, sharing is easy. (I mean non-commercial redistribution of exact copies.) So sharing ought to be legal, and preventing sharing is no excuse to make e-books into handcuffs for readers. If e-books mean that readers' freedom must either increase or decrease, we must demand the increase.

43 Who Does That Server Really Serve?

On the internet, proprietary software isn't the only way to lose your freedom. Service as a Software Substitute, or SaaSS, is another way to let someone else have power over your computing.

SaaSS means using a service implemented by someone else as a substitute for running your copy of a program. The term is ours; articles and ads won't use it, and they won't tell you whether a service is SaaSS. Instead they will probably use the vague and distracting term "cloud," which lumps SaaSS together with various other practices, some abusive and some OK. With the explanation and examples in this page, you can tell whether a service is SaaSS.

Background: How Proprietary Software Takes away Your Freedom

Digital technology can give you freedom; it can also take your freedom away. The first threat to our control over our computing came from *proprietary software*: software that the users cannot control because the owner (a company such as Apple or Microsoft) controls it. The owner often takes advantage of this unjust power by inserting malicious features such as spyware, back doors, and Digital Restrictions Management (DRM) (referred to as "Digital Rights Management" in their propaganda).[1]

Our solution to this problem is developing *free software* and rejecting proprietary software. Free software means that you, as a user, have four essential freedoms: (0) to run the program as you wish, (1) to study and change the source code so it does what you wish, (2) to redistribute exact copies, and (3) to redistribute copies of your modified versions. (See the free software definition (p. 3).)

With free software, we, the users, take back control of our computing. Proprietary software still exists, but we can exclude it from our lives and many of us have done so. However, we now face a new threat to our control over our computing: Service as a Software Substitute (SaaSS). For our freedom's sake, we have to reject that too.

---

[1] Please join our campaign against DRM, at `DefectiveByDesign.org`.

For more on this issue, see also "The Bug Nobody Is Allowed to Understand," at `http://gnu.org/philosophy/bug-nobody-allowed-to-understand.html`.

This essay was originally published in the online edition of the *Boston Review*, on 8 March 2010, under the title "What Does That Server Really Serve?" This version is part of *Free Software, Free Society: Selected Essays of Richard M. Stallman*, 3rd ed. (Boston: GNU Press, 2015).

How Service as a Software Substitute Takes away Your Freedom

Service as a Software Substitute (SaaSS) means using a service as a substitute for running your copy of a program. Concretely, it means that someone sets up a network server that does certain computing tasks—for instance, modifying a photo, translating text into another language, etc.—then invites users to do computing via that server. A user of the server would send her data to the server, which does *her own computing* on the data thus provided, then sends the results back to her or acts directly on her behalf.

The computing is *her own* because, by assumption, she could, in principle, have done it by running a program on her own computer (whether or not that program is available to her at present). When this assumption is not so, it isn't SaaSS.

These servers wrest control from the users even more inexorably than proprietary software. With proprietary software, users typically get an executable file but not the source code. That makes it hard to study the code that is running, so it's hard to determine what the program really does, and hard to change it.

With SaaSS, the users do not have even the executable file that does their computing: it is on someone else's server, where the users can't see or touch it. Thus it is impossible for them to ascertain what it really does, and impossible to change it.

Furthermore, SaaSS automatically leads to consequences equivalent to the malicious features of certain proprietary software.

For instance, some proprietary programs are "spyware": the program sends out data about users' computing activities.[2] Microsoft Windows sends information about users' activities to Microsoft. Windows Media Player reports what each user watches or listens to. The Amazon Kindle reports which pages of which books the user looks at, and when. Angry Birds reports the user's geolocation history.

Unlike proprietary software, SaaSS does not require covert code to obtain the user's data. Instead, users must send their data to the server in order to use it. This has the same effect as spyware: the server operator gets the data—with no special effort, by the nature of SaaSS. Amy Webb, who intended never to post any photos of her daughter, made the mistake of using SaaSS (Instagram) to edit photos of her. Eventually they leaked from there.[3]

Some proprietary operating systems have a universal back door, permitting someone to remotely install software changes. For instance, Windows has a universal back door with which Microsoft can forcibly change any software on the machine. Nearly all portable phones have them, too. Some proprietary

---

[2] For a growing list of the ways in which surveillance has spread across industries, see `http://gnu.org/philosophy/proprietary/proprietary-surveillance.html`.

[3] Amy Webb, "Congratulations, You Found a Photo of My Daughter Online," 12 September 2013, `http://slate.com/articles/technology/data_mine_1/2013/09/privacy_facebook_kids_don_t_post_photos_of_your_kids_on_social_media.html`.

applications also have universal back doors; for instance, the Steam client for GNU/Linux allows the developer to remotely install modified versions.

With SaaSS, the server operator can change the software in use on the server. He ought to be able to do this, since it's his computer; but the result is the same as using a proprietary application program with a universal back door: someone has the power to silently impose changes in how the user's computing gets done.

Thus, SaaSS is equivalent to running proprietary software with spyware and a universal back door. It gives the server operator unjust power over the user, and that power is something we must resist.

SaaSS and SaaS

Originally we referred to this problematical practice as "SaaS," which stands for "Software as a Service." It's a commonly used term for setting up software on a server rather than offering copies of it to users, and we thought it described precisely the cases where this problem occurs.

Subsequently we became aware that the term SaaS is sometimes used for communication services—activities for which this issue is not applicable. In addition, the term "Software as a Service" doesn't explain *why* the practice is bad. So we coined the term "Service as a Software Substitute," which defines the bad practice more clearly and says what is bad about it.

Untangling the SaaSS Issue from the Proprietary Software Issue

SaaSS and proprietary software lead to similar harmful results, but the mechanisms are different. With proprietary software, the mechanism is that you have and use a copy which is difficult and/or illegal to change. With SaaSS, the mechanism is that you don't have the copy that's doing your computing.

These two issues are often confused, and not only by accident. Web developers use the vague term "web application" to lump the server software together with programs run on your machine in your browser. Some web pages install nontrivial, even large JavaScript programs into your browser without informing you. When these JavaScript programs are nonfree,[4] they cause the same sort of injustice as any other nonfree software. Here, however, we are concerned with the issue of using the service itself.

Many free software supporters assume that the problem of SaaSS will be solved by developing free software for servers. For the server operator's sake, the programs on the server had better be free; if they are proprietary, their owners have power over the server. That's unfair to the server operator, and doesn't help the users at all. But if the programs on the server are free, that doesn't protect *the server's users* from the effects of SaaSS. These programs liberate the server operator, but not the server's users.

Releasing the server software source code does benefit the community: it enables suitably skilled users to set up similar servers, perhaps changing the

[4] See "The JavaScript Trap" (p. 230) for more information on this issue.

software. We recommend using the GNU Affero GPL as the license for programs often used on servers.[5]

But none of these servers would give you control over computing you do on it, unless it's *your* server. It may be OK to trust your friend's server for some jobs, just as you might let your friend maintain the software on your own computer. Outside of that, all these servers would be SaaSS for you. SaaSS always subjects you to the power of the server operator, and the only remedy is, *Don't use SaaSS!* Don't use someone else's server to do your own computing on data provided by you.

This issue demonstrates the depth of the difference between "open" and "free." Source code that is open source is, nearly always, free.[6] However, the idea of an "open software" service,[7] meaning one whose server software is open source and/or free, fails to address the issue of SaaSS.

Services are fundamentally different from programs, and the ethical issues that services raise are fundamentally different from the issues that programs raise. To avoid confusion, we avoid describing a service as "free" or "proprietary."[8]

Distinguishing SaaSS from Other Network Services

Which online services are SaaSS? The clearest example is a translation service, which translates (say) English text into Spanish text. Translating a text for you is computing that is purely yours. You could do it by running a program on your own computer, if only you had the right program. (To be ethical, that program should be free.) The translation service substitutes for that program, so it is Service as a Software Substitute, or SaaSS. Since it denies you control over your computing, it does you wrong.

Another clear example is using a service such as Flickr or Instagram to modify a photo. Modifying photos is an activity that people have done in their own computers for decades; doing it in a server instead of your own computer is SaaSS.

Rejecting SaaSS does not mean refusing to use any network servers run by anyone other than you. Most servers are not SaaSS because the jobs they do are not the user's own computing.

The original idea of web servers wasn't to do computing for you, it was to publish information for you to access. Even today this is what most web sites do, and it doesn't pose the SaaSS problem, because accessing someone's

---

[5] See "How to Choose a License for Your Own Work" (p. 174) for our licensing recommendations.

[6] See "How Free Software and Open Source Relate as Categories of Programs," at `http://gnu.org/philosophy/free-open-overlap.html` for more information.

[7] For the "Open Software Service Definition," see `http://opendefinition.org/ossd/index.html`.

[8] For more information, see my article "Network Services Aren't Free or Nonfree; They Raise Other Issues," at `http://gnu.org/philosophy/network-services-arent-free-or-nonfree.html`.

published information isn't doing your own computing. Neither is publishing your own materials via a blog site or a microblogging service such as Twitter or StatusNet. (These services may have other problems, of course.) The same goes for other communication not meant to be private, such as chat groups.

In its essence, social networking is a form of communication and publication, not SaaSS. However, a service whose main facility is social networking can have features or extensions which are SaaSS.

If a service is not SaaSS, that does not mean it is OK. There are other ethical issues about services. For instance, Facebook distributes video in Flash, which pressures users to run nonfree software; it requires running nonfree JavaScript code; and it gives users a misleading impression of privacy while luring them into baring their lives to Facebook. Those are important issues, different from the SaaSS issue.

Services such as search engines collect data from around the web and let you examine it. Looking through their collection of data isn't your own computing in the usual sense—you didn't provide that collection—so using such a service to search the web is not SaaSS. However, using someone else's server to implement a search facility for your own site *is* SaaSS.

Purchasing online is not SaaSS, because the computing isn't *your own*; rather, it is done jointly by and for you and the store. The real issue in online shopping is whether you trust the other party with your money and other personal information (starting with your name).

Repository sites such as as Savannah and SourceForge are not inherently SaaSS, because a repository's job is publication of data supplied to it.

Using a joint project's servers isn't SaaSS because the computing you do in this way isn't your own. For instance, if you edit pages on Wikipedia, you are not doing your own computing; rather, you are collaborating in Wikipedia's computing. Wikipedia controls its own servers, but organizations as well as individuals encounter the problem of SaaSS if they do their computing in someone else's server.

Some sites offer multiple services, and if one is not SaaSS, another may be SaaSS. For instance, the main service of Facebook is social networking, and that is not SaaSS; however, it supports third-party applications, some of which are SaaSS. Flickr's main service is distributing photos, which is not SaaSS, but it also has features for editing photos, which is SaaSS. Likewise, using Instagram to post a photo is not SaaSS, but using it to transform the photo is SaaSS.

Google Docs shows how complex the evaluation of a single service can become. It invites people to edit a document by running a large nonfree JavaScript program,[9] clearly wrong. However, it offers an API for uploading and downloading documents in standard formats. A free software editor can do so through this API. This usage scenario is not SaaSS, because it uses Google Docs as a mere repository. Showing all your data to a company is bad, but that is a matter of privacy, not SaaSS; depending on a service for access to your data is bad, but that is a matter of risk, not SaaSS. On the other hand, using the service for

[9] See "The JavaScript Trap" (p. 230) for more on this issue.

converting document formats *is* SaaSS, because it's something you could have done by running a suitable program (free, one hopes) in your own computer.

Using Google Docs through a free editor is rare, of course. Most often, people use it through the nonfree JavaScript program, which is bad like any nonfree program. This scenario might involve SaaSS, too; that depends on what part of the editing is done in the JavaScript program and what part in the server. We don't know, but since SaaSS and proprietary software do similar wrong to the user, it is not crucial to know.

Publishing via someone else's repository does not raise privacy issues, but publishing through Google Docs has a special problem: it is impossible even to *view the text* of a Google Docs document in a browser without running the nonfree JavaScript code. Thus, you should not use Google Docs to publish anything—but the reason is not a matter of SaaSS.

The IT industry discourages users from making these distinctions. That's what the buzzword "cloud computing" is for. This term is so nebulous that it could refer to almost any use of the internet. It includes SaaSS as well as many other network usage practices. In any given context, an author who writes "cloud" (if a technical person) probably has a specific meaning in mind, but usually does not explain that in other articles the term has other specific meanings. The term leads people to generalize about practices they ought to consider individually.

If "cloud computing" has a meaning, it is not a way of doing computing, but rather a way of thinking about computing: a devil-may-care approach which says, "Don't ask questions. Don't worry about who controls your computing or who holds your data. Don't check for a hook hidden inside our service before you swallow it. Trust companies without hesitation." In other words, "Be a sucker." A cloud in the mind is an obstacle to clear thinking. For the sake of clear thinking about computing, let's avoid the term "cloud."

Dealing with the SaaSS Problem

Only a small fraction of all web sites do SaaSS; most don't raise the issue. But what should we do about the ones that raise it?

For the simple case, where you are doing your own computing on data in your own hands, the solution is simple: use your own copy of a free software application. Do your text editing with your copy of a free text editor such as GNU Emacs or a free word processor. Do your photo editing with your copy of free software such as GIMP. What if there is no free program available? A proprietary program or SaaSS would take away your freedom, so you shouldn't use those. You can contribute your time or your money to development of a free replacement.

What about collaborating with other individuals as a group? It may be hard to do this at present without using a server, and your group may not know how to run its own server. If you use someone else's server, at least don't trust a server run by a company. A mere contract as a customer is no protection unless you could detect a breach and could really sue, and the company probably writes its contracts to permit a broad range of abuses. The state can subpoena your data from the company along with everyone else's, as Obama has done to phone companies, supposing the company doesn't volunteer them like the US phone companies that illegally wiretapped their customers for Bush. If you must use a server, use a server whose operators give you a basis for trust beyond a mere commercial relationship.

However, on a longer time scale, we can create alternatives to using servers. For instance, we can create a peer-to-peer program through which collaborators can share data encrypted. The free software community should develop distributed peer-to-peer replacements for important "web applications." It may be wise to release them under the GNU Affero GPL, since they are likely candidates for being converted into server-based programs by someone else.[10] The GNU Project is looking for volunteers to work on such replacements. We also invite other free software projects to consider this issue in their design.

In the meantime, if a company invites you to use its server to do your own computing tasks, don't yield; don't use SaaSS. Don't buy or install "thin clients," which are simply computers so weak they make you do the real work on a server, unless you're going to use them with *your* server. Use a real computer and keep your data there. Do your own computing with your own copy of a free program, for your freedom's sake.

---

[10] See "Why the Affero GPL," at `http://gnu.org/licenses/why-affero-gpl.html`, for a full explanation.

Part VII: Value Community and Your Freedom

44 Avoiding Ruinous Compromises

On September 27, 1983, I announced a plan to create a completely free operating system called GNU—for "GNU's Not Unix." To mark the 25th anniversary of the GNU system, I wrote this article to show how our community could avoid ruinous compromises. In addition to avoiding such compromises, there are many ways you can help GNU and free software. One basic way is to join the Free Software Foundation as an Associate Member.[1]

The free software movement aims for a social change: to make all software free[2] so that all software users are free and can be part of a community of cooperation. Every nonfree program gives its developer unjust power over the users. Our goal is to put an end to that injustice.

The road to freedom is a long road.[3] It will take many steps and many years to reach a world in which it is normal for software users to have freedom. Some of these steps are hard, and require sacrifice. Some of them become easier if we make compromises with people that have different goals.

Thus, the Free Software Foundation makes compromises—even major ones. For instance, we made compromises in the patent provisions of version 3 of the GNU General Public License (GNU GPL) so that major companies would contribute to and distribute GPLv3-covered software and thus bring some patents under the effect of these provisions.

The Lesser GPL's purpose is a compromise: we use it on certain chosen free libraries to permit their use in nonfree programs because we think that legally prohibiting this would only drive developers to proprietary libraries instead. We accept and install code in GNU programs to make them work together with common nonfree programs, and we document and publicize this in ways that encourage users of the latter to install the former, but not vice versa. We support specific campaigns we agree with, even when we don't fully agree with the groups behind them.

---

1 You can support the FSF through a membership at `http://my.fsf.org/join`.

2 "Free" as in "freedom." See p. 3 for the full definition of free software.

3 See FSF executive director John Sullivan's 2008 article "The Last Mile Is Always the Hardest," at `http://fsf.org/bulletin/2008/spring/the-last-mile-is-always-the-hardest`, for his perspective on this issue.

A similar point in a different area of life: "'Nudge' Is Not Enough, It's True. But We Already Knew That" (Jonathan Rowson, 19 July 2011, `http://guardian.co.uk/commentisfree/2011/jul/19/nudge-is-not-enough-behaviour-change`) says that "changes in attitudes and perspectives" are needed as well as "nudges."

This essay was originally published on `http://gnu.org`, in 2008. This version is part of *Free Software, Free Society: Selected Essays of Richard M. Stallman*, 3rd ed. (Boston: GNU Press, 2015).

But we reject certain compromises even though many others in our community are willing to make them. For instance, we endorse only the GNU/Linux distributions that have policies not to include nonfree software or lead users to install it.[4] To endorse nonfree distributions would be a ruinous compromise.

Compromises are ruinous if they would work against our aims in the long term. That can occur either at the level of ideas or at the level of actions.

At the level of ideas, ruinous compromises are those that reinforce the premises we seek to change. Our goal is a world in which software users are free, but as yet most computer users do not even recognize freedom as an issue. They have taken up "consumer" values, which means they judge any program only on practical characteristics such as price and convenience.

Dale Carnegie's classic self-help book, *How to Win Friends and Influence People,* advises that the most effective way to persuade someone to do something is to present arguments that appeal to his values. There are ways we can appeal to the consumer values typical in our society. For instance, free software obtained gratis can save the user money. Many free programs are convenient and reliable, too. Citing those practical benefits has succeeded in persuading many users to adopt various free programs, some of which are now quite successful.

If getting more people to use some free programs is as far as you aim to go, you might decide to keep quiet about the concept of freedom, and focus only on the practical advantages that make sense in terms of consumer values. That's what the term "open source" and its associated rhetoric do.

That approach can get us only part way to the goal of freedom. People who use free software only because it is convenient will stick with it only as long as it is convenient. And they will see no reason not to use convenient proprietary programs along with it.

The philosophy of open source presupposes and appeals to consumer values, and this affirms and reinforces them. That's why we do not support open source.

To establish a free community fully and lastingly, we need to do more than get people to use some free software. We need to spread the idea of judging software (and other things) on "citizen values," based on whether it respects users' freedom and community, not just in terms of convenience. Then people will not fall into the trap of a proprietary program baited by an attractive, convenient feature.

To promote citizen values, we have to talk about them and show how they are the basis of our actions. We must reject the Dale Carnegie compromise that would influence their actions by endorsing their consumer values.

This is not to say we cannot cite practical advantage at all—we can and we do. It becomes a problem only when the practical advantage steals the scene and pushes freedom into the background. Therefore, when we cite the practical advantages of free software, we reiterate frequently that those are just *additional, secondary* reasons to prefer it.

---

[4] You can find the full list of the Free System Distribution Guidelines (GNU FSDG) at `http://gnu.org/philosophy/free-system-distribution-guidelines.html`.

It's not enough to make our words accord with our ideals; our actions have to accord with them too. So we must also avoid compromises that involve doing or legitimizing the things we aim to stamp out.

For instance, experience shows that you can attract some users to GNU/Linux if you include some nonfree programs. This could mean a cute nonfree application that will catch some user's eye, or a nonfree programming platform such as Java[5] (formerly) or the Flash runtime (still), or a nonfree device driver that enables support for certain hardware models.

These compromises are tempting, but they undermine the goal. If you distribute nonfree software, or steer people towards it, you will find it hard to say, "Nonfree software is an injustice, a social problem, and we must put an end to it." And even if you do continue to say those words, your actions will undermine them.

The issue here is not whether people should be *able* or *allowed* to install nonfree software; a general-purpose system enables and allows users to do whatever they wish. The issue is whether we guide users towards nonfree software. What they do on their own is their responsibility; what we do for them, and what we direct them towards, is ours. We must not direct the users towards proprietary software as if it were a solution, because proprietary software is the problem.

A ruinous compromise is not just a bad influence on others. It can distort your own values, too, through cognitive dissonance. If you have certain values, but your actions imply other, conflicting values, you are likely to change your values or your actions so as to resolve the contradiction. Thus, projects that argue only from practical advantages, or direct people toward some nonfree software, nearly always shy away from even *suggesting* that nonfree software is unethical. For their participants, as well as for the public, they reinforce consumer values. We must reject these compromises if we wish to keep our values straight.

If you want to move to free software without compromising the goal of freedom, look at the FSF's resources area, at `http://www.fsf.org/resources`. It lists hardware and machine configurations that work with free software, totally free GNU/Linux distros to install, and thousands of free software packages[6] that work in a 100 percent free software environment. If you want to help the community stay on the road to freedom, one important way is to publicly uphold citizen values. When people are discussing what is good or bad, or what to do, cite the values of freedom and community and argue from them.

A road that lets you go faster is not better if it leads to the wrong place. Compromise is essential to achieve an ambitious goal, but beware of compromises that lead away from the goal.

---

[5] See `http://gnu.org/philosophy/java-trap.html` for more on this.

[6] The Free Software Directory, at `http://directory.fsf.org`, lists all the free software we know about.

45 Overcoming Social Inertia

Almost two decades have passed since the combination of GNU and Linux first made it possible to use a PC in freedom. We have come a long way since then. Now you can even buy a laptop with GNU/Linux preinstalled from more than one hardware vendor—although the systems they ship are not entirely free software. So what holds us back from total success?

The main obstacle to the triumph of software freedom is social inertia. It exists in many forms, and you have surely seen some of them. Examples include devices that only work on Windows and commercial web sites accessible only with Windows. If you value short-term convenience instead of freedom, you might consider these reason enough to use Windows. Most companies currently run Windows, so students who think short-term want to learn how to use it and ask their schools to teach it. Schools teach Windows, produce graduates that are used to using Windows, and this encourages businesses to use Windows.

Microsoft actively nurtures this inertia: it encourages schools to inculcate dependency on Windows, and contracts to set up web sites that then turn out to work only with Internet Explorer.

A few years ago, Microsoft ads argued that Windows was cheaper to run than GNU/Linux. Their comparisons were debunked, but it is worth noting the deeper flaw in their argument, the implicit premise which cites a form of social inertia: "Currently, more technical people know Windows than GNU/Linux." People who value their freedom would not give it up to save money, but many business executives believe ideologically that everything they possess, even their freedom, should be for sale.

Social inertia consists of people who have given in to social inertia. When you surrender to social inertia, you become part of the pressure it exerts on others; when you resist it, you reduce it. We conquer social inertia by identifying it, and resolving not to be part of it.

Here a weakness holds our community back: most GNU/Linux users have never even heard the ideas of freedom that motivated the development of GNU, so they still judge matters based on short-term convenience rather than on their freedom. This makes them vulnerable to being led by the nose by social inertia, so that they become part of the inertia.

To build our community's strength to resist, we need to talk about free software and freedom—not merely about the practical benefits that open source supporters cite. As more people recognize what they need to do to overcome the inertia, we will make more progress.

This essay was originally published on `http://gnu.org`, in 2007. This version is part of *Free Software, Free Society: Selected Essays of Richard M. Stallman*, 3rd ed. (Boston: GNU Press, 2015).

46 Freedom or Power?

Written by Bradley M. Kuhn and Richard Stallman.

The love of liberty is the love of others; the love of power is the love of ourselves.

—William Hazlitt

In the free software movement, we stand for freedom for the users of software. We formulated our views by looking at what freedoms are necessary for a good way of life, and permit useful programs to foster a community of goodwill, cooperation, and collaboration. Our criteria for free software[1] specify the freedoms that a program's users need so that they can cooperate in a community.

We stand for freedom for programmers as well as for other users. Most of us are programmers, and we want freedom for ourselves as well as for you. But each of us uses software written by others, and we want freedom when using that software, not just when using our own code. We stand for freedom for all users, whether they program often, occasionally, or not at all.

However, one so-called freedom that we do not advocate is the "freedom to choose any license you want for software you write." We reject this because it is really a form of power, not a freedom.

This oft overlooked distinction is crucial. Freedom is being able to make decisions that affect mainly you; power is being able to make decisions that affect others more than you. If we confuse power with freedom, we will fail to uphold real freedom.

Making a program proprietary is an exercise of power. Copyright law today grants software developers that power, so they and only they choose the rules to impose on everyone else—a relatively small number of people make the basic software decisions for all users, typically by denying their freedom. When users lack the freedoms that define free software, they can't tell what the software is doing, can't check for back doors, can't monitor possible viruses and worms, can't find out what personal information is being reported (or stop the reports, even if they do find out). If it breaks, they can't fix it; they have to wait for the developer to exercise its power to do so. If it simply isn't quite what they need, they are stuck with it. They can't help each other improve it.

Proprietary software developers are often businesses. We in the free software movement are not opposed to business, but we have seen what happens when

[1] See p. 3 for the full list of these criteria.

This essay was originally published on `http://gnu.org`, in 2001. This version is part of *Free Software, Free Society: Selected Essays of Richard M. Stallman*, 3rd ed. (Boston: GNU Press, 2015).

a software business has the "freedom" to impose arbitrary rules on the users of software. Microsoft is an egregious example of how denying users' freedoms can lead to direct harm, but it is not the only example. Even when there is no monopoly, proprietary software harms society. A choice of masters is not freedom.

Discussions of rights and rules for software have often concentrated on the interests of programmers alone. Few people in the world program regularly, and fewer still are owners of proprietary software businesses. But the entire developed world now needs and uses software, so software developers now control the way it lives, does business, communicates, and is entertained. The ethical and political issues are not addressed by the slogan of "freedom of choice (for developers only)."

If "code is law,"[2] then the real question we face is: who should control the code you use—you, or an elite few? We believe you are entitled to control the software you use, and giving you that control is the goal of free software.

We believe you should decide what to do with the software you use; however, that is not what today's law says. Current copyright law places us in the position of power over users of our code, whether we like it or not. The ethical response to this situation is to proclaim freedom for each user, just as the Bill of Rights was supposed to exercise government power by guaranteeing each citizen's freedoms. That is what the GNU General Public License is for: it puts you in control of your usage of the software while protecting you from others who would like to take control of your decisions.[3]

As more and more users realize that code is law, and come to feel that they too deserve freedom, they will see the importance of the freedoms we stand for, just as more and more users have come to appreciate the practical value of the free software we have developed.

---

[2] William J. Mitchell, *City of Bits: Space, Place, and the Infobahn* (Cambridge, Mass.: MIT Press, 1995), p. 111, as quoted by Lawrence Lessig in *Code and Other Laws of Cyberspace, Version 2.0* (New York, NY: Basic Books, 2006), p. 5.

[3] See "Why Copyleft?" (p. 187) for more on this issue.

47 Imperfection Is Not the Same as Oppression

When a free program lacks capabilities that users want, that is unfortunate; we urge people to add what is missing. Some would go further and claim that a program is not even free software if it lacks certain functionality—that it denies freedom 0 (the freedom to run the program as you wish) to users or uses that it does not support. This argument is misguided because it is based on identifying capacity with freedom, and imperfection with oppression.

Each program inevitably has certain functionalities and lacks others that might be desirable. There are some jobs it can do, and others it can't do without further work. This is the nature of software.

The absence of key functionality can mean certain users find the program totally unusable. For instance, if you only understand graphical interfaces, a command line program may be impossible for you to use. If you can't see the screen, a program without a screen reader may be impossible for you to use. If you speak only Greek, a program with menus and messages in English may be impossible for you to use. If your programs are written in Ada, a C compiler is impossible for you to use. To overcome these barriers yourself is unreasonable to demand of you. Free software really ought to provide the functionality you need.

Free software really ought to provide it, but the lack of that feature does not make the program nonfree, because it is an imperfection, not oppression.

Making a program nonfree is an injustice committed by the developer that denies freedom to whoever uses it. The developer deserves condemnation for this. It is crucial to condemn that developer, because nobody else can undo the injustice as long as the developer continues to do it. We can, and do, try to rescue the victims by developing a free replacement, but we can't make the nonfree program free.

Developing a free program without adding a certain important feature is not doing wrong to anyone. Rather, it's doing some good but not all the good that people need. Nobody in particular deserves condemnation for not developing the missing feature, since any capable person could do it. It would be ungrateful, as well as self-defeating, to single out the free program's authors for blame for not having done some additional work.

What we can do is state that completing the job calls for doing some additional work. That is constructive because it helps us convince someone to do that work.

If you think a certain extension in a free program is important, please push for it in the way that respects our contributors. Don't criticize the people who contributed the useful code we have. Rather, look for a way to complete the job.

This version of this essay is part of *Free Software, Free Society: Selected Essays of Richard M. Stallman*, 3rd ed. (Boston: GNU Press, 2015).

You can urge the program's developers to turn their attention to the missing feature when they have time for more work. You can offer to help them. You can recruit people or raise funds to support the work.

48 How Much Surveillance Can Democracy Withstand?

Thanks to Edward Snowden's disclosures, we know that the current level of general surveillance in society is incompatible with human rights. The repeated harassment and prosecution of dissidents, sources, and journalists in the US and elsewhere provides confirmation. We need to reduce the level of general surveillance, but how far? Where exactly is the *maximum tolerable level of surveillance,* which we must ensure is not exceeded? It is the level beyond which surveillance starts to interfere with the functioning of democracy, in that whistleblowers (such as Snowden) are likely to be caught.

Faced with government secrecy, we the people depend on whistleblowers to tell us what the state is doing.[1] However, today's surveillance intimidates potential whistleblowers, which means it is too much. To recover our democratic control over the state, we must reduce surveillance to the point where whistleblowers know they are safe.

Using free/libre software, as I've advocated for 30 years, is the first step in taking control of our digital lives, and that includes preventing surveillance. We can't trust nonfree software; the NSA uses[2] and even creates[3] security weaknesses in nonfree software to invade our own computers and routers. Free software gives us control of our own computers, but that won't protect our privacy once we set foot on the internet.[4]

[1] Maira Sutton, "We're TPP Activists: Reddit Asked Us Everything," 21 November 2013, `https://www.eff.org/deeplinks/2013/11/reddit-tpp-ama`.
[2] Glyn Moody, "How Can Any Company Ever Trust Microsoft Again?" 17 June 2013, `http://www.computerworlduk.com/blogs/open-enterprise/how-can-any-company-ever-trust-microsoft-again-3569376/`.
[3] James Ball, Julian Borger and Glenn Greenwald, "Revealed: How US and UK Spy Agencies Defeat Internet Privacy and Security," 6 September 2013, `http://theguardian.com/world/2013/sep/05/nsa-gchq-encryption-codes-security`.
[4] Bruce Schneier, "Want to Evade NSA Spying? Don't Connect to the Internet," 7 October 2013, `http://www.wired.com/2013/10/149481/`.

A version of this article was first published on the `Wired` web site under the same title (*Wired*, 14 October 2013, `http://www.wired.com/opinion/2013/10/a-necessary-evil-what-it-takes-for-democracy-to-survive-surveillance`). This version is part of *Free Software, Free Society: Selected Essays of Richard M. Stallman*, 3rd ed. (Boston: GNU Press, 2015).

Bipartisan legislation to "curtail the domestic surveillance powers"[1] in the US is being drawn up, but it relies on limiting the government's use of our virtual dossiers. That won't suffice to protect whistleblowers if "catching the whistleblower" is grounds for access sufficient to identify him or her. We need to go further.

The Upper Limit on Surveillance in a Democracy

If whistleblowers don't dare reveal crimes and lies, we lose the last shred of effective control over our government and institutions. That's why surveillance that enables the state to find out who has talked with a reporter is too much surveillance—too much for democracy to endure.

An unnamed US government official ominously told journalists in 2011 that the US would not subpoena reporters because "We know who you're talking to."[2] Sometimes journalists' phone call records are subpoenaed[3] to find this out, but Snowden has shown us that in effect they subpoena all the phone call records of everyone in the US, all the time, from Verizon[4] and from other companies too.[5]

Opposition and dissident activities need to keep secrets from states that are willing to play dirty tricks on them. The ACLU has demonstrated the US government's systematic practice of infiltrating peaceful dissident groups[6] on the pretext that there might be terrorists among them. The point at which surveillance is too much is the point at which the state can find who spoke to a known journalist or a known dissident.

---

1 Dan Roberts, "Patriot Act Author Prepares Bill to Put NSA Bulk Collection 'Out of Business,'" 10 October 2013, `http://theguardian.com/world/2013/oct/10/nsa-surveillance-patriot-act-author-bill`.

2 Lucy Dalglish, "Lessons from Wye River," *The News Media & the Law* (Summer 2011): p. 1, `http://www.rcfp.org/browse-media-law-resources/news-media-law/news-media-and-law-summer-2011/lessons-wye-river`.

3 Washington Agencies, "Yemen leak: former FBI man admits passing information to Associated Press," 24 September 2013, `http://www.theguardian.com/media/2013/sep/24/yemen-leak-sachtleben-guilty-associated-press`.

4 See "Verizon forced to hand over telephone data—full court ruling" (6 June 2013), at `http://www.theguardian.com/world/interactive/2013/jun/06/verizon-telephone-data-court-order`, for the Foreign Intelligence Surveillance Court under which the US government "is collecting the phone records of millions of US customers of Verizon."

5 Siobhan Gorman, Evan Perez, and Janet Hook, "NSA Data-Mining Digs into Networks Beyond Verizon," 7 June 2013, `http://www.marketwatch.com/story/nsa-data-mining-digs-into-networks-beyond-verizon-2013-06-07`.

6 ACLU, "Policing Free Speech: Police Surveillance And Obstruction of First Amendment-Protected Activity," 29 June 2010, `https://www.aclu.org/files/assets/Spyfiles_2_0.pdf`.

Information, Once Collected, Will Be Misused

When people recognize that the level of general surveillance is too high, the first response is to propose limits on access to the accumulated data. That sounds nice, but it won't fix the problem, not even slightly, even supposing that the government obeys the rules. (The NSA has misled the FISA court, which said it was unable to effectively hold the NSA accountable.)[7] Suspicion of a crime will be grounds for access, so once a whistleblower is accused of "espionage," finding the "spy" will provide an excuse to access the accumulated material.

In addition, the state's surveillance staff will misuse the data for personal reasons. Some NSA agents used US surveillance systems to track their lovers—past, present, or wished-for—in a practice called "LOVEINT."[8] The NSA says it has caught and punished this a few times; we don't know how many other times it wasn't caught. But these events shouldn't surprise us, because police have long used their access to driver's license records to track down someone attractive, a practice known as "running a plate for a date."[9]

Surveillance data will always be used for other purposes, even if this is prohibited. Once the data has been accumulated and the state has the possibility of access to it, it can misuse that data in dreadful ways, as shown by examples from Europe[10] and the US.[11]

Personal data collected by the state is also likely to be obtained by outside crackers that break the security of the servers, even by crackers working for hostile states.[12]

Governments can easily use massive surveillance capability to subvert democracy directly.[13]

Total surveillance accessible to the state enables the state to launch a massive fishing expedition against any person. To make journalism and democracy safe, we must limit the accumulation of data that is easily accessible to the state.

---

[7] David Kravets, Kim Zetter, Kevin Poulsen, "NSA Illegally Gorged on U.S. Phone Records for Three Years," 10 September 2013, `http://www.wired.com/2013/09/nsa-violations/`.

[8] Adam Gabbatt and agencies, "NSA Analysts 'Wilfully Violated' Surveillance Systems, Agency Admits," 24 August 2013, `http://theguardian.com/world/2013/aug/24/nsa-analysts-abused-surveillance-systems`.

[9] M. L. Elrick, "Cops Tap Database to Harass, Intimidate," 31 July 2001, `http://sweetliberty.org/issues/privacy/lein1.htm#.VeQiuxcpDow`.

[10] Rick Falkvinge, "Collected Personal Data Will Always Be Used against the Citizens," 17 March 2012, `http://falkvinge.net/2012/03/17/collected-personal-data-will-always-be-used-against-the-citizens/`.

[11] Consider, for instance, the US internment of Japanese Americans during WWII.

[12] Mike Masnick, "Second OPM Hack Revealed: Even Worse Than the First," 12 June 2015, `https://www.techdirt.com/articles/20150612/16334231330/second-opm-hack-revealed-even-worse-than-first.shtml`.

[13] Joanna Berendt, "Macedonia Government Is Blamed for Wiretapping Scandal," 21 June 2015, `http://www.nytimes.com/2015/06/22/world/europe/macedonia-government-is-blamed-for-wiretapping-scandal.html?_r=0`.

Robust Protection for Privacy Must Be Technical

The Electronic Frontier Foundation and other organizations propose a set of legal principles designed to prevent the abuses of massive surveillance.[14] These principles include, crucially, explicit legal protection for whistleblowers; as a consequence, they would be adequate for protecting democratic freedoms—if adopted completely and enforced without exception forever.

However, such legal protections are precarious: as recent history shows, they can be repealed (as in the FISA Amendments Act), suspended, or ignored.[15]

Meanwhile, demagogues will cite the usual excuses as grounds for total surveillance; any terrorist attack, even one that kills just a handful of people, can be hyped to provide an opportunity.

If limits on access to the data are set aside, it will be as if they had never existed: years' worth of dossiers would suddenly become available for misuse by the state and its agents and, if collected by companies, for their private misuse as well. If, however, we stop the collection of dossiers on everyone, those dossiers won't exist, and there will be no way to compile them retroactively. A new illiberal regime would have to implement surveillance afresh, and it would only collect data starting at that date. As for suspending or momentarily ignoring this law, the idea would hardly make sense.

First, Don't Be Foolish

To have privacy, you must not throw it away: the first one who has to protect your privacy is you. Avoid identifying yourself to web sites, contact them with Tor, and use browsers that block the schemes they use to track visitors. Use the GNU Privacy Guard to encrypt the contents of your email. Pay for things with cash.

Keep your own data; don't store your data in a company's "convenient" server. It's safe, however, to entrust a data backup to a commercial service, provided you put the files in an archive and encrypt the whole archive, including the names of the files, with free software on your own computer before uploading it.

For privacy's sake, you must avoid nonfree software since, as a consequence of giving others control of your computing, it is likely to spy on you.[16] Avoid service

---

[14] "International Principles on the Application of Human Rights to Communications Surveillance," last modified May 2014, `https://en.necessaryandproportionate.org/text`.

[15] Eric Lichtblau and James Risen, "Officials Say U.S. Wiretaps Exceeded Law," 15 April 2009, `http://nytimes.com/2009/04/16/us/16nsa.html`.

[16] For decades, the free software movement has been denouncing the abusive surveillance machine of proprietary software companies such as Microsoft and Apple. For a growing list of the ways in which surveillance has spread across industries, not only in the software business, but also in the hardware and—away from the keyboard—in the mobile computing industry, in the office, at home, in transportation systems, and in the classroom, see `http://gnu.org/philosophy/proprietary/proprietary-surveillance.html`.

as a software substitute;[17] as well as giving others control of your computing, it requires you to hand over all the pertinent data to the server.

Protect your friends' and acquaintances' privacy, too. Don't give out their personal information[18] except how to contact them, and never give any web site your list of email or phone contacts. Don't tell a company such as Facebook anything about your friends that they might not wish to publish in a newspaper. Better yet, don't be used by Facebook at all. Reject communication systems that require users to give their real names, even if you are going to give yours, since they pressure other people to surrender their privacy.

Self-protection is essential, but even the most rigorous self-protection is insufficient to protect your privacy on or from systems that don't belong to you. When we communicate with others or move around the city, our privacy depends on the practices of society. We can avoid some of the systems that surveil our communications and movements, but not all of them. Clearly, the better solution is to make all these systems stop surveilling people other than legitimate suspects.

We Must Design Every System for Privacy

If we don't want a total surveillance society, we must consider surveillance a kind of social pollution, and limit the surveillance impact of each new digital system just as we limit the environmental impact of physical construction.

For example: "smart" meters for electricity are touted for sending the power company moment-by-moment data about each customer's electric usage, including how usage compares with users in general. This is implemented based on general surveillance, but does not require any surveillance. It would be easy for the power company to calculate the average usage in a residential neighborhood by dividing the total usage by the number of subscribers, and send that to the meters. Each customer's meter could compare her usage, over any desired period of time, with the average usage pattern for that period. The same benefit, with no surveillance!

We need to design such privacy into all our digital systems.

---

17 See "Who Does That Server Really Serve?" (p. 243) for more information on this issue.

18 Nicole Perlroth, "In Cybersecurity, Sometimes the Weakest Link Is a Family Member," 21 May 2014, `http://bits.blogs.nytimes.com/2014/05/21/in-cybersecurity-sometimes-the-weakest-link-is-a-family-member/`.

Remedy for Collecting Data: Leaving It Dispersed

One way to make monitoring safe for privacy is to keep the data dispersed and inconvenient to access. Old-fashioned security cameras were no threat to privacy.[19] The recording was stored on the premises, and kept for a few weeks at most. Because of the inconvenience of accessing these recordings, it was never done massively; they were accessed only in the places where someone reported a crime. It would not be feasible to physically collect millions of tapes every day and watch them or copy them.

Nowadays, security cameras have become surveillance cameras: they are connected to the internet so recordings can be collected in a data center and saved forever. This is already dangerous, but it is going to get worse. Advances in face recognition may bring the day when suspected journalists can be tracked on the street all the time to see who they talk with.

Internet-connected cameras often have lousy digital security themselves, so anyone could watch what the camera sees.[20] To restore privacy, we should ban the use of internet-connected cameras aimed where and when the public is admitted, except when carried by people. Everyone must be free to post photos and video recordings occasionally, but the systematic accumulation of such data on the internet must be limited.

Remedy for Internet Commerce Surveillance

Most data collection comes from people's own digital activities. Usually the data is collected first by companies. But when it comes to the threat to privacy and democracy, it makes no difference whether surveillance is done directly by the state or farmed out to a business, because the data that the companies collect is systematically available to the state.

The NSA, through PRISM, has gotten into the databases of many large internet corporations.[21] AT&T has saved all its phone call records since 1987 and makes them available to the DEA[22] to search on request. Strictly speaking, the US government does not possess that data, but in practical terms it may as well possess it.

The goal of making journalism and democracy safe therefore requires that we reduce the data collected about people by any organization, not just by the

---

19 I assume here that the security camera points at the inside of a store, or at the street. Any camera pointed at someone's private space by someone else violates privacy, but that is another issue.

20 Ms. Smith, "CIA Wants to Spy On You through Your Appliances," 18 March 2012, `http://networkworld.com/article/2221934/microsoft-subnet/cia-wants-to-spy-on-you-through-your-appliances.html`.

21 Jon Queally, "Latest Docs Show Financial Ties between NSA and Internet Companies," 23 August 2013, `http://www.commondreams.org/news/2013/08/23/latest-docs-show-financial-ties-between-nsa-and-internet-companies`.

22 Scott Shane and Colin Moynihan, "Drug Agents Use Vast Phone Trove, Eclipsing N.S.A.'s," 1 September 2013, `http://www.nytimes.com/2013/09/02/us/drug-agents-use-vast-phone-trove-eclipsing-nsas.html?_r=0`.

state. We must redesign digital systems so that they do not accumulate data about their users. If they need digital data about our transactions, they should not be allowed to keep them more than a short time beyond what is inherently necessary for their dealings with us.

One of the motives for the current level of surveillance of the internet is that sites are financed through advertising based on tracking users' activities and propensities. This converts a mere annoyance—advertising that we can learn to ignore—into a surveillance system that harms us whether we know it or not. Purchases over the internet also track their users. And we are all aware that "privacy policies" are more excuses to violate privacy than commitments to uphold it.

We could correct both problems by adopting a system of anonymous payments—anonymous for the payer, that is. (We don't want the payee to dodge taxes.) Bitcoin is not anonymous,[23] though there are efforts to develop ways to pay anonymously with Bitcoin. However, technology for digital cash was first developed in the 1980s;[24]we need only suitable business arrangements, and for the state not to obstruct them.

A further threat from sites' collection of personal data is that security breakers might get in, take it, and misuse it. This includes customers' credit card details. An anonymous payment system would end this danger: a security hole in the site can't hurt you if the site knows nothing about you.

Remedy for Travel Surveillance

We must convert digital toll collection to anonymous payment (using digital cash, for instance). License-plate recognition systems recognize all license plates, and the data can be kept indefinitely;[25] they should be required by law to notice and record only those license numbers that are on a list of cars sought by court orders. A less secure alternative would record all cars locally but only for a few days, and not make the full data available over the internet; access to the data should be limited to searching for a list of court-ordered license numbers.

The US "no-fly" list must be abolished because it is punishment without trial.[26]

It is acceptable to have a list of people whose person and luggage will be searched with extra care, and anonymous passengers on domestic flights could

---

[23] Dan Kaminsky, "Let's Cut through the Bitcoin Hype: A Hacker-Entrepreneur's Take," 3 May 2013, `http://wired.com/2013/05/lets-cut-through-the-bitcoin-hype/`.

[24] Steven Levy, "E-Money (That's What I Want)," *Wired*, 2.12 (December 1994), `http://archive.wired.com/wired/archive/2.12/emoney_pr.html`.

[25] Richard Bilton, "Camera Grid to Log Number Plates," last updated on 22 May 2009, `http://news.bbc.co.uk/2/hi/programmes/whos_watching_you/8064333.stm`.

[26] Nusrat Choudhury, "Victory! Federal Court Recognizes Constitutional Rights of Americans on the No-Fly List," 29 August 2013, `https://www.aclu.org/blog/victory-federal-court-recognizes-constitutional-rights-americans-no-fly-list`.

be treated as if they were on this list. It is also acceptable to bar non-citizens, if they are not permitted to enter the country at all, from boarding flights to the country. This ought to be enough for all legitimate purposes.

Many mass transit systems use some kind of smart cards or RFIDs for payment. These systems accumulate personal data: if you once make the mistake of paying with anything but cash, they associate the card permanently with your name. Furthermore, they record all travel associated with each card. Together they amount to massive surveillance. This data collection must be reduced.

Navigation services do surveillance: the user's computer tells the map service the user's location and where the user wants to go; then the server determines the route and sends it back to the user's computer, which displays it. Nowadays, the server probably records the user's locations, since there is nothing to prevent it. This surveillance is not inherently necessary, and redesign could avoid it: free/libre software in the user's computer could download map data for the pertinent regions (if not downloaded previously), compute the route, and display it, without ever telling anyone where the user is or wants to go.

Systems for borrowing bicycles, etc., can be designed so that the borrower's identity is known only inside the station where the item was borrowed. Borrowing would inform all stations that the item is "out," so when the user returns it at any station (in general, a different one), that station will know where and when that item was borrowed. It will inform the other station that the item is no longer "out." It will also calculate the user's bill, and send it (after waiting some random number of minutes) to headquarters along a ring of stations, so that headquarters would not find out which station the bill came from. Once this is done, the return station would forget all about the transaction. If an item remains "out" for too long, the station where it was borrowed can inform headquarters; in that case, it could send the borrower's identity immediately.

Remedy for Communications Dossiers

Internet service providers and telephone companies keep extensive data on their users' contacts (browsing, phone calls, etc.). With mobile phones, they also record the user's physical location.[27] They keep these dossiers for a long time: over 30 years, in the case of AT&T. Soon they will even record the user's body activities.[28] It appears that the NSA collects cell phone location data in bulk.[29]

Unmonitored communication is impossible where systems create such

---

[27] Kai Biermann, "Betrayed by Our Own Data," 26 March 2011, `http://www.zeit.de/digital/datenschutz/2011-03/data-protection-malte-spitz`.

[28] Sara M. Watson, "The Latest Smartphones Could Turn Us All into Activity Trackers," 10 October 2013, `http://wired.com/2013/10/the-trojan-horse-of-the-latest-iphone-with-the-m7-coprocessor-we-all-become-qs-activity-trackers/`.

[29] Patrick Toomey, "It Sure Sounds Like the NSA Is Tracking Our Locations," 30 September 2013, `https://aclu.org/blog/it-sure-sounds-nsa-tracking-our-locations`.

dossiers. So it should be illegal to create or keep them. ISPs and phone companies must not be allowed to keep this information for very long, in the absence of a court order to surveil a certain party.

This solution is not entirely satisfactory, because it won't physically stop the government from collecting all the information immediately as it is generated—which is what the US does with some or all phone companies.[30] We would have to rely on prohibiting that by law. However, that would be better than the current situation, where the relevant law (the PAT RIOT Act) does not clearly prohibit the practice. In addition, if the government did resume this sort of surveillance, it would not get data about everyone's phone calls made prior to that time.

For privacy about who you exchange email with, a simple partial solution is for you and others to use email services in a country that would never cooperate with your own government, and which communicate with each other using encryption. However, Ladar Levison (owner of the mail service Lavabit that US surveillance sought to corrupt completely) has a more sophisticated idea for an encryption system through which your email service would know only that you sent mail to some user of my email service, and my email service would know only that I received mail from some user of your email service, but it would be hard to determine that you had sent mail to me.

But Some Surveillance Is Necessary

For the state to find criminals, it needs to be able to investigate specific crimes, or specific suspected planned crimes, under a court order. With the internet, the power to tap phone conversations would naturally extend to the power to tap internet connections. This power is easy to abuse for political reasons, but it is also necessary. Fortunately, this won't make it possible to find whistleblowers after the fact, if (as I recommend) we prevent digital systems from accumulating massive dossiers before the fact.

Individuals with special state-granted power, such as police, forfeit their right to privacy and must be monitored. (In fact, police have their own jargon term for perjury, "testilying,"[31] since they do it so frequently, particularly about protesters and photographers.[32]) One city in California that required police to

---

30 Glenn Greenwald, "NSA Collecting Phone Records of Millions of Verizon Customers Daily," 6 June 2013, `http://www.theguardian.com/world/2013/jun/06/nsa-phone-records-verizon-court-order`.

31 See, for instance, the articles "Testilying: Cops Are Liars Who Get Away with Perjury" (Nick Malinowski, 3 February 2013, `http://vice.com/read/testilying-cops-are-liars-who-get-away-with-perjury`) and "Detective Is Found Guilty of Planting Drugs" (Tim Stelloh, 1 November 2011, `http://nytimes.com/2011/11/02/nyregion/brooklyn-detective-convicted-of-planting-drugs-on-innocent-people.html?pagewanted=all&_r=0`), for examples of the extent to which this practice has been normalized.

32 See the *Photography Is Not a Crime* web site, at `http://photographyisnotacrime.com/`, for more on this issue.

wear video cameras all the time found their use of force fell by 60 percent.[33] The ACLU is in favor of this.

Corporations are not people, and not entitled to human rights.[34] It is legitimate to require businesses to publish the details of processes that might cause chemical, biological, nuclear, fiscal, computational (e.g., DRM[35]) or political (e.g., lobbying) hazards to society, to whatever level is needed for public well-being. The danger of these operations (consider the BP oil spill, the Fukushima meltdowns, and the 2008 fiscal crisis) dwarfs that of terrorism.

However, journalism must be protected from surveillance even when it is carried out as part of a business.

Digital technology has brought about a tremendous increase in the level of surveillance of our movements, actions, and communications. It is far more than we experienced in the 1990s, and far more than people behind the Iron Curtain experienced in the 1980s,[36] and proposed legal limits on state use of the accumulated data would not alter that.

Companies are designing even more intrusive surveillance. Some project that pervasive surveillance, hooked to companies such as Facebook, could have deep effects on how people think.[37]Such possibilities are imponderable; but the threat to democracy is not speculation. It exists and is visible today.

Unless we believe that our free countries previously suffered from a grave surveillance deficit, and ought to be surveilled more than the Soviet Union and East Germany were, we must reverse this increase. That requires stopping the accumulation of big data about people.

---

[33] Kevin Drum,"Ubiquitous Surveillance, Police Edition," 22 August 2013, `http://motherjones.com/kevin-drum/2013/08/ubiquitous-surveillance-police-edition`.

[34] Public Citizen, "Call Your Representative: Tell Her or Him to Co-Sponsor a Constitutional Amendment to Overturn *Citizens United* and Restore Democracy to the People," accessed August 2015, `http://action.citizen.org/p/dia/action3/common/public/?action_KEY=12266`.

[35] See the related section in "Words to Avoid (or User with Care)" (p. 95) for more on this.

[36] James Allworth, "Your Smartphone Works for the Surveillance State," 7 June 2013, `https://hbr.org/2013/06/your-iphone-works-for-the-secret-police`.

[37] Evan Selinger and Brett Frischmann, "Will the Internet of Things Result in Predictable People?" 10 August 2015, `http://theguardian.com/technology/2015/aug/10/internet-of-things-predictable-people`.

A: A Note on Software

Written by Richard E. Buckman and Joshua Gay.

This section is intended for people who have little or no knowledge of the technical aspects of computer science. It is not necessary to read this section to understand the essays and speeches presented in this book; however, it may be helpful to those readers not familiar with some of the jargon that comes with programming and computer science.

A computer *programmer* writes software, or computer programs. A program is more or less a recipe with *commands* to tell the computer what to do in order to carry out certain tasks. You are more than likely familiar with many different programs: your Web browser, your word processor, your email client, and the like.

A program usually starts out as *source code.* This higher-level set of commands is written in a *programming language* such as C or Java. After that, a tool known as a *compiler* translates this to a lower-level language known as *assembly language.* Another tool known as an *assembler* breaks the assembly code down to the final stage of *machine language*—the lowest level—which the computer understands *natively.*

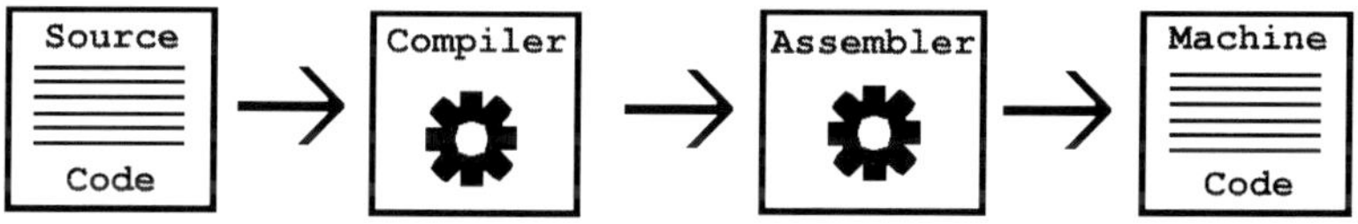

For example, consider the "hello world" program, a common first program for people learning C, which (when compiled and executed) prints "Hello World!" on the screen.[1]

[1] In other programming languages, such as Scheme, the *Hello World* program is usually not your first program. In Scheme you often start with a program like this:

```
(define (factorial n)
  (if (= n 0)
      1
      (* n (factorial (- n 1)))))
```

This computes the factorial of a number; that is, running `(factorial 5)` would output 120, which is computed by doing 5 * 4 * 3 * 2 * 1 * 1.

This note was originally published in 2002, in the first edition. This version is part of *Free Software, Free Society: Selected Essays of Richard M. Stallman*, 3rd ed. (Boston: GNU Press, 2015).

```
int main(){
    printf(''Hello World!'');
    return 0;
}
```

In the Java programming language the same program would be written like this:

```
public class hello {
    public static void main(String args[]) {
        System.out.println(''Hello World!'');
    }
}
```

However, in machine language, a small section of it may look similar to this:

```
1100011110111010100101001001001010101110
0110101010011000001111001011010101111101
0100111111111100101101100000000010100100
0100100001100101011011000110110001101111
0010000001010111011011110111001001101100
0110010000100001010000100110111101101111
```

The above form of machine language is the most basic representation known as binary. All data in computers is made up of a series of 0-or-1 values, but a person would have much difficulty understanding the data. To make a simple change to the binary, one would have to have an intimate knowledge of how a particular computer interprets the machine language. This could be feasible for small programs like the above examples, but any interesting program would involve an exhausting effort to make simple changes.

As an example, imagine that we wanted to make a change to our "Hello World" program written in C so that instead of printing "Hello World" in English it prints it in French. The change would be simple; here is the new program:

```
int main() {
    printf(''Bonjour, monde!'');
    return 0;
}
```

It is safe to say that one can easily infer how to change the program written in the Java programming language in the same way. However, even many programmers would not know where to begin if they wanted to change the binary representation. When we say "source code," we do not mean machine language that only computers can understand—we are speaking of higher-level languages such as C and Java. A few other popular programming languages are C++, Perl, and Python. Some are harder than others to understand and program in, but they are all much easier to work with compared to the intricate machine language they get turned into after the programs are compiled and assembled.

Another important concept is understanding what an *operating system* is. An operating system is the software that handles input and output, memory allocation, and task scheduling. Generally one considers common or useful programs such as the *Graphical User Interface* (GUI) to be a part of the operating system. The GNU/Linux operating system contains a both GNU and non-GNU software, and a *kernel* called *Linux*. The kernel handles low-level tasks that applications depend upon such as input/output and task scheduling. The GNU software comprises much of the rest of the operating system, including GCC, a general-purpose compiler for many languages; GNU Emacs, an extensible text editor with many, many features; GNOME, the GNU desktop; GNU libc, a library that all programs other than the kernel must use in order to communicate with the kernel; and Bash, the GNU command interpreter that reads your command lines. Many of these programs were pioneered by Richard Stallman early on in the GNU Project and come with any modern GNU/Linux operating system.

It is important to understand that even if *you* cannot change the source code for a given program, or directly use all these tools, it is relatively easy to find someone who can. Therefore, by having the source code to a program you are usually given the power to change, fix, customize, and learn about a program—this is a power that you do not have if you are not given the source code. Source code is one of the requirements that makes a piece of software *free*. The other requirements will be found along with the philosophy and ideas behind them in this collection.

B: Translations of "Free Software" and "Gratis Software"

This is a list of recommended unambiguous translations for the term "free software" ("free as in freedom") into various languages, along with translations for the term "gratis software," in a separate column, to show how to make the contrast. The parenthesized phrases in Latin letters after some of the entries are transliterations (with vowels added where relevant).

en	English	free software	gratis software
af	Afrikaans	vrye sagteware	gratis sagteware
ar	Arabic	برمجيات حرة *(barmajiyat ḥorrah)*	
be	Belarusian	свабоднае праграмнае забесьпячэньне *(svabodnae pragramnae zabes'pjachen'ne)*	
bg	Bulgarian	свободен софтуер *(svoboden softuer)*	безплатен софтуер *(bezplaten softuer)*
bn	Bengali	স্বাধীন সফটওয়্যার *(swadhin software)*	
ca	Catalan	programari lliure	programari gratuït
cs	Czech	svobodný software	bezplatný software
cy	Welsh	meddalwedd rydd	
da	Danish	fri software *or* frit programmel	gratis software
de	German	freie Software	Gratis-Software *or* kostenlose Software
el	Greek	ελεύθερο λογισμικό *(elefthero logismiko)*	δωρεάν λογισμικό *(dorean logismiko)*
eo	Esperanto	libera programaro *or* programo	
eu	Basque	software librea	doako softwarea
es	Spanish	software libre	software gratuito
et	Estonian	vaba tarkvara	tasuta tarkvara
fa	Persian (Farsi)	نرم‌افزار آزاد *(narmafzar azad)*	نرم‌افزار رایگان *(narmafzar raygan)*
fi	Finnish	vapaa ohjelmisto	ilmainen ohjelmisto

The most current list of translations and transliterations is maintained at `http://gnu.org/philosophy/fs-translations.html`. Please send any additional translations or corrections to the list to `web-translators@gnu.org`.

This version of the list is part of *Free Software, Free Society: Selected Essays of Richard M. Stallman*, 3rd ed. (Boston: GNU Press, 2015).

fr	French	logiciel libre	logiciel gratuit
ga	Irish	saorbhogearraí	bogearraí saora in aisce
he	Hebrew	תוכנה חופשית *(tochna chofshit)*	תוכנה חינמית *(tochna chinamit)*
hi	Hindi	मुक्त सॉफ्टवेयर *(mukt software)*	मुफ़्त सॉफ्टवेयर *(muft software)*
hr	Croatian	slobodan softver	besplatan softver
hu	Hungarian	szabad szoftver	ingyenes szoftver *or* ingyen szoftver
hy	Armenian	ազատ ծրագիր/ծրագրեր *(azat tsragir/tsragrer)*	
ia	Interlingua	libere programmage *or* libere programmario	
id	Indonesian	perangkat lunak bebas	
io	Ido	libera programaro	
is	Icelandic	frjáls hugbúnaður	
it	Italian	software libero	software gratuito
ja	Japanese	自由ソフトウェア *(jiyū-sofutouea)*	無料ソフトウェア *(muryō-sofutouea)*
ka	Georgian	თავისუფალი პროგრამები *(tavisupali programebi)*	უფასო პროგრამები *(upaso programebi)*
ko	Korean	자유 소프트웨어 *(ja-yu software)*	
lt	Lithuanian	laisva programinė įranga	nemokama programinė įranga
lv	Latvian	brīva programmatūra	bezmaksas programmatūra
mk	Macedonian	слободен софтвер *(sloboden softver)*	бесплатен софтвер *(besplaten softver)*
ml	Malayalam	സ്വതന്ത്രസോഫ്റ്റ്‌വെയർ *(svatantrasophttveyar)*	സൗജന്യസോഫ്റ്റ്‌വെയർ *(soujanyasophttveyar)*
ms	Malay	perisian bebas	
nl	Dutch	vrije software	gratis software
no	Norwegian	fri programvare	
pl	Polish	wolne oprogramowanie	darmowe oprogramowanie
pt	Portuguese	software livre	
ro	Romanian	programe libere	programe gratuite
ru	Russian	свободные программы *(svobodnie programmi)*	бесплатные программы *(besplatnie programmi)*
sc	Sardinian	software liberu	
si	Sinhala	නිදහස් මෘදුකාංග *(nidahas mṛdukāṅga)*	
sk	Slovak	slobodný softvér	

sl	Slovenian	prosto programje	
sq	Albanian	software i lirë	software falas
sr	Serbian	слободни софтвер *or* slobodni softver	бесплатни софтвер *or* besplatni softver
sv	Swedish	fri programvara *or* fri mjukvara	
sw	Swahili	software huru *or* programu huru za kompyuta	
ta	Tamil	கட்டற்ற மென்பொருள் *(kaṭṭaṟṟa meṉpoñaḷ)*	இலவச மென்பொருள் *(illavasa menporul)*
th	Thai	ซอฟต์แวร์เสรี *(sofotwerseri)*	
tl	Tagalog (Filipino)	malayang software	
tr	Turkish	özgür yazılım	
uk	Ukrainian	вільне програмне забезпечення *(vil'ne prohramne zabezpechen-nja)*	
ur	Urdu	آزاد سافٹ ویئر *(azad software)*	مفت سافٹ ویئر *(muft software)*
vi	Vietnamese	phần mềm tự do	
zh-cn	Chinese (simplified)	自由软件 *(zi-you ruan-jian)*	免费软件 *(mian-fei ruan-jian)*
zh-tw	Chinese (traditional)	自由軟體 *(zih-yo)*	免費軟體 *(mien-fei)*
zu	Zulu	isoftware ekhululekile	

C: The Free Software Song

The lyrics of "The Free Software Song" are sung to the melody of the Bulgarian folk song "Sadi moma bela loza." To listen to a recording of the piece accompanied by Bulgarian instruments played in traditional style, please visit `http://gnu.org/music/FreeSWSong.ogg`.

This song is in a rhythm of 7/8; those unaccustomed to odd rhythms often take the unevenness to be a mistake. The meter can be analyzed into three subgroups as slow quick quick or 3-2-2. Such meters in Bulgarian music can often be stretched, and some musicians analyze this song as 3-2-3 instead; however, the last "3" is not as long as the first. Yves Moreau, who collected and taught the dance, endorses the rhythm of 7.

Richard Stallman wrote the lyrics above in 1991. This version of the score is published in *Free Software, Free Society: Selected Essays of Richard M. Stallman*, 3rd ed. (Boston: GNU Press, 2015).

Index

D

E

F

G

H

M

Q

R

S

T

X

Y